LAND OF EXTRACTION

Land of Extraction

*Property, Fracking, and
Settler Colonialism*

Rebecca R. Scott

NEW YORK UNIVERSITY PRESS
New York

NEW YORK UNIVERSITY PRESS
New York
www.nyupress.org

Library of Congress Cataloging-in-Publication Data
Names: Scott, Rebecca R., author. Title: Land of extraction : property, fracking, and settler
colonialism /   Rebecca R. Scott.
Description: New York: New York University Press, [2024] | Includes bibliographical refer-
ences and index.
Identifiers: LCCN 2023022570 | ISBN 9781479821259 (hardback ; alk. paper) | ISBN
9781479821266 (paperback ; alk. paper) | ISBN 9781479821280 (ebook   other) | ISBN
9781479821297 (ebook)
Subjects: LCSH: Mineral industries--Social aspects--West Virginia. | Real   property--West
Virginia. | Environmentalism--West Virginia. | Hydraulic   fracturing--West virginia.
Classification: LCC HD9506.U63 W427 2024 | DDC 338.209754--dc23/20230623
LC record available at https://lccn.loc.gov/2023022570

This book is printed on acid-free paper, and its binding materials are chosen for strength
and durability. We strive to use environmentally responsible suppliers and materials to the
greatest extent possible in publishing our books.

Manufactured in the United States of America

10 9 8 7 6 5 4 3 2 1

Also available as an ebook

For my parents

CONTENTS

Prologue

Solastalgia

It's summer on the Greenbrier River, around 1977. In a canoe with my parents, Mom in the front, paddling, Dad in the back, steering, Becky sitting in the middle. Rushing over "Tumblin' Rock," a famously risky spot, spilling the canoe, and laughing in the sun and cool fresh. Anthony Creek. A tributary of the Greenbrier, cold as ice, especially cold in the swimming holes, with shallows abounding with minnows and crawdads. These waters were my home away from home. The water is greeny-brown and reflects the forested mountainsides that rise up on either bank, reflects the blue sky and clouds above. A close look through the clear water shows the colorful smooth sandstone river rocks on the bottom, speckling with sunlight through the ripples. The creek, the river, the water is alive, and its spirit makes Greenbrier County the best place on Earth; everyone knows that. A natural river undammed and wild, it can also cause harm.

The Mountain Valley Pipeline has plans to dig under the river and blast through the bedrock, on a quiet southern stretch of the river between a steep forested hillside and open fields in Summers County. The Atlantic Coast Pipeline once threatened the same on a northern stretch near the headwaters of the river in Pocahontas County. Company geologists and consultants say this is no big deal. Friends of the river say if the pipeline company truly blasts away the bedrock of the Greenbrier River, they will not be accountable for their actions. By any means necessary. Defending the sacred. My brother says, "The day hydrocarbons come down the Greenbrier River is the day I don't want to live any more. If they mess with your mother, then what do you have to live for?" I used to believe we were safe. Mountaintop removal mining? Not in Greenbrier County! But yes, in Greenbrier County. Fracking? Not in Greenbrier County! Not yet in Greenbrier County, but rights have been leased, explorations launched. May they find nothing. But now, pipelines under the river.

It's summer, 2018, I'm in West Virginia doing research. Many interviews, meetings, and other explorations take me from one side of the state to the other. But my favorite places are the ones close to home. Monroe County is southwest of Greenbrier County, and it is like part of the family. The land is karst, gentle rolling hills and farmland. Underneath lays "Big Lime," the Greenbrier Limestone. One day, my travels take me from Peterstown, on the far end of Monroe County at the border of Virginia, all the way to Renick, toward the northern end of Greenbrier County. I realize the names of the towns along US Route 219, called the Seneca Trail, form a litany of my youth. Of home and remembrance. Union, Pickaway, Organ Cave, Ronceverte (Greenbrier in French), Fairlea, Lewisburg, Maxwelton, Clendenenville, Frankford, Renick, Hillsboro, Marlinton. I haven't lived here in 24 years, but the litany of the towns along this "old Indian Path" named for the Seneca people (self-name Onödowaʼgaːʼ), who belong to the Haudenosaunee, a federation of six nations whose laws provided a model for the US Constitution, albeit rewritten without a role for women,[1] return me to a comforting sense of home and belonging. I know this road like the back of my hand.

But there is trouble. Outside Peterstown sits a huge pipe yard, acres of limestone gravel piled high with stacks of 50-foot-long, 42-inch-diameter steel segments of pipe. Man camps appear in fields nearby, and the motel in Alderson (along the Greenbrier River) advertises rooms for pipeline workers. Pickup trucks with company logos. Tractor trailers with pipeline segments pushing cars off the road. Creek water roils with muddy runoff from the pipeline ditches and limestone gravel. A right-of-way for the pipeline cuts through a farm, leaving a big 8-foot-deep gash, and, in the steepest sections of the pipelines' pathways, piles of Quikrete bags are stacked up on the near-vertical hillsides to prevent erosion on the pipeline route. All they do is, they stack the bags of Quikrete up like a wall on the slope, then wait for it to rain and make concrete. The plastic sacks themselves will wear away eventually.

Introduction

Fracking Property

I stand in alliance with relatives—both human and other-than-human—who suffer across the planet from the violence that is the American Dream. In order to sustain good relations among all the beings that inhabit these lands, we must undercut settler (property) relations. Instead of killing the Indian to save the man, we must turn the ontological table. The twenty-first-century mantra must be to kill the settler and save us all.

—Kimberly TallBear

West Virginia has been known as "Almost Heaven" ever since John Denver wrote its unofficial anthem. My personal bias is that the rolling hills and forests, clear rivers and creeks, and scenic views of the southeastern areas of the state especially fit this description. My home county, Greenbrier County, is a beautiful place, mostly farms and forests, practically untouched by extractive industry. Recently, however, the rural tranquility of places like Greenbrier County has been disrupted. Mary, whose organic farm lies in the path of a natural gas pipeline, commented, "Sometimes I think . . . I'm just having a nightmare and I'm going to wake up any minute. Cause . . . nothing like this ever happened here that we've ever had to go through. It's just always been a farming area, and you know, quiet and peaceful."[1]

With tractor trailers carrying stacks of 50-foot-long, 42-inch-diameter pipe segments, influxes of heavy equipment for digging deep trenches through fields, forests, and waterways, company trucks and worker traffic crowding the narrow roads, and construction sites across multiple roadways following a serpentine path through the mountains, the pipelines have brought unfamiliar disruption to quiet communities around the state. The pipelines are being built to transport highly pressurized natural gas, so that even after their construction is completed, the peace and quiet that parts of West Virginia are famous for will be undermined by a background level of unease. Pipelines break. It's what they do. Natural gas pipelines explode.[2] As Mary expressed, the place has "been a really . . . nice place to live. That's the reason we stayed . . . But now . . . it's just going to ruin a whole way of life. It's sad."

In Mary's case, her specific concern is about the destruction of her beloved organic farm. Pipelines are infrastructure, and their construction is therefore overseen by the Federal Energy Regulatory Commission (FERC), the agency in charge of the interstate transportation of electricity, oil, and gas. FERC regulates the storage and transportation of natural gas from the privately owned hydraulic fracturing wells, compressor stations, and storage facilities through the privately owned and constructed pipeline network.[3] FERC is armed with the power of eminent domain to force landowners to sell their property in the name of the public good. Eminent domain is the federal power described in the Fifth Amendment, which specifies that the government has the power to (re)claim private property for projects supporting the public good. As part of the oversight of the construction of natural gas extraction and transport, FERC is able to use eminent domain to forcibly take a right-of-way across an individual property holding provided the owner is fairly compensated for this taking according to the market value of the land.[4]

Mary and her husband don't want to sell the right-of-way, but they are out of luck because their neighbors sold as soon as they got an offer. Although the future of these pipelines is currently a political question, Mary's property could be taken eventually whether she likes it or not. This situation leads to a feeling of powerlessness that is not supposed to be part of the American Dream. Due to this unexpected feeling of powerlessness and dispossession, many pipeline opponents have remarked on the apparent similarities between the experience of US landowners in the way of extractive development and the historical dispossession of Indigenous Peoples in what is currently known as North America.[5] However, Mary's loss is the loss of a family's property, a loss that will cause a transformation in a community. The dispossession of Indigenous lands by settlers and extractive industry contributes to the destruction of an entire network of caretaking relations within the traditional territory of a People.[6] These distinctions highlight the contradiction between, on the one hand, Mary's awareness that "the Native Americans had the right . . . [idea] . . . to protect the environment; they still do. And . . . we should be protecting our environment," and, on the other hand, how settler property relations restrict her ability to do so. Discussions about fracking and pipelines are always already discussions of property: surface and mineral rights, eminent domain, and rights-of-way. The individualistic property regime of capitalist settler culture is set up for extraction.[7] Individual private property is a defining characteristic of the United States as a settler colonial and capitalist project.[8]

Settler Colonialism, Extraction, and Environmental Destruction

I'm proceeding from a lens centering the United States as a settler colony, so I will start with some notes on my use of language. Indigenous people, in the US context, are those who belong to one of the many Nations of Turtle Island (i.e., that place which is currently known as North America) that preexist colonization by Europeans. This is therefore a political designation referring to belonging to a People, rather than a racial identity.[9] Many others of us are settlers, a term that refers to non-Indigenous people whose selves, parents, or forebearers joined the settler colonial project more or less willingly or who have benefited by joining it. Many are also what Jodi Byrd (Chickasaw Nation) named as arrivants, or those whose forebearers were brought here by force and who do not experience the full privileges of citizenship in the settler state.[10] These categories are not exclusive; indeed, they frequently overlap and fail to capture all circumstances, but they are nevertheless useful to draw distinctions that are necessary to emphasize in this context.

In this text, I have identified Indigenous scholars and some settler scholars according to their publicly available self-identification. In other references to the original nations of what is currently known as North America, I have identified people to the best of my ability depending on the context as Native or Indigenous Peoples, by the self-name of their nation, which is preferred, or by another commonly recognized name used historically in the United States. The politics of naming are critical for a project that seeks to center settler colonialism in an analysis of contemporary American social problems. The lack of recognition of Indigenous self-names in contemporary America represents a significant source of "colonial unknowing" and Indigenous erasure.[11] I capitalize the word Indigenous in this text for related reasons, to show respect for people, identities, collective relations, and ways of life that have been the object of colonial campaigns of disrespect, destruction, and genocide for the last 500 years.[12]

To say that the United States is a settler colony means that it is a nation characterized by settler colonialism, which refers to the appropriation of Indigenous territory by an occupying state and its citizens, coupled with the attempt to eliminate Indigenous Peoples and lifeways and replace them with settler ones.[13] Instead of representing a historical event that is over and done with, that is, "Land gets stolen, that's how it works,"[14] Indigenous and critical settler scholars argue that the United States is an ongoing settler colonial project in the present. Simultaneously, the settler colonial structure produces various new cultural/economic/political forms, appropriates (as American heritage) Indigenous land and life, and aims to eliminate Indigenous ways of life.[15] Currently existing settler colonialism is also a structure of feeling.[16] In other words, it is an *experienced* system, whose "affective networks need to be explored as part of understanding how settler colonial governmentality comes to be lived as the self-evident condition of possibility for (settler) being."[17] These structures of feeling produce a sense of inevitability for a never-ending future of the settler state. Thus, an effective analysis or critique of the state of contemporary US politics must include a recognition of "the constitutive role of settler colonialism in American political development."[18] The institution of individual private property in land is at the root of the social, cultural, economic, and political structures of settler colonialism, and therefore shapes its effects on the land and people. As Brett A. Chapman (Pawnee) remarked on Twitter, it was only 30 years after Frederick Jackson Turner's declaration of the closing of the frontier [i.e., the near total conversion of land in the United States to private or government property] that the "delicate, ancient ecosystem that sustained vast herds of buffalo for centuries" became "a barren desert in the worst man-made environmental disaster in U.S. history—the Dust Bowl."[19]

The material effects of settler culture, including "the 'ugliness' of settler infrastructure," the production of wastelands and sacrifice zones,
and the mad dash to exploit natural resources for quick profit highlight
the unsustainability of our current politics of disposability.[20] For these
reasons, this book seeks to open space for its settler readers to think
about how environmental politics might unfold if these "'settled expectations' and self-evident 'settler states of feeling'" were denaturalized and
decentered.[21] I single out settler readers here because this book represents my grappling with how things I grew up taking for granted, such
as individual private property ownership as the epitome of the American
Dream, help set the stage for environmental crisis in the United States.
These settler structures of political economics and feeling are what this
book is about. Political economic and affective structures are interwo-
ven in the institution of private property and all that it entails for individual life chances, gendered and sexual expectations, and sense of
personhood.[22] Indigenous people and others shut out from the American Dream are perhaps all too familiar with these perspectives, whereas
they may be less familiar for those of us positioned as settlers. I use the
pronouns "us" and "we" advisedly in the text to refer to my own social
location, that of a middle-class white settler in what is currently known
as North America, who has been raised in an atmosphere of settler state
hegemony, American exceptionalism, and Indigenous erasure.[23] For
these reasons, the book focuses its critical lens on settler structures and
practices, not because they are the only cause of our current predicament, but in order to acknowledge some of the ordinarily unspoken sub-
structures of American social and environmental problems.

Colonizing relationships depend on a willful unknowing on the part
of the colonizer, a refusal to recognize the knowledge, perspectives, and
reality of the colonized.[24] "Settler memory" is a cultural formation that
works to limit "the scope of one's sense of obligation to others and to the
world" by confining the Indigenous history of the United States to an as-
terisk or footnote. This happens for example when historical texts offer
a brief reference to historical settler violence against Indigenous people
and quickly move on to more seemingly relevant material.[25] Challenges
to settler memory such as We Are All Treaty People, and No One Is Illegal on Stolen Land offer the possibility for questioning the legitimacy of
the settler state.[26] The first phrase should remind us that treaties are not

bills of sale but agreements between two (or more) groups. Therefore, treaties not only affect the Indigenous signatories and descendants, but also exert responsibilities on the settler state that also signed the treaty, and on its members.[27] The second puts into question the right of some (settlers) to deny entry to others to land that was stolen in the first place. These phrases draw on the knowledge explained by Leanne Betasamosake Simpson (Michi Saagiig Nishaabeg) that in Nishnaabeg thought, "the opposite of dispossession is not possession, it is deep, reciprocal, consensual *attachment*."[28] These relations and attachments to nonhumans and other humans are rooted in true, informed, and freely given consent, generating autonomy and self-determination for the individual that possessive extractivism promises but does not deliver.[29]

Settlers in what is currently called the United States and Canada have chosen to largely disregard and ignore Indigenous principles of the human relationship to each other, nonhumans, and land. Indigenous understandings of treaties as frameworks for relationships instead of as contracts of sale, and other aspects of Indigenous social and political life, if recognized by settlers and the settler state, would have altered or could alter the course of history.[30] This possibility is rendered unthinkable by the practices of settler memory that confine Indigenous history to a footnote in a story of modernization and progress that leaves the so-called traditional past behind.[31] Nevertheless, things didn't have to be this way, it could have been, could be, otherwise. Throughout the conquest and colonization of North America, there have been countertrends and opponents to settler colonial structures and violence.[32]

The Seven Fires Prophesy, given to the Anishinaabe long ago, foretells a time when settlers in what is currently called North America will have to choose between two divergent paths, one leading toward renewed brotherhood and the Eighth Fire (an historical era of peace), the other toward continued destruction for all Earth's people.[33] Currently, concepts drawn from Indigenous traditions, such as Mni Wiconi (Water Is Life),[34] the emergent embrace of thriving through mutual responsibilities rather than individual rights, and the ever more apparent entanglement of human life in the more-than-human[35] are becoming increasingly prominent ideas in US public culture. In the twenty-first century it has become more difficult for settlers to ignore that "Indigenous relational practices and agency can evade or overcome 'elimina-tionist' endeavours" and that these relational practices offer generative forms of leadership in the current crisis.[36]

Despite these transformations and challenges to settler hegemony, American history is characterized by settler culture attempting to elimi-nate Indigenous relational practices and replace them with property as the primary and seemingly most rational method of relating to land, nature, and other people.[37] Robert Nichols explains:

> Property does not refer to a set of things. Rather it refers to a species of *relations*. To claim property in something is in effect to construct a relationship with others, namely, a relation of exclusion. Most often, to assert property in something is to make an enforceable claim to exclude someone from access to something.[38]

Explaining a distinction between settler and Indigenous relations, Sisseton Wahpeton Oyate scholar Kimberly Tallbear notes that property "undercuts Indigenous kinship and attempts to replace it. It objectifies the land and water and other-than-human beings as potentially owned resources."[39] Property is "a bundle of decentered ways of speaking about the world, of mapping it, and of telling stories about it" that produce social identities and material consequences.[40] The property structure of settler relations exists in part through individuals' histories of intergen-erational inheritance and family property, which in turn reinforces white supremacist patriarchal kinship, and relies on compulsory monogamy and heterosexuality.[41]

Property operates as a technology of empowerment for some indi-viduals and disempowerment for others, creating social hierarchies. At the same time, it inflicts similarly violent effects on the more-than-human worlds we share. Currently, some of the material consequences of property relations are reverberating in the intensification of fossil fuel extraction in what is currently called North America. Mountaintop removal coal mining, tar sands oil extraction, and hydraulic fractur-ing for natural gas destroy massive quantities of water and ecosystems while worsening the climate crisis.[42] This intensive extraction shakes the foundations of some of the basic ideological underpinnings of settler culture—progress, freedom, and the eternalization of settler futurity.[43] Therefore, in the context of this book, *fracking* represents both an extractive practice and a metaphor for the effects of this historical moment that offers the potential for shaking up "the dominant narrative of a multicultural and supposedly progressive (always progressing toward greater good) settler state."[44]

"Fracking" doubles as a literal term for the intensification of fossil fuel extraction through so-called nonconventional means and as the effect of this expansion of extractive industry on the industry's own foundational assumptions. Fracking serves as a figurative reference to the cracking foundations of the private property regime and its destructive relationship to nonhuman nature. This relationship is rooted in real estate, or private property in land, which is "not a material object but a mediating device, a conceptual and legal category that serves to relate humans to 'nature' and to each other in a particular, proprietary manner."[45] Private property underlies American notions of citizenship and rights and offers property owners the fantasy of perfect liberal freedom.[46] Natural gas extraction represents a material and symbolic fracturing of some of the certainties of white American belonging: Through its flowing and seeping materiality underground, it represents an indeterminacy of property claims that are "severed" or forcibly "pooled," and the unsettling of property rights effected by its extraction and transportation.[47] Fracking is also the somewhat pejorative name for the extraction technology of hydraulic fracturing and horizontal drilling. This technical achievement, in which impermeable shale rock, a mile underground, is cracked open by a stream of highly pressurized sand, water, and a proprietary mixture of chemicals, allows access to deep pools of natural gas such as those in the Marcellus Shale and the Utica Shale gas plays.

Private property is the scaffolding upon which natural gas extraction depends in the United States. Under US law, the split estate doctrine severs property rights horizontally between the surface and underground. Surface ownership gives the right to surface use and transformation. Holding access to underground deposits of coal, oil, or natural gas, etc., is known as holding mineral rights, and because the owner must be able to access this property, these usually entail the right to disrupt the surface owner's use.[48] Although most mineral rights in the western United States are held by the government and leased to individuals or corporations, this severing occurred piecemeal in the eastern states where individual (surface) owners can retain ownership of their rights or lease or sell them to others.[49] These leases or sales can affect future surface owners long after the mineral rights were originally leased or sold. Mineral rights that are severed from the surface can be owned or leased by individual entrepreneurs or corporations who then can use the land for wells, mines, or frack pads regardless of the surface owner's preferences. The fact that infrastructure projects like pipelines on which the gas industry depends also rely on the state's power to claim eminent domain highlights the fact that, despite its naturalization in American culture, the US government's sovereignty shapes, supports, and limits individual private property.

Tracing the connections between fracking that shale and the shaky cultural and environmental politics of private property is the goal of this book. In this book, I follow these connections through popular culture, politics, and the contradictions inherent in using private property as the paradigmatic structure of the human relationship to land.[50] Like many residents of this continent, I inhabit these contradictions, and this book represents my effort to bring that subjectivity into dialogue with the structural bind that private property places on contemporary American environmental politics. In its theoretical approach and framing, the book is located most firmly within the tradition of critical whiteness and critical settler colonial studies, which are lenses that demand a relentless critique of the harmful structures that lead to environmental and social destruction. However, I augment this critique with lessons from Indigenous studies, feminist theories, and affect theories about how stories, juxtaposition, and creativity contribute to the kind of holistic thinking that can open up new perspectives for those of us who inhabit these structures of feeling.[51]

I was raised in the region currently known as Appalachia on the shared territories of the Tsalagi, Yesáng, Moneton, Haudenosaunee, and other Indigenous Peoples.[52] This territory that is and has been in relation to many different Indigenous nations is currently divided into pieces of property and controlled by the sovereignty of several states and the federal government. I have always considered the small family farm where I grew up as my homeplace; however, both its dimensions and my access to it rely on property law.[53] The larger region currently known as Appalachia (a name derived from the French name for an Indigenous community, Apalache, in what is currently known as Florida)[54] is the shared territory of numerous Indigenous nations, including the Shawano (Shawnee) and Haudenosaunee among others.[55]

In discussions of land and politics in West Virginia it is common for white Appalachians to remark that their family has "been in these hills forever," or "for six generations."[56] I learned growing up that my family was "Scotch-Irish," descended from Protestant Scots who helped colonize Ireland before coming to America. However, I heard no specific stories along the lines of the "six generations" reported by some West Virginians. Turning to the genealogy website Ancestry.com, I found a series of links to a possible Scotch-Irish ancestor, James Burnes. According to their information, he was born in Ireland after his parents left Scotland to settle there. From Ireland, he immigrated to America as a young man. He was shot and killed by "Indians" at Fort Donnally in what is currently Greenbrier County, West Virginia, in 1778, a few miles from my family homeplace.[57] The Native people in this story were identified as Shawnee, and they were defending their land from encroaching American settlements. This man, who was possibly my fourth great-grandfather, James Burnes, was reportedly shot in the road while attempting to reach the shelter of the fort, having only had time to marry and reproduce himself (a son, also named James Burns) before his death.

This "Fort Donnally Massacre" is a famous Greenbrier County incident that occurred during the "Indian Wars" of the early Republic. The Royal Proclamation of 1763, which claimed the Eastern Seaboard for Britain and left all land west of the Shenandoah ridge to the Indigenous nations, was re-negotiated in the Treaty of Fort Stanwix in 1768, which was said to "cede" all land in what is currently Pennsylvania, West Virginia, and Kentucky to the British.[58] The treaty was negotiated with the Haudenosaunee, and the Shawnee were not a party to it, nor did they agree with it. Their raid on the fort in 1778 was an effort by the Shawnee to defend their land.[59] Besides the personal interest of the involvement of my (possible) fourth great-grandfather, this incident raises several points important to this book. The Treaty of Fort Stanwix was a document negotiated in an epistemological fog, if not in outright bad faith. The treaty forcibly attributed alienable property ownership (i.e., the possibility of severing a People's relationship to land and selling it to others) to people who didn't conceive of land as a commodity to sell, but rather thought of human beings as existing in relation to the more-than-human life and landforms of a place.[60] Through the treaty process the British, and later the United States, also cut other interested parties out of negotiations entirely, attributing singular "ownership" of the place to only one group, thereby serving the interest of the settlers and their colonizing project. As Gina Starblanket (Star Blanket Cree and Saulteaux) and Heidi Stark (Turtle Mountain Ojibwe) argue, whereas settlers viewed these treaties as contracts, or even better, as bills of sale marking the end of Indigenous possession, Indigenous people understood them as the beginning point for a relationship of mutual respect and coexistence in a territory with which more than one nation or People is in relation.[61] However, the promise of American independence and "free land" for any "free man" who could come and take it overran any possibility of coexistence. "Civilizing" the wilderness meant its conversion to private property.[62]

This concrete ancestral connection to settler colonial violence in Greenbrier County, West Virginia, should not have been surprising; however, I found this information startling and strangely affecting. The common expression in Appalachia of "having been here" for multiple generations reveals the foreshortening of history in settler time. For some settlers in the United States, unlike many other people in the world, 200 years seems practically to represent "time immemorial." Ancestry.com markets our ancestors to us in a way that reveals their lack of everyday relevance in settler time and settler culture.[63] The orientation to the new, to progress and mobility, and the general American lack of place attachment result in a situation where many settlers don't pay much attention to their ancestors on an everyday basis.[64] When I found James Burnes's story on Ancestry.com, I was excited to learn of a concrete connection to what appears (from a settler perspective) to be ancient history, but at the same time I also felt a growing awareness of the instability of "this historically brief, highly disruptive moment."[65] My own excitement about this seemingly "ancient history" enabled me to see how settler hegemony works through the eternalization of settler state sovereignty, the negation of history's relevance to the present, and the naturalization of property. In other words, the settling of Greenbrier County by Europeans becomes the "beginning" of the story. The violence of that settlement is not seen as fundamentally impactful to the unfolding of US history, although it is the individual properties claimed by or granted to these individual settlers that have structured the environmental, political economic, and cultural history of the settler state.[66] The genealogical facts marketed by Ancestry.com exist within a cultural frame where history's relevance to the present is a relative novelty that has to be sought out, not an everyday assumption. However, one way that ancestry is salient in the everyday for (some) settlers is in terms of property and inheritance, and this usage contributes to the naturalization of the institution of property, the narrow lens of patriarchal kinship, and settler sovereignty.[67] "We've been here six generations" is often part of a claim to long-term property rights in a place, or of a claim to the rights of a stakeholder.[68] Again, the assumption that this long-term inhabitation is unusual contributes to reducing the history of the place to the time frame of Euro-American settlement.

In this context it is very interesting to note that the environmental and social effects of fracking seem to destabilize people's feelings of entitlement to private property rights in relation to the land.[69] Mineral rights owned by someone else who then has the right of access through one's property, or a pipeline that is forced across one's farm, run counter to an American citizen's expectations of what private property means. Intensive extractive industry also "unsettles" the expectations of certainty and "settler futurity" that characterize the settler state.[70] The damage to water and to land caused by mining or natural gas extraction and transportation puts the future inhabitation of a place into question. The rush to extract as much natural gas as possible from the Marcellus Shale in order to quickly generate profits and encourage continuing investment exemplifies the commodification of land in the interest of the market.[71] The free market as an engine for improvement envisions economic development as naturally seeking the highest purpose of any piece of land, and considers unprofitable land as "waste."[72] However, the intensive exploitation of these fictitious commodities (such as land, water, and air, which are not produced by human labor) runs counter to their long-term viability as conditions of continued production and inhabitation.[73] In short, seeking the highest, most profitable use for land (extraction) stands in contradiction to the future human inhabitation of that land, and the settled expectations of its inhabitants.

Over the course of the twentieth century, the seemingly endless power provided by fossil fuels fed an imagination of unlimited economic growth, no longer tied to territory, but to an ever increasing GNP.[74] However, the free-market drive to development has revealed a contradiction in *settler time*.[75] Settler time refers to a conception of time based on a linear progress narrative characteristic of settler culture, in which the future is understood as an abandonment of the past. Capitalism's drive toward ever greater technical efficiency and development is intrinsic to this settler temporality. Other cultural frameworks such as Indigenous cyclical temporalities are left out of the projected linear trajectory of settler time. Settler futurity encompasses both the eternalization of the settler state (which is imagined as extending without end into the future) and its assumption of absolute sovereignty (i.e., its natural place as local and global hegemon), as well as "the feeling of futurity as rupture, a disjunction between what was and what will be."[76] This feeling of futurity as difference also belongs to the modern market forces that demand the new and improved. More and more obviously, expanding sacrifice zones, speculation in energy futures, and a growing awareness of the unsustainability of capitalism reveal the costs of this contradiction, resulting in a proliferation of dystopian future imaginaries of apocalypse and extinction.[77]

Settler time, which abandons the past as something dead and gone, represents a way of imagining time that finds expression concretely and materially in the creation of environmental sacrifice zones.[78] In short, sacrifice zones are places and populations deemed disposable in the name of a so-called higher good, such as national security, economic development, or the GNP. These may be nuclear testing or waste disposal sites, uranium mines, or industrial sites placed in low-income neighborhoods.[79] This is a politics of disposability that treats entire populations and places as expendable, useless, and without value.[80] This results in a "Euro-American movement toward the future as necropolitical," in which the present life and future survival of some are sacrificed in the name of the private benefit of others in the present.[81] This necropolitical future of divergent prosperity and death is widely represented in contemporary science fiction, dystopian television, and cinema.

Mark Rifkin notes that, in Indigenous temporality, white settlers are cyclical "destroyers" whose accumulation strategies rely on "the attempted elimination of the conditions of life for countervailing social formations, particularly those of Indigenous peoples."[82] These countervailing social formations include the "ontology of care" and responsibility that underlies many Indigenous forms of sovereignty, which stem from valuing relationships between humans and nonhumans, rather than domination.[83] "The assertion, imposition, and maintenance of settler sovereignty" and temporality entail an increasingly global "chrononormativity" in which settler time spreads itself across the globe through the annihilation of noncapitalist space by linear time.[84] Narratives of "end times" and apocalypse signal the underlying logic of settler time, in which time is a one-way street, perhaps headed for a brick wall. Indigenous temporalities in which settlers are periodic destroyers, or in which settler colonialism is a dystopia where the apocalypse has already occurred (again), also reject the politics of disposability that enable the creation of sacrifice zones.[85]

To address these complicated interconnections, my critique of property structures brings together critical whiteness and settler studies, Indigenous and Native American studies, and related insights from environmental and materialist feminisms, science and technology studies, sociology, geography, and environmental justice, among other fields. The critical settler perspective offered here is not innocent, and throughout the book I use an autoethnographic approach to elicit what insights may come from exploring the connections between my own position and the events and representations I analyze.[86] Rather than remaining entirely within the familiar disciplinary space of sociology, tracing connections between property, my own and others' settler upbringing, and the structures of feeling underlying environmental protest, destruction, and terror in the United States requires me to range abroad into the territory of fiction and story.

This book reflects that I wasn't able to chart a one-way path through this terrain, and therefore it shifts between the social, cultural, and political to the emotional. In an effort to express and evoke a series of questions about the role of property in settler environmental destruction,

I offer these reflections which come together to expose something ordinary, "a shifting assemblage of practices and practical knowledges, a
scene of both liveliness and exhaustion," that slides away from a direct
attempt at measuring.[87] These chapters approach the subject of settler
culture and property from different directions, in a gesture toward an
anti-colonial "multidimensionality" of worlds where ideas and practices
are "intertwined," and the past and future overlap.[88] I navigate through
these contradictory entanglements of cultural imaginations of time,
property ownership, and development, tracing their linkages through
historical context, representational practices, and moment-in-time
snapshots of extraction, sacrifice, and settler culture. Rather than serving as a definitive "map" of this territory, these chapters suggest alternative paths and connections with the goal of opening space for thought.

Real Estate: Environmental Justice and the Problem of Property

Reflecting the goals and ideologies of the first European settlers seeking
upward social mobility on this continent, real estate is the cornerstone
of the American dream.[89] In the transition away from feudal landownership patterns, the privatization of land in early modern England (i.e.,
the enclosures of the common lands that had been shared by community
members) vested individual owners with a "'real interest' in the land,
. . . as 'real estate,' . . . to do with it as they will."[90] Known as "fee simple"
property, it is considered by Anglo-American law to be "the highest and
purest form of property."[91] Completely severed from traditional relationships or entanglements, fee simple property represents the rejection
of feudal holdovers like the entailed estate.[92] Fee simple ownership of
real estate is the hyperlucid standard of clarity and fixity in the North
American economy.[93] Owning a home of one's own is a critical part of an
ideal American life, and in the suburbanization of the postwar twentieth
century, a small patch of grass in the suburbs offered a paradigmatic
way to reach this dream. In the postwar twentieth century, suburban
houses were mass produced and these suburbs democratized the ideal
of land ownership that was exemplified by the plantation rich and the
western homesteaders of the previous century to a broadening white
middle class.[94] The expansion of homeownership to the white middle
class was also rooted in a tradition of idealizing the rural landowner as

the quintessential American citizen.[95] These suburban "estates" became a primary signifier for economic security, full cultural citizenship, and social dignity, as an individual homeowner and head of household became the "king of his castle."

Real estate is also referred to as real property, and in Marxian terms is the primary means of production—the basic source of subsistence for humans on Earth.[96] Currently, private property largely determines relations between humans and more-than-human nature in the United States. Property ownership or the lack thereof conditions individuals' experiences of space and place. Social, economic, and environmental justice hinges on these relationships. Land is life, whether that means arable land, forest, access to water, etc. A lack of access to these natural sources of subsistence leaves a person at the mercy of those who own various forms of property (farms, factories, and other productive organizations), as an employee who eats only if her labor produces value for capital. Of course, this situation only seems natural to most people in the contemporary United States. This is another situation in which Indigenous perspectives are revealing, because as many Indigenous land-rights activists will tell you, money is no substitute for land.[97] Removing people's access to land and other more-than-humans (like the buffalo, slaughtered almost to extinction by settlers in the late nineteenth century) has been instrumental in the attempt to destroy Indigenous lifeways and sovereignty and to force assimilation to the US economy.[98] The invasion and settling of the American continent have been orchestrated and organized on the basis of private property ownership, which has historically signified an individual relationship between a (white/European) man and an objectified piece of nature. This quintessential property relationship has been created through settler state sovereignty. The settler state holds individual property ownership to be the only legitimate claim to land and through owning the land, to full citizenship.[99]

Property shapes environmental justice (or injustice) through the ability of wealthy property owners to use their political and economic power to protect their homes, communities, and regions from locally unwanted land uses such as waste disposal, toxic industry, or extraction.[100] These undesirable and harmful land uses are relegated to less powerful communities.[101] At the same time, industrial exploitation (elsewhere) and the accumulation of capital it enables increase elites' wealth and

therefore increase their ability to protect themselves from such externalities.[102] However, environmental problems don't recognize national
borders or legal boundaries such as property lines. Radiation, persistent
organic pollutants, and the effects of climate chaos can cross all barriers,
leaving traces of flame-retardant chemicals in everyone's blood.[103]

What's more, owning a piece of land, as an alienable (sellable) bit of
property, is a legal fiction constantly muddled by environmental conditions that don't respect legal or political boundaries, not to mention
animals, weeds, and other so-called uncivilized entities that frustrate
property owners' desires for control and self-reliance.[104] Private property is the performative effect of bracketing away the complications that
muddy its apparent clarity and fixity.[105] The state sovereignty underlying
private property also further complicates property law. The split estate
doctrine, which severs below-the-surface mineral rights from surface
rights to land, is a legal structure that creates conflicts between surface
and mineral owners over access to valuable resources underground. Because the surface stands in the way, usually the mineral rights owner
has preference and can insist on a "reasonable accommodation."[106] Legal
rights to property are also limited by eminent domain, when "the public
interest" allows government or corporations to use and access property
despite the owners' wishes.[107] These uses and legal battles raise questions about what property is, what rights it provides, and who is guaranteed these rights. What forms of human activity are made possible, and
which are foreclosed by this property structure and the cultural context
that gives it shape? In other words, how specifically does the centrality of
property ownership as both a cultural, material, and financial structure
in contemporary America contribute to the social and environmental
crisis we find ourselves in?

The Crisis

Due in part to the exhaustion of "easy" fossil fuel deposits, including
wider coal seams and conventionally accessible oil and gas reserves,
the extraction of fossil fuels is increasingly extending into new "unconventional" extraction methods. One of these, hydraulic fracturing and
horizontal drilling, has opened vast natural gas "plays" to extraction in
places ranging from Texas to New York.[108] The Marcellus Shale is a rock

formation containing vast amounts of natural gas on average a mile below the surface of the Appalachian Mountains. The complex technological developments commonly referred to as hydraulic fracturing or fracking have enabled a boom in natural gas extraction in the region. In West Virginia, this has led to the development of a new, larger, and more intrusive gas industry both within and expanding out from the historically important sites of the oil and gas industry. The Ohio River Valley is also the planned home of a new Appalachian Storage Hub where industrialists and politicians in West Virginia hope to attract investment to capture some of the "downstream" profits of natural gas processing and storage by developing a petrochemical complex to rival that of Louisiana's Saint James Parish.[109] This industrial zone in Louisiana is known as Cancer Alley due to the high cancer rates that plague the low-income communities living among the many petrochemical complexes in that area.[110]

Thus far in West Virginia, the effects of the natural gas boom have been a proliferation of larger, multi-well frack pads with underground "legs" that stretch out for miles in all directions; large compressor stations that pressurize the gas in preparation for piping it out through an expanding network of pipelines; other so-called midstream facilities; waste processing plants; and cracker plants. The future plans for a petrochemical complex on the Ohio will include more cracker plants, which break ethane down into ethylene and resin, a basis for manufacturing plastics.[111] The excess natural gas and natural gas liquids produced by fracking the Marcellus Shale provide literal fuel for the treadmill of production—natural gas is being extracted so quickly, a market must be developed for its use.[112] Whether the gas is needed, or whether new plastic manufacturing is wise, the rush to get the gas out reflects the "energy logic" or "energopower" Cara Daggett sees as the driving force behind fossil fuels that "aims to put the world to work, and to sacrifice any and all who are in the way of that vision."[113]

The natural gas industry speaks in terms of flows and streams: Upstream is the well itself. Midstream storage and transportation companies service downstream processing plants. At the same time as the rush is on to construct a mid- and downstream market in the planned Appalachian Storage Hub, an array of pipelines is planned to carry the gas away in all directions: to destinations on the Eastern Seaboard, to Canada, and to power plants in the South. These pipelines are bringing diverse communities across several states together in the experience of being drawn into a "spider's web," as an activist called the spreading network of wells, pipelines, and petrochemical facilities in the area.[114] As of this writing, despite the best efforts of the pipeline companies, parts of this web have been canceled due to their own pyramid scheme–like finances and interminable legal battles, while other parts are still struggling through lawsuits to receive official authorization.[115]

Although natural gas is promoted as a cleaner-burning alternative for use in power plants and vehicles, the largest component of natural gas, methane, is itself a dangerous greenhouse gas. In the short term, methane holds more heat than carbon, although it decays quickly.[116] Emissions of methane from fossil fuel extraction are an important contributor to global warming that need to be controlled as much as carbon emissions do.[117] Cracker plants and other natural gas processing techniques release toxic volatile organic compounds (like formaldehyde) into the air.[118] The "clean natural gas" campaign[119] also generally ignores the involvement of natural gas in the petrochemical and plastics industries. As The Climate Reality Project points out, developing the infrastructure for natural gas deepens the already existing inertia of fossil fuel path dependency and impedes the transition to renewable energy.[120]

The natural gas boom is only a small part of the overwhelming array of attacks on environmental health occurring around the world. In West Virginia alone, it competes for attention with the ongoing disaster of mountaintop removal coal mining, a decades-long project to mine as much coal as quickly as possible at the expense of the land, forests, water, and human communities.[121] However, despite a presidential candidate's promises during the 2016 campaign, coal mining jobs are not coming back.[122] Despite the coal industry's turn to mechanization, natural gas is often blamed for the economic shift away from jobs in coal.[123] Natural gas is challenging industrial and residential reliance on electric power from coal, and at the same time, it is increasingly intruding into places previously unfamiliar with industrial exploitation. The situation in West Virginia, where the natural gas boom is helping to move coal mining (at least ideologically) into the past at the same time as it intensifies the state's status as a sacrifice zone, exemplifies events that are happening in communities around the United States.

The documentary *Gasland*, by Josh Fox, begins with a description of how the beautiful natural conditions of Josh's childhood home in rural Pennsylvania had been contaminated and endangered by fracking.[124] It was a shock, in this wooded and secluded neighborhood, to experience the callous exploitation of the fossil fuel industry. The shock led him on a nationwide tour of sites of fracking and natural gas processing, as well as into an investigation of the industry's influence on government and regulatory agencies. Fox's surprise has been repeated over and over in the last decade as even the wealthy and privileged are confronted with the negative effects of the extraction economy.[125] This is challenging some of the comforting stories that middle- and upper-middle-class Americans tell ourselves about industrial society, including that waste can be kept "away" and that these sacrifices contribute to the common good.[126]

We are in the midst of what some scientists are calling the sixth extinction.[127] This is an anthropogenic crisis, as the name indicates, caused by "Man," and is estimated to be the largest extinction event since the end of the dinosaurs. Earth loses countless species every day, essential pollinators are endangered, new zoogenic pathogens arise, oceans are threatened by carbonic acid and plastic, and of course the overarching threat of global climate chaos puts human survival at risk unless action is taken in the next decade.[128] Some have named this period the Anthropocene, reflecting the importance of humanity as a primary geological influence. But these Anthropocene narratives identify "human society" with western civilization, whiteness, and global capitalism.[129] The prefix "anthropo" harkens back to the nineteenth-century singular, capitalized Man, the European-male-identified human subject imagined to be climbing a linear ladder of development that supposedly leaves other social forms in history's dustbin.[130] This image relegates other existing human societies to the past and treats their continued existence as irrelevant to the one-way path of human development. To borrow an image from feminist geographers J.K. Gibson-Graham, in place of this narrow evolutionary ladder of the western imagination, Black, Indigenous, and other people of color futurisms offer a multiplicity of possibilities.[131] As settler scholars Audra Mitchell and Aadita Chaudhury argue:

[BIPOC futurisms] center diverse, plural subjectivities and forms of agency, undermining homogenous notions of "humanity"; attune to nonlinear temporalities; and embrace lively practices of mobility and hybridity. In so doing, they imagine multiple futures and alternatives to apocalypse.[132]

These alternative future imaginaries represent hope in the face of the end of the status quo. What liberatory possibilities emerge as we turn away from the cis-hetero patriarchal white supremacist capitalist present?[133] The imagined futures in these narratives (the end of "civilization as we know it" or the flowering of human possibility enabled by the end of the structures and ideologies of white supremacism) are important because they shape the limits and possibilities of action, whether they are science writing or science fiction.[134] As Daniel Heath Justice (Cherokee Nation) explains, stories help us learn how to be human, how to be in relation with other humans and nonhumans, and how to get along with those different from us.[135]

Representing Anthropos: Béatriz and the Man

Some time ago, on the first day of my environmental justice class, I showed a short, animated video called "Man," by Steve Cutts.[136] The video portrays a devastating vision of humanity. The singular figure, Man, appears in a bucolic setting wearing a t-shirt marked with the word "Welcome." He then struts callously through the video, pulling a pair of snakes onto his feet as boots in the first scene, and working up to a frenzy of consumption and death by the end, all set to the music of Edvard Grieg's "In the Hall of the Mountain King." We see Man slaughter everything in his wake; a bear becomes a coat; squawking chickens and innocent cows enter a merciless automated abattoir; bleating lambs lose their limbs for Man's rapacious feast. The music swells to a crescendo and Man reaches a climax of industrial consumption and destruction. The video concludes with Man sitting on a throne atop a pile of garbage on a dead planet. He smokes a cigar with smug self-satisfaction. Finally, a pair of aliens land their flying saucer on the garbage pile, look around at Man and his kingdom, drag him off the throne, and stomp him flat. My students were divided on whether the aliens were angry about what they found on Earth or if they were just replicating Man's previous actions toward the animals. After the stomping they take off in their ship and Man's t-shirt remains legible atop the pile of garbage like a welcome mat.

Interestingly, as my students noted, the video portrays humanity as a singular person, specifically a white man. As a class we reflected about whose relationship to nature it depicts. Some thought it represented "the Man," i.e., powerful corporations, the West, or global capitalism. We wondered how the video would change if it had had a nonwhite male "Man" as its focus. Despite the video's name, there is not a singular generic kind of relationship possible between "Man" and "nature." On the contrary, the video portrays a very specific relationship, albeit one that has become hegemonic and is identified with humanity itself, which is the voracious capitalist appetite for destruction that characterizes the current environmental crisis.

The musical climax in the video is suggestive of the libidinal economy of the human-nature relationship it portrays. The narcissism of Man enables him to take and use the other inhabitants of the planet as objects of his desire with no corresponding intersubjectivity (i.e., no relationship between subjects or actors).[137] His consumption of the objects of his desire is deadly rather than generative. This highlights the ironic final image of the video when his t-shirt has become a welcome mat on top of a garbage dump. The welcome that the emergent Man received from Earth—the potential plenitude of plants, animals, and their symbiosis— becomes an empty promise because his appetite laid waste to the place and left him as the only subject, the only actor.

The deus ex machina of the alien stomping was surely overkill because Man had already destroyed his means of life—the land, water, air, and other living things he needs to survive. It is notable, however, that in the video his demise comes from an apparently "higher" life-form who treats him in the same manner he treats others, rather than from slow starvation on the garbage dump. Perhaps this intervention by alien life-forms represents a settler "move to innocence" or an effort to deflect capitalist and settler guilt without questioning the existence of colonization.[138] As Suzanne Kite (Oglala Lakota) remarks, in the "imagining of the alien colonization of Earth, the Euro-American becomes 'indigenous' through the act of being attacked."[139]

Property per se is not featured in the "Man" video, but it conditions the possibilities for the story it tells. A singular human being is not strictly speaking possible; humanity is a collective project. We are all born into a community, no matter how small or how cruelly structured. Human life is a shared effort requiring culture: language, knowledge, and technology. However, individual private property enables a performance of hyper-individuality and personal agency.[140] Legally and representationally it puts forth its owner as the prime mover, whether that be of a family, of which he is the head, of servants, whose labor he buys, or a corporation, of which he is the owner or CEO.[141] This concept is clearly expressed in a famous quote from John Locke:

> Thus the grass my horse has bit; the turfs my servant has cut; and the ore I have digged in any place, where I have a right to them in common with others, become my property, without the assignation or consent of any body. The labour that was mine, removing them out of that common state they were in, hath fixed my property in them [sic].[142]

This hierarchical "covering" of dependent servants by the legal identity of a white male property owner, as in the Anglo-American common law doctrine of "coverture" in which the legal identity of a married woman was absorbed by her husband's, is behind the scenes in the video.[143] The abattoir, factory, and house in which he devastates the animals, reduced to resources around him, appear to be animated by his will alone, although in reality this destruction would happen through the actions of other people whose labor he directs.[144]

Neither the workers who carry out these actions nor human community members who resist these actions are visible in Cutts's video. On one hand, it could be argued that the blame is squarely placed on the types of individuals most responsible for environmental destruction. On the other hand, this blame is distributed universally through the ontologically expansive name "Man." This name attributes the responsibility for the crisis to "Mankind" or to the essence of human nature, in an "'All-Lives-Matter'-ing of the climate crisis."[145] This generalized blame is a common feature of what Mitchell and Chaudhury call white apocalypse narratives, which place the blame for the crisis on a supposedly capitalist human nature and then proceed to focus their attention on the survival of the pioneer-like subjects of western civilization.[146] These narratives (common in both fictional and nonfictional media) center the experience, lifestyle, and concerns of the wealthy global North while consigning the majority of human beings to the background, to the status of canaries in the coal mine, or to becoming spectacular victims. Similarly, the environmentalist message of the animated video "Man" erases less powerful human communities and the other human worlds that are being destroyed along with the more-than-humans who are shown in the video.[147] These other human worlds don't even seem to merit representation. This erasure also confines the future imaginary to a singular dead-end ladder of human development.

A feature film by Puerto Rican director Miguel Arteta, *Béatriz at Dinner*, repeats some of the themes from the animated video "Man." The story is told from the point of view of a Mexican immigrant and holistic healer (Béatriz, played by Salma Hayek) in coastal California who ends up unexpectedly joining a dinner party of super-wealthy white people when her car doesn't start after a massage appointment at a friendly client's house.[148] One member of the party, the most important one, is a hotel development financier (Doug, played by John Lithgow). Doug seems to be a representation of "the Man," a similar figure if not the same person who bought the land where Béatriz grew up. We are shown in flashbacks that a developer built a resort and displaced her community, leaving its members without access to clean water and other resources that had been their livelihood and causing them to make their way as immigrants to the United States. In the conversations before and during the dinner, it is clear Béatriz knows the value of things, while the others take life much less seriously.

Béatriz almost ruins the dinner party for the first time with her heartfelt critique of big game hunting. This exclusive entertainment for the very rich is enabled by wealth stemming from the kind of resort development that was implicated in the ruin of her family's homeplace. After getting "too emotional" at dinner, she is sent away to bed. Her ultimate powerlessness is revealed when her vivid fantasy of killing Doug fades away to inaction. Her critiques are erased by the privilege of entitled wealth to enjoy thoughtless entertainments at the expense of everyone else. After the jocular discussion of the hunt, and after Béatriz goes to bed, the partiers light illegal paper lanterns that use lit candles to float up into the sky and away over the drought-ridden California hills. When she returns to the party, Béatriz finally angers her client's husband, the party host, to the point that he kicks her out of the house. She is left to the mercy of a tow-truck driver, whom she will not be able to afford to pay, for a ride home. In the end she does the partygoers' work for them and swims out into the ocean, alone.

Béatriz can't make it in the world of the developer and his friends. A low-income holistic healer, she could be an invisible background character in the "Man" video who helps him manage the pains caused by overindulgence. Béatriz's suicide is a disappointing end to the film for the viewer, after being teased by the murder of Doug, which felt very justified even though that too could have ended her life. The film thus gives a voice but no power to the human victims of "Man," who share the suffering with the more-than-humans he destroys. The multimillion-dollar property of the client, a palatial gated property overlooking the Pacific Ocean that makes its owners virtually untouchable, frames the film and limits Béatriz's actions.

Béatriz at Dinner offers us what Tanana Athabascan scholar Dian Millon calls "felt theory," or the embodied emotional knowledge that is foreclosed by reductive western rationalism.[149] Like Béatriz's intuitive identification of Doug and big game hunting with the hotel developer who displaced her family, felt theory emphasizes the holistic knowledge that is rendered unsayable in techno-rational discourse. In the film, Béatriz demonstrates for the viewer the connections between hierarchical identity formations that structure the master/owner identity in western culture. The master identity is not limited to masculinity, whiteness, and property ownership, but it is formed by linking these identities and others in a hierarchical structure that opposes them to femininity, blackness, and indigeneity, and the nonpropertied among other things.[150] As the identifying characteristics of those who were enabled by the state to own property and have it defended, whiteness and maleness are tied up with the notion of property ownership. As property ownership was a prerequisite for democratic participation, it is also linked to rationality and self-governability.[151] Other ways of knowing, and other ways of relating to each other, to nonhumans, and land, were excluded and marked as female, domestic, and irrational through the violence of colonization.[152] This devaluation is a strategy of accumulation, shifting wealth and resources into the hands of an elite.[153] The land identified as "wilderness" or "waste" thus becomes a frontier for claiming and developing natural and human resources for profit.[154]

Whiteness, masculinity, and property are not only co-constitutive in US history, but they share a structural organization; they are similarly structured by negation, separation, and fixity. Whiteness (meaning the ideologies and structures of white supremacism) relies on notions of purity and separation, echoing the right of exclusion inherent in private property ownership. Whiteness and property are relations of domination that depend on asserting control over marginalized people and nature. This "mindset of the frontier" that seeks to assert control operates through the mobilization of a "paradigmatic Indianness."[155] This paradigmatic Indianness is an imagined state of primal freedom (embodied in "Indians"). In this imagination, there is no culture without private property, and therefore Indianness signifies the frontier fantasy of a freewheeling absence of fixed property structures and of hierarchical sociality, where "lawlessness" reigns and there seems to exist a possibility for freedom from the constraints of western culture. However, due to the racialized and gendered developmental ideology of settler culture, this frontier lawlessness promises lawless freedom for the masculine frontiersman but simultaneously foreshadows the supposedly inevitable imposition of "civilized" hierarchical structures and sociality through settlement and the establishment of white property.[156] The western tradition values this eternalized social hierarchy above the immediate and material relations of Indigenous Peoples existing in place and denies the importance of things and experiences marked subjective, concrete, and emotional.[157]

Standing Rock Sioux scholar Vine Deloria Jr. notes that the universalistic imagination of Christianity sees an eternal sacred *utopia* (no-place) as its scene of action and as its endpoint, whereas many of the practices considered under the umbrella of Indigenous spirituality are occupied with the maintenance of right relationships in place in the everyday.[158] Deloria thus suggests that one difference between Indigenous worldviews and that of European Christian settlers consists in the separation of "religion" and "morals" from other categorical sections of life, such as "business." These categorical separations in settler culture contradict the importance of the everyday practice of good relations in Indigenous traditions.[159] Settler scholar David Delgado Shorter further notes that the imposition of western categories such as "spirituality" onto Indigenous worldviews is another tool of colonization. "Spirituality," as a constrained category in western culture, erases the practical material and scientific knowledges contained in Indigenous worldviews. "Spirituality" as a label reduces "Indigenous traditions and land claims and wisdom tradition to sacred matters rather than rational science" which renders them insignificant from the point of view of settler politics.[160] He therefore urges the adoption of "relation" to describe the human and more-than-human worlds of Indigenous knowledges. Tallbear also emphasizes the importance of relations in creating flourishing life:

> Making or creating kin can call non-Indigenous people (including those who don't fit easily into the "settler" category) to be more accountable to Indigenous lifeways long constituted in intimate relation with this place. Kinship might inspire change, new ways of organizing and standing together in the face of state violence against both humans and the land.[161]

As the above discussion suggests, ownership of land paradoxically represents both an effort at fixity and an abstraction from materiality. On the one hand, owning nature is a foolish attempt to nail down an ever-changing landscape shaped by geological and climatological forces.[162] On the other hand, capitalist property remains necessarily alienable. This means that as a commodity, it always already exists within an abstract system of value measured against other equivalent properties or other commodities for which it can be traded.[163] Through property, the human relation to land becomes more personal in the sense that the piece of land is said to be owned by one individual person (or group). At the same time, it becomes less personal in that it is an object (a piece of real estate) equivalent to other objects (other pieces of real estate), without intersubjectivity (or relationship) between that person and itself.[164]

This one-sided relationship between owner and land is analogous to related forms of social organization. Its structural affinity with the nuclear family contributed to the growth of homeownership especially among white, middle-class Americans in the mid-twentieth century.[165]

Each ideal American nuclear family is hierarchically organized from the head of household down to the children and their pets, and owns their own small "estate," with lawn and garden. Monogamous marriage offers each partner "property" in the other, although traditionally this property relation was also one-sided.[166] Each family operates independently and promotes itself through a kind of entrepreneurialism of economic productivity, healthy middle-class hygiene, and patriotic consumption.[167] As Talcott Parsons described it, this independent breadwinner/caretaker family suits the needs of the economy. Its organizational hierarchy and geographic flexibility allow each family to "find its place" in the economic structure, similar to how each nation-state was said to find its place in the postwar global order of economic modernization.[168] The isolated household enabled by federally subsidized homeownership and automobility furthered this imagined independence. These new households also contributed to the demand for an ever-expanding consumer culture fueled by petroleum and petrochemical products—aiming toward a Jetsons-like future of high mass consumption, heteronormativity, and space suburbs.[169]

In addition to the imagined independence of the nuclear family household, settler culture is characterized by a sense of entitlement to nature (i.e., manifest destiny) according to settler scholar Eva Mackey. This sense of entitlement to nature and natural resources is co-constituted by wholly unfounded expectations of certainty (for example, in the name of "a good business climate").[170] This cultural imagining relies on a notion of inert, passive nature (an object) and the singular importance of human agency. Such ideologies that naturalize both the process of industrial modernization and the nuclear family rely on a human/nature dualism. French science studies scholar Bruno Latour argues that (western) modernity ideologically separates the matters of the world into the political or social on one hand (i.e., the human), and the natural on the other. Nature then stands in for objectivity and underlines the morality of the social order (i.e., through Natural Law).[171] The social is seen as the realm of human control over the natural world, as reflected in the video "Man." This peculiar (western) modernity is defined by the hyper-exploitation of the biophysical world, and the denial of complexity in the relation between biophysical nature and the human social world. The pervasive denial of the interdependency between humans and the more-than-human is demonstrated effectively in Cutts's video; Man seems to be doing fine until he is killed by the aliens. It would have been more realistic for him to simply starve to death due to the destruction of his habitat, and perhaps that image would have offered a more effective environmentalist message. However, the apparently necessary intervention by a "higher" life-form illustrates the video's representational investment in the independence of "Man" from the biosphere. Similarly, although Béatriz suffers the consequences of her encounter with the wealthy dinner guests, her hosts and their guests themselves appear to be invulnerable to the flames they send out over the dry California hills.

For Latour, this conceptual ordering of the social as separate from objectified nature has enabled a flourishing of social-natural hybrid "monsters"—like the climate crisis, the automobile-dependent suburb, and the pipeline—that are increasingly escaping human control.[172] These out-of-control "monsters" grow unchecked because the relationship between nature and culture is repressed and denied.[173] However, in relationships between equals, the effects of actions on all parties must be considered, and it is not possible for one party to control the actions of another.[174] This openness to others' autonomy represents precarity as defined by Anna Tsing, "the condition of being vulnerable to others," which is a baseline of "collaborative survival."[175] Modern attempts to control and objectify more-than-human nature enable its exploitation and destruction along with the associated effects of this attempted control on human social forms.[176] Regardless of the (western) modern investment in separating the social from the natural, Earthly relations extend beyond the human to more-than-human entities and landforms.[177] Living in right relation is a way of respecting the webs of indeterminant interdependency that support life on Earth.[178] Represented by Béatriz's sensitivity in the film, these interdependencies are narrated in many Indigenous knowledge systems in terms of ecologies, cosmologies, kinships, or trickster figures who crisscross the modern partitioning of human/nonhuman, life/death, and past/present.[179] Indigenous knowledges reflect practices that occur in places, rather than abstractions away from the particular.[180] The divergent understandings of treaty, discussed above, as a contract or bill of sale as opposed to a guide to new relations in place, illustrate the same distinction. The settler signatories saw their Indigenous counterparts, and the landforms the settlers were bent on conquering, as objects to be dominated instead of as possible relations.[181]

Another characteristic of the western dualistic illusion is its universalist self-image, or the characteristically white colonizing "ontological expansiveness" that expects entry everywhere, and access to all knowledge.[182] Whereas all Peoples have knowledge about how the world works, the supposed "confusion" between humanity and nature (or in other words the respect for these interdependencies) that characterizes so-called nonscientific worldviews undermines their claims to scientific knowledge in the "modern" sense.[183] Moderns have "the Truth" (objective science), and the supposedly "backward" ideas of the rest are relegated to the past.[184] However, the distinctiveness of modern (western) societies' knowledges is of course illusory; we all share the same entanglements of the human and more-than-human in how we live and how we understand. The difference is in how we organize these entanglements in more or less sustainable ways. Discursive materialism explores how cultural categories determine our perceptions and interactions with other humans and more-than-humans and how these others in turn shape human cultural practices.[185] The crisis of climate change makes it ever more evident that the nature/culture dualism dominant in science and the larger US social formation limits our understanding of both social and more-than-human processes.[186]

Representations of settler time and western developmentalism like the video "Man" impose a one-way ordering on knowledge that places non-Indigenous people at the forefront, and therefore it may be necessary to underline the fact that Indigenous knowledges from Turtle Island and elsewhere have been, are, and will be critical to world politics, science, and technology, especially in light of the current crisis.[187] Indigenous knowledges are not fixed in the past as they are portrayed in settler culture, but live and develop in conversation with other knowledges in fluid relation with contemporary issues.[188] What Glen Coulthard (Yellowknives Dene) calls grounded normativity refers to the practical reasoning that grows though experiences in place. These experiences reveal the importance of reciprocal interdependencies between humans and more-than-humans.[189] The new materialisms that have emerged from the (re)discovery of subject-object entanglements in western thought are often inspired by Indigenous knowledges, worldviews, and scholars—although sometimes without recognition.[190] Mutual aid, consent-based ethics, and respect for human and nonhuman relations are both the means and ends of this process.[191]

Plan of the Book

The chapters in this book are focused on various aspects of private property as a structure of settler culture in the United States. The book is, in other words, an exploration of a world shaped by private property. As human beings we experience a biophysical reality too vast and open-ended to be contained in a single story.[192] But we require stories to shape the worlds we are born into "to help us find ways of meaningful being in . . . whatever contexts we've inherited."[193] A story builds a perceivable "world" through an aesthetic ordering imposed on the open-endedness of biophysical reality, and private property is an essential aesthetic and political ordering principle of settler worlds.[194] Stories offer holistic knowledge of worlds and their inner logics, and in this book I seek to trace connections between everyday lives and experiences of property in the current environmental crisis and the stories that we use to help make sense of these lives and this crisis.[195]

This book takes a critical settler perspective in an attempt to denaturalize the story of private property and problematize the existence of the United States as a settler colony and erstwhile global hegemon. This perspective draws from Indigenous materialism, which involves recognizing the agency of the nonhuman.[196] It also decenters the ideology of modernization that drives the treadmill of production and the privatization, industrialization, and financialization that contribute to the contemporary ecological crisis. The modern imperative of work, productivism, and efficiency has led to a perception that "all energy exchanges on Earth that are not being exploited by human industry can be considered waste, including waterfalls and each ray of sunlight."[197] Productivism was integral to the ideology of "terra nullis" which justified the theft of Indigenous territory on this continent and in Australia; all that was not owned and exploited fell under this umbrella of waste.[198] When settlers observed Indigenous social forms, they perceived sustainable subsistence practices as inefficient because these practices neither centered individual property ownership nor maximized production, and they deemed sustainable reproductive strategies immoral because these strategies neither controlled women's sexuality nor maximized family size.[199]

The chapters in this book offer an exploration from various directions of how private property and the settler cultures it shapes underlie the current unsustainable and damaging set of relations between the US state, its human inhabitants, and the more-than-human beings around us. I proceed through triangulation to trace the role of property in our collective environmental crisis. Tracing the connecting threads between different cases, scales, and registers draws out the embeddedness of settler culture and property in everyday structures of feeling. Drawing on Dian Million's felt theory and Avery Gordon's *Ghostly Matters*, this approach aims to elicit notice of what is apparently absent in positivist analysis.[200] The tools I've assembled for this examination include an analysis of cases of environmental injustice involving marginal and privileged property, and a consideration of the limitations of white-centered politics in controversies about control of land or other natural resources. I also follow the traces of property through fictional narratives of the (white) apocalypse which contain various future imaginaries of the settler state, in an exploration of how these narratives of the future reveal anxieties around the environment and extractive industry.

Finally, I draw on ethnographic fieldwork in West Virginia, to illuminate the role of property in the natural gas fracking and pipeline boom. Two ethnographic snapshots bring the themes of the previous chapters together and are drawn from 24 open-ended interviews and observations conducted in 2017–18 in nine West Virginia counties. Participants included property owners, health and cultural professionals, activists, and industry associates. All were white; 13 were men and 11 women. I also attended public meetings, talks, and actions conducted by pipeline opponents and their organizations. I learned directly about the role of property in this development from area residents and others who oppose fracking and the pipeline projects, as well as from media coverage of groups like Appalachians Against Pipelines, who support more radical actions including tree sitting and blockades. However, rather than representing an ethnography of fracking in West Virginia, these chapters focus on the entanglements of settler culture and private property in the creation of a sacrifice zone, and how the contradictions raised in conflicts over natural gas extraction and transportation reveal fault lines in the foundations of these structures.[201]

Hegemonic conceptions of settler time (western history) as a universal category for human experience limit our imagination of other possible future trajectories. This imagination remains fixed on the limited forms of agency authorized by settler legal formations, which pretend to encompass all of human possibility, and which enable extractive capitalism.[202] Reflecting on "settler common sense" about the inevitability of the settler state, its legal arrangements, and its definition of sovereignty enables an exploration of the limits of this "whitestream" worldview.[203] This exploration contributes to the conditions of possibility for thinking differently about the future of this continent, specifically through Land Back, or the movement for return of territory to Indigenous sovereignty.[204] The chapters in this book illustrate the damages, contradictions, and impossibilities imposed by contemporary settler culture, which increasingly make clear the necessity for (non-metaphorical) decolonization.[205] Settler colonialism attempts to render other possible ways of living unimaginable. In this book, I am offering a critique of the property structures that naturalize settler colonialism and its effects on this continent.

In the words of Vine Deloria Jr., white settler culture, based as it is on individual property ownership and capitalist market relations, depends "primarily upon the exploitation of land, people, and life itself."[206] Decolonization means returning land to Indigenous sovereignties and transforming the individualistic property regimes of land use and conservation in favor of systems more closely aligned with both human and more-than-human *thrivance*.[207] Therefore these chapters represent a small utopian demand, in the spirit of Cara Daggett, who argues:

> The utopian demand must [offer] . . . some measure of practicality—it should be achievable (even if difficult) in the present—while also opening humans up to radically different visions of life. Importantly, the purpose of the utopian demand is not to map out the precise contours of a future society or set of policies. Rather, it is in the very act of making utopian demands that humans engage in a process of becoming different, of becoming new kinds of political subjects.[208]

Chapter 1 examines how property, as the cornerstone of both social and political organization in the US settler-colonial system, generates protection for some and vulnerability for others. Property is linked with personhood, national identity, and rights, and yet in some cases can be so marginal that it begins to function as a form of necropolitics in which the state disinvests in populations whose property works against the logic of patriarchal personhood.[209] These marginalized populations are excluded from neoliberal civil society.[210] Thus, ownership of some forms of property contributes to the economic marginalization and vulnerability of the owners. However, the legal personhood of wealthy citizens and property owners is enhanced by the property they own and the collective capital represented by their privileged neighborhoods. Nevertheless, the chapter makes the case that the biopolitics of property that are reflected in NIMBY[211] movements are fundamentally at odds with the extractive economy of late fossil fuel society.

Chapter 2 examines three cases of "white" environmental protest: the Bundy ranch standoff and subsequent takeover of the Malheur Nature Preserve, the Sierra Club's involvement in the anti-mountaintop removal campaign in West Virginia, and grassroots environmentalism in that state against MTR, fracking, and pipelines. These movements are fraught with contradictory and irreconcilable tensions due to their underpinnings in settler colonialism and white supremacism. The alienation from other humans and from nature which underlies settler culture and the property relation forces the cases of white protest under consideration here into a binary logic of expressing white saviorism or racialized injury. I argue that anti-capitalist and anti-colonial environmental movements need to take these settler cultural structures into account.

Chapter 3 shifts the scene to popular culture, examining three narratives of settler futurity to reveal contemporary anxieties about fossil fuels and extraction. Eschatology, or the theological study of the end times, figures largely in each of these "petro-melancholic" stories. These include a short story, "People of Sand and Slag" (2004), the TV show *Revolution* (NBC 2012–14), and the Netflix movie *Cargo* (2018). Each of these three narratives explores a dystopic future in which the conditions of life in fossil fuel–addicted settler society result in various apocalyptic scenarios: the total destruction of recognizable life, a reconstruction of the American frontier, and finally, the elimination of the settler from

Australia. Contrasting these with the examples of Indigenous science fiction writers, this chapter demonstrates how these imaginaries limit the range of imaginable actions in the interest of sustainable economies and cultures. The elements of settler culture explored in these imaginaries pave the way for the ethnographic explorations in the last section of the book.

Chapter 4 examines the conditions of an expanding sacrifice zone in West Virginia. In 2017, it became known that Chinese investors had signed a memorandum of understanding with political and industry leadership in West Virginia, with the goal of building a petrochemical complex on the Ohio River, known as the Appalachian Chemical Storage Hub.[212] This, as well as the expansion through a spider web–like arrangement of pipelines exporting the fracked gas from the state, has made it clear that the industrial exploitation of West Virginia is far from finished even if coal declines in importance. Moreover, this web of natural gas extraction, transportation, and processing is expanding into previously bucolic, peaceful, "almost heaven" West Virginia, where farmers and back-to-the-land flower children have lived in relative serenity while other parts of the state were blasted apart for coal. The intensification of West Virginia's long-term status as a sacrifice zone thus leads to a problematization of settler futurity, as residents face the forcible interruption of their property rights and expectations.

Chapter 5 examines some of the cracks that are emerging in the foundations of settler culture, which provide a window into that culture as well as, optimistically, the possibility for decolonization and right relationship. Metaphors and comparisons to Indigenous dispossession and the theft of Indigenous land are prevalent in anti-pipeline and fracking politics. But these politics also mobilize a discourse of constitutional property rights that reflect people's affective belonging to the settler state. In this chapter, I trace three contradictions in settler culture brought out by the stresses of fracking and the pipeline boom. What can we make of these contradictions? What possibilities for new forms of environmental politics and liberation could emerge from a serious consideration of the role of private property in our current environmental crisis?

The conclusion centers on an Indigenous story of a settler apocalypse, *Moon of the Crusted Snow*, by Anishinaabe writer Waubgeshig Rice.[213] This story of a fictional Anishinaabe community in what is currently known as northern Ontario highlights some of the alternative future imaginaries and forms of sovereignty that make a different relationship to this continent possible. This is a story of how Anishinaabe traditions of resistance and "Original Instructions" fill the gap left by the failure of settler infrastructure, values, and material culture when the power suddenly goes out for good.[214]

1

Keystone, Flint, and Porter Ranch

The Property Bind

If an object you . . . control is bound up in your future plans
or in your anticipation of your future self, and it is partly
these plans for your own continuity that make you a person,
then your personhood depends on the realization of these
expectations.
—Margaret Jane Radin

The concept of private property in land is a useful focal point for thinking about cultural ideas about personhood and citizenship, political
economic ideas about market interactions, and the environmental
effects of industrial development. Private property is key to the capitalist mode of production, but also to its "mode of life."[1] What does
property have to do with our self-concepts, with how we imagine the
market functioning, and with how these interact and leave us exposed
to environmental toxins? In this chapter I dive into a consideration
of the role of property as a foundational structure underpinning
culture, politics, and environmental catastrophe. Property figures
significantly in a tension that has existed since the earliest days of the
post-revolutionary United States between two ideals of the body politic.
In part, the political project of the United States represented a reflection of the radical republican notion of commonwealth, of equality, and
anti-hierarchy. Characters like Natty Bumppo from James Fenimore
Cooper represented the humble everyman who was supposed to thrive
in the fledgling United States, learning from and replacing the Indigenous inhabitants. However, this more radical notion of (limited, white)
brotherhood as a characteristic of the US polity was rapidly surpassed
by an elite and liberal market rationality based on competitive and possessive individualism.[2]

The classical liberal capitalist logic of the free market, peopled by property-owning white men pursuing their own self-interest, became the primary political theory that expressed the most significant ideas about what freedom could entail in the United States by the end of the nineteenth century.[3] In other words, Natty Bumppo was replaced by Andrew Carnegie. Property ownership emerged not only as the substance of citizenship but as the major source of rights (i.e., what kinds of protections one could expect from the government) in the legal structure during this time.[4] Today, property ownership is a cornerstone of American political, economic, and cultural citizenship, with the identity of "homeowner" expressing a key element of the American dream of independence, freedom, and material comfort.[5] Ironically, homeowning became a possibility for much of the white middle class only due to the social programs of the postwar era, including the GI Bill and other federal subsidies. Since the 1970s, a rebirth of the classical liberal free-market ideals has brought waves of deregulation, privatization, and disinvestment in public goods. Known as neoliberalism, this philosophy has reinforced the idealization of property ownership and centered the free market as the primary or preferred form of human activity, while increasing the gap between rich and poor.[6]

In the European monarchies from which many early settlers originated, white male property owners were the only subjects with full civil, political, and economic rights, because they were the only people who were seen as "independent," that is, not dependent on another person's patronage.[7] This understanding of political participation as being properly limited to "independent" white men migrated along with settlers to the United States and institutionalized their race, gender, and class privilege in legal and cultural structures such as universal white male suffrage and the concept of the "head of household."[8] Today, the historical consequences of this privilege are visible in the fact that poor women of color bear an unequal burden of environmental risk as a result of intersecting environmental racism and other forms of institutional racism, sexism, and classism.[9] In the social sciences, property ownership is understood to be related most obviously to the sociological categories of class or socioeconomic status. However, as discussed in the introduction, property can be considered more holistically as a complex material and ideological framework that shapes and constrains the human relation to other humans and nonhuman nature. Ownership or the lack of property creates relationships between families and between individuals in families and concretizes structural racism and sexism.[10] As such, it provides a window into the mutual constitution of multiple, intersecting forms of inequality.[11] What's more, property has a material agency or causative force in determining the life chances of differently propertied individuals and groups. We can see "her shape and his hand" or the traces of the historical agency of owners and the erasure of those treated as property, in the contemporary evidence provided by radically different conditions of life.[12] Therefore, used as a lens of analysis, property provides an opportunity to dissect the environmental, material, or biophysical construction of these intersecting forms of inequality.

Intersectionality is a concept that expresses the experience of Black women, whose perspectives are erased from abstract categorical analyses of gender, race, or class.[13] Intersectionality is a theory of social inequality that emphasizes the mutual construction and interdependency of concepts that have been treated as theoretically distinct categories in social science. For example, when the term environmental racism was coined following the publication of the United Church of Christ's report *Toxic Wastes and Race in the United States* in 1987, scholars began to debate the cause of the disproportionate siting of locally unwanted land uses (LULUs, i.e., toxic waste dumps, landfills, and other toxic facilities) in poor communities of color.[14] This debate centered on which abstract category (race or class) was responsible for this pattern of siting toxic industries or disposal sites in communities of color.[15] In other words, is it really racism, or is it simply market forces that determine where these facilities are located and the concentration of Black people and other people of color near these toxic sites? An intersectional lens reveals how focusing on the binary question of race versus class obscures the mutual construction of race and class formations in the United States, where the history of property ownership (and therefore wealth) is racialized, where the racially segmented labor market restricts opportunities, and where residential segregation enforces racialized geographies that make it impossible to separate the two categories in understanding environmental inequalities.[16] This intersectional complexity is also expressed in the multifaceted grassroots activism of women of color and others who defy the limits of labels (such as environmentalist, concerned citizen, or civil rights activist) in their fight to protect their communities and children from the combined effects of social, cultural, political, and economic factors that lead to diminished life chances.[17]

The very complexity of environmental inequalities, whether they stem from workplace exposures, from LULUs near residential communities, or from toxic "accidents" such as oil spills or chemical leaks, or some combination of such causes, reflects the difficulty of labeling Environmental Justice (EJ) activism in traditional political terms. Many of these groups of "concerned citizens" must do identity politics, class politics, and environmental politics simultaneously to account for the complex causes of environmental injustices.[18] Laura Senier and colleagues have called for an analysis of what they term the socio-exposome, a concept that encapsulates the cumulative, socially generated exposures to environmental risks and amenities over the course of time for an individual or community. This terminology reflects the problem's highly complex and multiscalar nature. Various forms of discrimination, daily stress, and features of the built environment are just a few of the factors that contribute to unequal health outcomes for communities.[19]

What Patricia Hill Collins calls "Eurocentric masculinist thought" represents the dominant paradigm of knowledge production in the western modernist tradition.[20] Like the debate over whether race or class is to blame for the disproportionate exposure of communities of color to toxins, this paradigm relies on abstract categories that reflect so-called objective facts, and often invokes a property fence or "bright line" between categories, disciplines, or types of knowledge.[21] This type of intellectual segmentation between categories of things that are labeled spiritual or scientific, environmental or economic, social or political, creates barriers to holistic comprehension.[22] The tradition that Collins names Black feminist thought disrupts this "colonial agnosia," or conditioned unrecognition, that resists seeing patterns, contexts, and connections.[23]

This chapter uses the lens of property to conduct a discursive materialist contextual analysis of environmental inequalities. Considering the ideological and material effects of US legal property systems on the construction of individuals as rights-bearing citizens may reveal how overlapping layers of legal, cultural, and material structures are implicated in environmental politics. As a cultural ideal, real estate ownership is normally considered to be an addition to personal power or agency, either through wealth accumulation or through heightened social mobility. However, despite the fact that real property ownership implies a commitment to place (i.e., owning a specific piece of land or fixed property), that piece of property must provide at least the possibility of mobility in order to be effective as an augmentation of personal agency. This underscores the centrality of the abstract terrain of the idealized free market to ideas of sociality and freedom.

The three case studies considered here are interesting because they don't have much in common on the surface. Each offers a distinct form of environmental harm in a very different context, from a lack of water infrastructure in the West Virginia coalfields, to the municipal water crisis of Flint, Michigan, to the natural gas leak in Porter Ranch, California. The fact that the cases appear unrelated and unconnected to each other disguises their underlying structural similarity. Despite their differences, they are all cases of environmental injustice in which property ownership specifically plays a central role in empowerment or disempowerment. This analysis may shed light on both how environmental injustices are structurally produced and how these political structures may be transformed in the future.

Property as a Material and Ideological Framework of Identity and Inequality

The institution of property in land is one of the most basic technologies structuring the relationships of humans to their biophysical surroundings. Rather than stemming from natural law (as argued by Locke), property is constructed by state-sponsored techniques including precise and standardized measurements, cadastral surveys, cartography, and accounting, and it relies on these to shape routines, land use, and the market in land.[24] Sacrosanct in the liberal tradition, individual private property is at the heart of Anglo-American law and notions of justice. For much of American history, political and economic rights were conceived of as stemming from property ownership, and property ownership was largely limited to white men.

Despite the existence of diverse Indigenous and colonial property regimes in the so-called New World, the US Constitution conceived of and institutionalized political and economic rights as stemming primarily from individual fee simple property ownership, specifically the rights to manage, control, and sell real property.[25] These rights to buy and sell (or alienate) real property are citizenship rights that stem from the underlying primacy of state sovereignty (the Crown in Canada, the federal government in the United States). This settler state sovereignty claims the ultimate right to be the source and guarantor of property rights and superior jurisdictional authority.[26] The distribution of property reflects the historical institutionalization of privilege discussed above; in 2001, white Americans owned 98 percent of the agricultural land in the United States, and in 2012, 86.3 percent of such land was owned by men.[27]

The legal institution of property embodied in these clusters of rights increases the individual property owner's agency through the ability to enlist the state in maintaining these rights, and this enhanced agency or personal power is an important part of everyday white American culture. This augmented agency is observable in the form of "Stand your ground" laws and the castle doctrine which permit deadly violence in the defense of white individuals and their property.[28] For settler scholar Kevin Bruyneel, this exemplifies settler memory, in which the naturalized right of the historical settler to "circle the wagons" and defend the (often illegal) settlement from (Indigenous) attackers is both evoked and minimized in everyday language.[29] The limits of this agency for nonwhite people is also clear, as evidenced by the cases of Siwatu-Salama Ra and Philando Castile, among many others.[30] The institution of property can thus be considered a constitutive element of white masculinity in the United States, or in Steve Garlick's words, as part of a "technology of embodiment that functions to stabilize the self . . . [signifying that] control over nature is central . . . to the ontological security offered by [white] masculinity."[31]

Reflecting this need for control and perhaps anticipating the incompatibility of unlimited extractive development with human habitation of the continent, elements of the US environmental movements of the late nineteenth century launched a limited challenge to the ideal of individually held property. Specifically, the preservationist movement at least raised the question of the ecological sustainability of the market in land and natural resources when it began to argue for the necessity of removing wilderness and other resources from the market for their protection. Ironically, because of Fredrick Jackson Turner's frontier thesis, which theorized that it was the wilderness as proving ground that created Americans' exceptional character, the health, independence, and vigor of white masculinity and the family structure it maintained were profound motivators for this preservationist movement.[32] Accordingly, the question of who belongs to the "public" of public land ownership was essential to the idea of protecting nature. Racialized and classed notions of who were appropriate users characterized the development of the National Park Service and Forest Service, and this remains a persistent question in the present.[33]

Land use and ownership were central to the first stirrings of environmental consciousness in the US settler state. The preservationist "wilderness idea" mapped a system of exploitability and value onto North America in which sites of industrialization and development were cognitively separated from sites with a perceived inherent value. This reflected the human/nature dualism that obscures the interconnection of human health and well-being with so-called environmental pollution.[34] These distinctions are evident in the cases under consideration. In the late nineteenth century, burgeoning industrial exploitation in the form of the emergent coal, oil, and gas industries in West Virginia, and the timber and meatpacking industries of the Midwest, contrasted with the bucolic ranchlands characteristic of the San Fernando Valley.[35] In the mid-twentieth century, growing concern with the effects of chemicals on human health, expressed in Rachel Carson's *Silent Spring*, refocused the US environmental movement on the connections between environmental health and human well-being.[36] However, the most immediate victims of the environmental crisis were workers or poor residents of industrial areas, and these vulnerable communities have often been rendered invisible in debates over environmental regulation and protection.

This reflects what Michael McIntyre and Heidi Nast refer to as the dialectic of biopolitics and necropolitics.[37] This historical materialist perspective forces a consideration of the dispossessions caused by slavery and settler colonialism as intrinsic to the modern American institution of property.[38] In both, the suffering and hyper-exploitation of Black and Indigenous people served as "racial subsidies" for white American property accumulation, which today structures the wealth and property hierarchies reflected in the United Church of Christ's report mentioned above.[39] Biopolitics represent an investment by the state in the health of populations, in the interest of a healthy and productive society. In neoliberalism the free market becomes the model for all human activity, thus public health becomes the responsibility of individuals and their consumer activity. The biopolitics of neoliberalism, which compels individual participation in a routine of self-surveillance, self-improvement, and healthism (i.e., the moral imperative to be healthy) relies on the notion that the individual has value to the market.[40] Healthism is an ideology that equates good health with moral worthiness, and conversely, sees poor health as an individual failing. This moral worthiness is the key to national belonging, or to being accepted as an upstanding member of society. By contrast, those who are excluded or who exclude themselves from the nation are seen as excessive or wasteful. Whether as intermittent or permanent surplus populations, these dispossessed people are subjected to a necropolitics in which their shortened life expectancies, mortality, and morbidity become an externality to the market.[41] This is evident in patterns of toxic extraction and waste disposal.[42] These externalities then support the continued accumulation of wealth (and biopolitical fitness) by elites and the middle classes.

Indeed, as Andrew Szasz documents in *Shopping Our Way to Safety*, environmental politics can become lodged in a language of an inverted quarantine: the protection of private spaces from outside contamination through green consumption that contributes to that outside contamination.[43] Thus, in this chapter I trace how a common thread—property ownership—leads through environmental disaster, liberal environmentalism, and environmental racism. Private property shapes the individual's relation not only to a piece of land which they are said to "own" but also to other beings and processes that are denied, reduced, or minimized in the concept of private property. The thread of private property ownership through environmental destruction is exposed through the more radical critiques of the environmental justice movement, which necessarily move beyond a focus on property-based rights into a discourse of community, human rights, and human dignity.[44] Indigenous peoples' environmental justice activism and ecological knowledge challenge conventional settler categories of politics and individual property-based rights to health and well-being.[45]

The environmental justice movement's roots in the grassroot struggles of communities of color and Indigenous communities has reoriented environmental activism and scholarship through the use of analytical tools such as sacrifice zones, job blackmail, and environmental racism.[46] For example, a sacrifice zone is a place or community that has been deemed expendable, in environmental or health terms, in service of a supposedly higher purpose, often in the name of the security of the settler state or of its economic health.[47] Sacrifice zones also imply a cultural imperative to move, to leave behind the polluted or dangerous place, despite any desire a community might have to remain. A classic example of such a place is the nuclear testing area of the southwestern United States, where the valuelessness of the desert landscape in the eyes of the settler state is both affirmed and confirmed by its sacrifice in the name of national security.[48] The Western Shoshone have been said to have the distinction of being the most bombed nation on Earth.[49] The image of the desert as a valueless landscape, because of its nonproductive status and its undesirability as private property, contributes to the attempted erasure of its complex webs of existence and Indigenous nonproperty relations, symbolically in the eyes of the public and materially through the enactment of this sacrifice. The sacrifice thus destroys (or attempts to destroy) the ability of people to remain in place and live healthy lives.

As a precursor to the contemporary environmental crisis and its disproportionate impact on poor communities, communities of color, and Indigenous Peoples, it is useful to consider the settler colonial policy of allotment (e.g., the Dawes Act of 1887). This was a policy seeking termination of the special status of tribes and their rights to collectively hold land. Indigenous-held lands and reservations were divided and assigned as private property to individual men in Indigenous communities, in order to force assimilation to the liberal ideal of gendered individualism and private property.[50] This genocidal policy attempted to render Indigenous relations to community, place, and land obsolete and replace them with a relationship shaped by the logic of *homo economicus*. As property, land is no longer considered to be in relation to a community or group but becomes perceived as a commodity for exchange owned by an individual. The nominal empowerment of individual heads of households through allotments of property actually aimed to reduce community security and to make individuals more vulnerable to job blackmail (being forced to accept harmful work to survive) and other types of economic coercion. The property relation now shapes the conditions of possibility for environmental policymaking and environmental activism, by filtering environmental harm through the lens of property. The traces of the imposition of private property are visible in each of the cases under consideration in this chapter.

Intersectional and material feminism's theoretical tools enable a consideration of the overdetermination of experience, or the complexity of causes and effects in any social phenomenon. These approaches also emphasize the critical importance of contextualized analysis in which the universal only ever exists in the particular and deploy an "oppositional consciousness" that traces the connections between divergent social categories.[51] Informed by intersectionality, this analysis doesn't reify the existence of categories such as private property, but instead, looks at what property structures are *doing* in a particular case. Known as anti-foundationalism, this approach doesn't take the nature of social categories as a given, but instead investigates the production and use of categories in context. These tools are invaluable in the analysis of environmental injustice. Indigenous, anti-foundationalist, and intersectional feminisms emphasize the necessity of context and specificity in understanding oppression and liberation struggles.[52] Taken-for-granted analytical categories, such as class, if treated as objective truths, can limit empirical analysis and direct it in predetermined ways.[53] Reductive categories of analysis can oversimplify the causes of environmental inequalities while enabling generalization, as suggested by the debate about the role of race versus class in environmental justice scholarship. Indigenous and ecological feminisms, queer ecologies, and "new" materialisms have raised similar questions about how everyday structures such as the private property–wielding nuclear family and its gendered and spatialized structures of production and consumption contribute to the perpetuation of environmental harms to marginalized people and communities.[54]

Denaturalized, property reveals the construction of multiple mutually constitutive systems of inequality, including class, gender, race, and place.[55] An anti-foundational conception of property can be a lens into the multiple logics of oppression at work in different contexts of industrial exploitation and environmental harm. It is possible to understand the basic formulation of environmental policy in the United States as being constructed around the axis of property. Other rights not linked to property ownership are often imagined as distinct from what we consider environmental issues, due to a narrow definition of political and economic freedom as freedom from direct coercion. Thus, on the one hand, the political and economic domination of a poor community by a polluting industry that hurts its population's health and damages its property has not traditionally been understood as impinging on the civil rights of the inhabitants. This is reflected in the history of the environmental justice platform of the EPA; in the almost 30 years since its inception, only one civil rights case has been successfully prosecuted under that policy.[56] However, on the other hand, property owners are understood as having a vested interest in protecting the value of their property, and indeed, when their property holds a lot of value, they do have that power, often, to say NIMBY,[57] and relegate environmentally harmful practices elsewhere.[58]

Property, broadly conceived, is a category that has historically shaped personhood, identity, and industrialization in the United States, and which has only increased in importance in an age of neoliberalism. Property provides a thread that can theoretically link widely divergent cases in a larger story of environmental injustice. Using a critical settler lens and drawing on the intersectional and materialist feminisms of Patricia Hill Collins, Donna Haraway, and others, I am defining property as a flexible technology of identity and inequality. As critical legal scholar Patricia Williams explains, property, as a bedrock of law and personhood, fundamentally shapes identity and experience in the United States.[59] A "bright line" that creates clear categories for policy and legal proceedings, property contributes to the social life and "social death" of subjects empowered or erased in various ways by its existence.

Drawing on current media accounts and analyses, public documents, and previous research, this chapter explores how property is involved in environmental injustice in three cases. First will be the case of the southern West Virginia coalfields, where property ownership is problematic due to an overwhelming corporate presence and the split estate doctrine. Property in this case can function simultaneously as an advantage and a detriment due to the contradictory nature of such a legal attachment to place in the context of coal. McDowell County, West Virginia has a relatively high proportion of owner-occupied housing, but the county lacks adequate infrastructure for water, resulting in residents of the town of Keystone having lacked drinkable water in their taps for a decade. This situation is structurally similar in some ways to the second case, in Flint, Michigan, where the poisoning of children through negligent governance made it a national symbol of environmental racism. Homeowners in Flint found that their very homes were poisoning their children, and lost trust in the benefits of owning property. In both cases, the historical and contemporary structure of property ownership, and its relative granting of legal personhood, mobility, and agency, have produced complex environmental injustices born most significantly by poor communities and people of color. Finally, as a counterpoint, the last case is the Porter Ranch gas leak in southern California. The wealthy residents of neighborhoods displaced by a leaking natural gas storage facility in the hills around suburban Los Angeles stand in contrast to the usual victims of environmental disasters, and contradict the first rule of risk society à la Ulrich Beck—pollution follows the poor.[60] How does an environmental disaster unfold in a place where the well-to-do "live, work, play, and worship?"[61] What insights can this counterexample reveal about the structural constraints faced by marginalized people in the face of environmental harms?

"The curse of Keystone": Coal Mining and Real Estate in the Former Billion Dollar Coalfield

Private property can seem like an obsession in rural places like the southern West Virginia coalfields. Posted signs warn trespassers away from private farms and wooded lots. Second Amendment fans declare their willingness to use firearms to protect their homes, while coal companies place fences, large warning signs, and guardhouses at the edges of their mines to prevent unauthorized access. Genealogies of property are also a major thread in stories of property once owned and lost, or in statements such as "we've been in these hills forever." Place names marking Native American heritage, like Pocahontas, Mingo, and Logan, underline the settler colonial history of the region, while white residents often claim a native-like status based on long-term inhabitation.[62] Historical fact and familial resentment merge in the often-repeated stories of land theft by the slick agents of the coal, railroad, and land companies who came seeking resource wealth at the end of the nineteenth century. The agents bought land or mineral rights from vulnerable settler subsistence farmers, ensuring the region's future as a sacrifice zone.[63]

Not every coalfield resident has this long local history of property ownership. Another story often told is how the coal camps that lined the narrow mountain hollows were created by coal companies, rented by them, and subsequently became private property. Once a company owned a mine and its surroundings, it was necessary to import and house the requisite labor. The sparse local population didn't suffice for the heavy demands of early coal mining, so immigrants from Southern Europe and migrants from the Southern United States were welcomed into the newly formed coal camps. Coal companies rented cheaply built houses to workers, and provided a company store, company doctor, and so on, for their families. Many of these coal camps were scattered in the narrow hollows of McDowell County, West Virginia, which was known in the early twentieth century as the Billion Dollar Coalfield. Booming, racially-diverse-but-segregated communities housed immigrants from Europe and the South, making McDowell Country one of the most diverse counties in West Virginia.[64] Today it still has a more racially diverse population than many West Virginia counties, at about 8 percent African American and 91 percent white.[65]

In the coal camp, the company controlled most aspects of life, from the colors the houses were painted, to the segregation patterns of the workplace and community. However, as Henry Caudill described in *Night Comes to the Cumberlands*, when mines were worked out, it was no longer in the company's interest to own the property.[66] Selling off the tiny individual lots to mining families was instrumental in creating marginal property.[67]

Marginal property binds its owner in the name of the American Dream. Unlike the ideal property owner of Jefferson's yeoman democracy, marginal property does not enhance its owner's agency and capacity, but instead disempowers. Former coal camp houses were sold off in "postage stamp lots" too small for a septic tank and too rural for public services.[68] Abandoned by the company and without local services, the former coal camps became spaces of poverty and stigma. The plumbing left behind by the coal companies suffered years of neglect and disrepair. In the early years of the twenty-first century, the town of Keystone in McDowell County had no access to the equipment necessary to repair their broken water system, leaving residents without access to drinkable water from their home faucets for a decade.[69]

With a per capita annual income of about $15,500, McDowell County is one of the poorest places in the United States, yet with a higher owner-occupied housing rate than the average (80 percent versus 64 percent for the United States).[70] This particular form of rural poverty is characterized by marginal property—homeownership in the absence of a market or demand. Valueless, property cannot be sold, but can only be abandoned. The problem is thus emphatically not a lack of property, but that in owning certain forms of property, people can be too poor to move. The median value of owner-occupied housing in 2019 was about $33,800, but no one was buying because people were not moving to the area. On the contrary, the population decreased by almost 18 percent between 2010 and 2018.[71] In 2016, the Walmart in McDowell County closed, leaving a food desert. In the wake of these events, local activists and cooperatives have been mobilizing to fill these needs and rebuild community infrastructure.[72]

If we compare McDowell County with nearby Logan County, West Virginia, we find a trace of something we might call white privilege. Much the same in terms of age and decline in population, racially Logan County is almost 97 percent white alone, and only 2 percent African American alone.[73] The owner-occupied rate is similar. At an average home value of $90,100, the economic edge Logan has over McDowell reflects historical and geographic factors that are embodied in racialized communities.[74] In the first decades of the twenty-first century, the former Billion Dollar Coalfield (McDowell County) has experienced a desertion by capital. High rates of disability and drug addiction reveal the desolation of these abandoned sacrifice zones.[75] But Logan County is more fortunate, in a manner of speaking, because however transformed through automation, coal mining is still ongoing there, especially mountaintop removal (MTR, defined below). The Walmart hasn't closed yet, and several fast-food franchises offer employment, in addition to the schools and hospitals.

Yet if we look through an intersectional- and context-focused lens, we see that the investment in a broadly defined idealized whiteness as characterized by middle-class property ownership and nuclear families is relatively fragile. The most valued form of local employment, mining, often entails work that requires destroying the landscape. The specter of poverty looms, leading aspiring middle-class people to distance themselves from the poor. This often takes the form of a commentary on property, its upkeep, and how these reflect on the owners who may not have work. As much as local communities self-police against derogatory images of poverty, Appalachian poverty also plagues the US national self-image as a progressive settler state. A form of exceptional white poverty in a nation where it is imagined that whiteness equals wealth, it seems to beg for explanation.[76] For more than a century, white American writers have periodically examined the case of white poverty in Appalachia and found the region's hillbilly culture to have explanatory power.[77] However, images of hillbillies in "tarpaper shacks" aside, in Keystone, what acting Mayor Vondalere Scott referred to as the "curse of Keystone" is the pattern of extraction that leaves the region with nothing but the costs of coal.[78]

Thus, the sacrifice zone encompasses the human residents as well as the geographical space. The quality of property ownership as a sign of American citizenship is fragile and exists in the shadow of the effects of resources extraction. Residents' bodies, as well as the landscape, bear the signs of sacrifice, through black lung, disabilities from working underground, and poor health caused by the pollution of water and air.[79] It is in making that sacrifice, of their lungs, backs, or landscape, in the name of economic development, that coalfield residents maintain their membership in the American public as people who work.[80] The fragility of this belonging is apparent, however, in the spatial domination of coal. MTR is a surface mining technique that intensifies the impact of coal mining on the landscape and community. Explosives reduce the mountains, enormous equipment removes the "overburden" and the coal, and the topography is left permanently flattened. Nearby homes often suffer damages due to the blasting and dust from the mine. While the mine is not legally permitted to blast in a way that affects people's homes, in practice, the explosions and dust regularly impact nearby communities. At this point, to avoid trouble, the company often offers to buy people's homes, thus pushing them out and freeing their property for use by the mine.[81]

Here the catch-22 of marginal property is clear, because even the remaining coal economy leaves the homeowners of Logan County with few resources to work with in the contemporary housing market if they are forced to sell their house to a coal company or choose to sell and succeed in doing so. However, those who prefer to stay and resist the company's offer can end up with property that is both unlivable and valueless that they cannot escape.[82] Thus they may find themselves in a situation more like that of McDowell County, in the aftermath of coal. In the space of "six generations," settler colonialism converted the land to property, transformed the landscape, and generated poverty for the residents despite the natural wealth of the area.

"As good as trapped in this poisoned city": Flint, Michigan and Post-Industrial Disinvestment

Shifting context to an urban case of environmental injustice, Flint, Michigan has been in the news for the last decade as a textbook case of environmental racism. There are many differences between the situation in Flint and the rural poverty of the coalfields of West Virginia, yet they both operate as sacrifice zones. Despite their differences, underlying property structures shape experiences in both places. Both sites bear the traces of settler colonial relations, in everyday place names, the marks of historical violence and exclusion, and the ongoing exploitation and structural violence enabled by the institution of property. In West Virginia, family stories often claim a distant relation to the Cherokee, and people like Chief Logan and Pocahontas are remembered by white Americans as part of their own history.[83] Flint also has a history of dispossession of Indigenous people. In 1819, under duress, 100 Anishinaabeg signed the Saginaw Treaty, "ceding" more than 6 million acres of land to the US government.[84]

The area currently known as Flint was divided into allotments meant for the Native American descendants of a fur trader and interpreter, Jacob Smith, who had both Anishinaabe and white children. Regardless of the way these allotments were intended, the land ended up in the hands of the white sons of the fur trader. Later allotments further weakened tribal collective property. The Saginaw Chippewa Indian tribe was eventually able to purchase 500 acres of land east of Mt. Pleasant, Michigan, which is their current reservation.[85] As Native studies scholar Dylan Miner (Métis) reports, Flint's historic Stockton House Museum at Spring Grove, built in 1879, is located on "Plot Eight of the 'Reservation on Flint River,' [which] was awarded to Smith's [white] daughter Maria Reed Smith and her husband Colonel Thomas Stockton."[86] The museum's website remarks on the "naturally flowing spring behind their newly built home," which they called "Spring Grove," and notes simply that "Maria inherited a large tract of land along the banks of Thread/Swartz Creek and the Flint River."[87] This Victorian house, now a museum, represents the transformation of the area from Indigenous inhabitation, to individual white property, and now to post-industrial sacrifice zone. Starting with logging in the 1830s, the Flint River became integral to the industrial development of the area. The Flint River has been a dumping ground for automobile factories, paper and packaging companies, meatpacking plants, fertilizers used on farms upstream, and legal and illegal landfills for more than a century. Until recently, it had been considered far too polluted to be used as a source for the city's water.[88]

Richard Sadler and Andrew Highsmith outline the history of Flint in an article tracing the long-term causes of the water crisis.[89] Like the coalfields of southern West Virginia, Flint was a destination in the early twentieth century for Black people leaving the South to seek industrial employment. Like the Black people who migrated to the coalfields, they found residential segregation in their new communities. General Motors was the primary employer in Flint, and the company created separate housing for its white workers while leaving Black migrants to make do in poorly served urban neighborhoods.[90] As Sadler and Highsmith recount, these white communities were developed along existing sewer lines, and initially had more access to public services than either the Black neighborhoods or the unincorporated, largely white, rural communities surrounding the city.

The Flint case makes abundantly clear the role of public goods in the construction of property as a value. The unincorporated rural property became devalued in the context of GM's capital-driven development in the area, and then GM was able to appropriate that land into its company town. GM's success led to rapid growth in the postwar era, which resulted in the development of suburbs around the city. Although the infrastructure for these communities was provided by the city of Flint for the benefit of GM, these white-only suburbs sought separate incorporation to protect their tax base. Urban development was governed at the time, and to an extent still is, by the assumptions that local governments work most efficiently by competing with each other for residents. Here we see how the public goods offered by governments (in exchange for the taxes citizens choose to pay by living there) are imagined as purchasable commodities on the market. This imagination endows property (real estate) with a mystical value ideologically severed from its social origins. Conforming to the policy of fragmented governance, numerous small local municipalities sprang up around the city of Flint. White flight, discriminatory housing policies, and forgotten infrastructural interdependencies led to the isolation of Flint among a sea of wealthier white suburbs. As Sadler and Highsmith point out, this theory of urban development as market competition not only assumes freedom of movement between rival municipalities, it also assumes relocating takes place without cost.

However, many of the low-income residents of Flint who have suffered the poisoning of their water are stuck in place just like the residents of Keystone, West Virginia. The story of the poisoning is complex. As Sadler and Highsmith point out, the historical structural situation of the city, isolated and increasingly impoverished, surrounded by hostile suburbs, precipitated events. The municipal fragmentation of cities and suburbs in Michigan led to a situation in which many cities faced financial crises. The Michigan state government's response to these crises was punitive. First, they reduced revenue sharing to cities, exacerbating the crisis. Then cities in crisis, all of which are majority Black, were subjected to undemocratic rule by city managers.[91] It was Flint's city manager who decided in 2014 that shifting from the more expensive Detroit water supply to the Flint River, without accounting for the decontamination such a source requires, was a reasonable cost-saving measure for the city. Many local, state, and federal officials are implicated in the disaster that followed, where frightened parents reported children breaking out in rashes from their showers, and lead poisoning cases skyrocketed.

After initial apparent impunity, a decade later the former governor and other officials are still facing indictments despite setbacks and challenges that make the outcome of these cases uncertain, including the appointment of a new prosecutor.[92]

Despite parents' concerns, no corrective measures were taken until a study by Dr. Mona Hanna-Attisha revealed the degree of lead exposure in children and a team from Virginia Tech tested the water and demonstrated its violation of EPA regulations.[93] Local activists, including concerned mothers like LeeAnne Walters and then eight-year-old Mari Copeny, took action that brought national attention and federal aid to Flint.[94] Years later, some Flint residents still don't have clean water and still rely on purchasing bottled water. Given that the water is still not trusted, some Flint residents resent their record-breaking water bills, especially in light of the phaseout of state subsidies.[95] Worst of all, children have been impacted for life by their exposure to harmful amounts of lead that can lead to developmental problems and other lifelong consequences.

The potentially life-altering lead exposures children have suffered during the crisis are compounded by the weight of marginal property. Residents reported feeling "as good as trapped in this poisoned city."[96] As one resident put it, "People feel absolutely trapped. We feel like prisoners in our own homes. We're being poisoned by the very homes we live in."[97] Another resident said, "I couldn't rent out my house now if I wanted to. Who would want to move to Flint?"[98] Housing prices declined in 2017 to an average of $14,000, but even slumlords were passing up those opportunities. In 2017, Flint had the highest vacancy rate in the country, at 1 in 14 houses. In the worst hit neighborhoods of the city center, the vacancy rate was one in five. Many of these required too much renovation to attract buyers, and lenders such as Fannie Mae need assurance of a safe water supply.[99] Here, whiteness, formed in part through the legal enactment of racially exclusive municipalities, is visibly intrinsic to the creation of property and wealth. The use of Flint as a growth engine, and then as a sink, represents a racial subsidy for the residents of its white suburbs. The relative value and disposability of places and communities reflect the biopolitics and necropolitics of settler colonial property ownership.

"It makes you question the long-term sustainability of a
carbon-based power system": The Ill-Fated Future of
Property as a Basis for Environmental Politics

The last case moves from some of the most disinvested rural and urban
neighborhoods in the United States to one of the wealthiest. Although
serving as a contrast to the marginal property structures of Keystone and
Flint, property still figures significantly in this story. The present-day
neighborhood of Porter Ranch, California, was part of a 120,000-acre
secularized mission sold to Eulogio de Celis in 1846 by the Alta California government. The land is the traditional territory of the Tongva
(Gabrieleno), Chumash, and Fernandeño Tataviam Peoples, and the
sale included responsibility for the Indigenous inhabitants, many of
whom de Celis nevertheless evicted.[100] In 1875, the property was facing
foreclosure and was sold to members of the Porter family, who traced
their ancestry to the Mayflower. It was once a bucolic scene of celebrity
ranches and film locations.[101] Even after its development as a suburb
in the 1960s, the neighborhood was known for "hiking trails and spectacular scenic views . . . reminiscent of . . . more rural days that are long
gone."[102]

The 2015 methane gas leak in Porter Ranch was the worst natural gas leak in US history. For five months, methane seeped out of the
large Aliso Canyon underground natural gas storage facility, owned by
the company Southern California Gas (SoCalGas).[103] It was a kind of
airborne, invisible version of the 2010 Deep Water Horizon disaster.
Symptoms were apparently caused by additives that give natural gas its
unpleasant smell, tertiary butyl mercaptan and tetrahydrothiophene, although benzene was also identified as a possible carcinogen in the gas.
Families in the Porter Ranch neighborhood started complaining about
an odor of rotten eggs, headaches, and nosebleeds.[104] Pets died, the air
became unbreathable, and children suffered burns and rashes.[105] Despite the leak caused by aging infrastructure, SoCalGas soon reopened
the facility.[106]

The community of Porter Ranch is frequently described by the media
as "upscale."[107] In 2019, the per capita income in Porter Ranch's zip code
(91326) was $58,385, and the population of the census tract was majority
white and Asian American, with 4 percent of the population identify-

ing as Black.[108] Although authorities decided that the gas leak did not require a mandatory evacuation, many residents wanted their families out. SoCalGas furnished alternative housing for almost 5,000 residents at a cost of "up to $250 a day or about $7,500 per month."[109] In addition, the gas company worked with the Los Angeles Police Department to provide additional police protection for the vacated homes.[110]

After the leak, Porter Ranch residents felt a loss of trust in the company and security in their homes. Families were afraid to allow their children to play outside. One long-term resident put it this way, "It's frightening. You have a home that you used to love. People move to Porter Ranch for the views, the camaraderie, and the community. Now we're seeing it destroyed."[111] The anxiety the Porter Ranch residents experienced, especially those with small children or preexisting medical conditions, echoes that of the residents of Flint. "I feel like I'm trapped. I'm stuck in a poisonous house," was one such comment.[112] After the disaster, the gas company furnished cleaning services for those whose property was impacted, including some cases of a "dark brown residue" that settled on cars and outdoor furniture.[113] Today it seems things were able to return to something like normal. Most people returned from their alternative housing, some have moved away, and others have stayed and continued to fight for the closure of the facility.[114] A community organization, Save Porter Ranch, was created to work on shutting down the Aliso Canyon natural gas storage facility and to educate the public about the dangers of fracking.[115]

Another at least temporary victim of the disaster was the aggregate property value of the community. After the gas leak, sales declined by 20 percent and the median price only rose by 5.7 percent. As one resident put it, "We just want to keep our value at the end of the day."[116] This concern is understandable in the highly leveraged southern California housing market, where exorbitant prices are offset by the promise of future gains in value. In 2015, the average home price in Porter Ranch was over $600,000.[117] In comparable neighborhoods, not affected by the leak, housing prices appreciated by 30 percent in the same period, perhaps benefiting from the misfortune of Porter Ranch.[118] The existence of the Aliso Canyon gas storage facility, largely unrecognized before the leak, threatened not only people's health, but also the status and standing of the "pristine, quasi-rural paradise."[119]

Conclusion

The existence of residential segregation is necessary for the continued existence of polluting industry.[120] The spatial separation of populations with high financial, political, and social capital from toxic industrialization and its related waste disposal processes has been necessary for the continued acceptance of these practices by those who benefit most from them. In spatially separated neighborhoods, those who bear the costs have less ability to fight locally unwanted land uses and less of a platform for their protests. Larger geographic processes of marginalization and the creation of sacrifice zones operate on the logic of regional differences that arise between highly valued and undervalued places. Property values further institutionalize the relative worth or worthlessness of places.

These spatial separations are translated into different ways of perceiving and compensating for harm. During the disaster in Porter Ranch, government agencies and the gas company at fault worked to protect not only people's health, but their property, their children's education, and their lifestyles. Even as their property values were shaken, the fundamental right of the residents to live in the manner to which they were accustomed was not questioned. In 2021, SoCalGas denied their guilt, but agreed to pay a settlement of up to $1.8 billion to the more than 35,000 victims for compensation for the past and continuing health effects of the disaster, medical bills, lost businesses, and lost home value.[121]

Meanwhile, Flint residents' complaints about the water were ignored while government offices quietly replaced the tap water with bottled water for their employees.[122] In this sense, the Flint water crisis is an event that reproduces the structure of the unequal school system, based on local property taxes, that subjects Michigan children in disinvested municipalities to unequal educational opportunities.[123] In 2021, a settlement of $626.25 million (most coming from the state of Michigan) was approved for 50,000 lawsuit participants, with most of the award going to children, who suffered the worst health impacts from the contamination.[124]

The Black residents of the southern West Virginia coalfields are often not even recognized when the region is scrutinized for its exceptional poverty, which is normally coded as white.[125] In Keystone, there's been no lawsuit or settlement, but a California nonprofit Dig Deep provided residents with hookups to the new water line installed by the state. The project manager of Dig Deep's Appalachian Water Project, Bob McKinney, grew up in McDowell County but had not realized the extent of his neighbors' trouble: "I was embarrassed to say that I didn't know we were in this kind of shape."[126]

Property threads through these distinctions. As ideal American middle-class consumers, the Porter Ranch residents were attracted to the amenities of their neighborhood. The property was an investment, not only in its worth, but in their personal "worth." They were promised a vibrant, luxurious community with rapidly appreciating value. It was a hidden and fatal flaw (the gas storage facility and its disintegrating 40-year-old equipment hidden underground) that was responsible for the disaster. There is a sense in media coverage of the leak that the residents of Porter Ranch were shortchanged by this turn of events or were the victims of a bad deal.

The survivors of the Flint water crisis, however, abandoned by industry, simply had another problem added to their already complicated predicament of social, economic, and political disinvestment in their communities. There is little talk of loss of value, or of losing out, in the coverage of Flint. Instead, there is a story of progressively worsening conditions caused by poor administrative choices, and a lack of institutional response on the part of responsible parties. Rather than being granted extra police protection, they have had a decade-long fight for a modicum of justice. Finally, the coalfields are out of sight and mind for most of America, and the cultural image of (white-owned) rural private property stands for a kind of conservative rural idyll, in which observers only sporadically perceive the ongoing environmental, social, and economic disaster being created and left behind by coal. The fact that this disaster is most acute in the most diverse coalfield communities makes the contradictions of rural property ownership in a non-economy even more apparent. Flint and Keystone belie the mantra of American prosperity. Their property doesn't protect them.

Notably, the Flint water crisis was at first characterized by official disinterest in the complaints and fears of low-income parents. Environmental inequality reflects the role of a property-based calculation of the values of lives that overlaps with an equivalence between whiteness and property. Racialization and spatial marginalization lead to exclusion of deindustrialized communities from the biopolitics of the nation, as disinvested spaces are blamed for their own problems. The baseline requirement of healthy surroundings for children is considered to be the sole responsibility of the parent, for example, leaving structural constraints on mobility out of the conversation. Deindustrialization makes clear that places are disposable, and mobility is expected.

This expected economic and geographic mobility is organized through the idealized heteronormative nuclear family unit, whose breadwinner finds "his" niche in the economy while the caretaker provides the affective glue that holds the unit together regardless of their geographical location. Historical labor market segmentation and other forms of discrimination made this idealized and rare family structure a form of property for many white middle-class and some white working-class Americans.[127] Especially in the absence of this idealized family structure, the inability or disinclination to move is part of what writes the communities of deindustrialized cities or extractive landscapes out of national belonging. Notably, the expectation of Porter Ranch homeowners that they would be able to leverage their home purchase in order to move (when and if they chose) was jeopardized by the existence of the gas storage facility.

Neoliberal discourses of personal responsibility assign blame to individuals and by extension, communities, that are unable to mobilize the resources necessary to relocate, to vote with their feet, or to protect their children by being able to afford the healthiest place to live.[128] Many of these factors were cited by homeowners in Porter Ranch to explain why they had bought there, why they were disappointed, and why they hoped to stay or go. In the contrasts between these sites, there is revealed a micro bio- and necropolitics expressed in the intimate daily acts of teams of house cleaners and police working to protect vacated property in one context, while in another context families must use bottled water to bathe their children. Yet there is also a confluence in the drift of environmental crisis across property lines. As the mayor of Porter Ranch explained, the gas leak "really puts into question the long-term sustainability of a carbon-based energy system."[129] The Porter Ranch disaster brought the environmental crisis "home" by bringing it into one of the most idealized spaces of American property and prosperity, a wealthy suburb of Los Angeles. This may reflect a heightening of the crisis and a resultant fracturing of the institution of property in late–fossil fuel society. This crossing of lines creates the conditions of possibility for an emergent environmental politics of *res publica*, the public good, beyond the scope of acquisitive individualism.

As the bedrock of settler culture and the colonizing process, the division of land into individual private property empowers some while disempowering others. It also enables the objectification of natural resources for extraction and the generation of industrial wealth. The coalfields and Flint bear the scars of industrialization, while Porter Ranch seems to represent the ideal of a commodified white upper-middle-class experience. In each case, property, its worth, and its condition are instrumental in constructing identity and biophysical conditions. Idealized nuclear families whose property must be defended are constructed against disinvested populations whose limited ability to control their circumstances is alleged to be a function of their dysfunction or dependency. Property is a material and ideological framework of identity intrinsic to the biopolitics of liberalism and neoliberalism.

In Garrett Hardin's fable of the tragedy of the commons, individual property owners (specifically livestock herders) are used to represent humanity, rather than communities, families, or other groups, a choice which presents an atomistic, acultural, and amoral vision of human nature.[130] The story recounts that each of Hardin's individual herders only sought to increase their own wealth by increasing their herds, eventually leading to overgrazing and destroying the fields they shared, in other words, the tragedy of the commons, a shared resource will inevitably be spoiled. Ironically, Hardin's fable was meant to prove that private property ownership would lead to more environmental protection, because people would seek to preserve their property. History seems to have made a different point. Hardin's fable calls to mind the imagined wild freedom, or "paradigmatic Indianness," of the frontier.[131] Like the frontier, the commons must inevitably be protected from its imagined amoral and acultural free-for-all by its conversion to property. Although there are many other ways of organizing the use of space, the division of land into private property is generative of wealth, whiteness, and masculinity. The corresponding commodification and disposability of places has been devastating for marginalized people and communities.

The property bind both creates environmental risks and limits how we can address them. However, as Porter Ranch's mayor's quote above suggests, the worsening environmental crisis may be putting into question the efficacy of property as a form of personal agency and environmental protection in the context of late fossil fuel society. In short, the situation in Porter Ranch increasingly echoes that of the coalfields and Flint, as the necropolitics of capital comes home to roost.

2

The Contradictions of "White" Protest

Settler Culture, Property, and Alienation

The Bundys assert a property right which was only made possible through the genocide of indigenous peoples and the continued occupation of our lands by the same government they claim to fight. Their white supremacist ideology is the foundation of the settler state, and their ranching would not be possible without it.
—Ladonna Bravebull Allard

What does the Bundy family have in common with grassroots environmentalists in West Virginia, or a Big Green organization like the Sierra Club? The Bundy family is famous for their anti-government protests at Cliven Bundy's Nevada ranch and the Malheur National Wildlife Refuge in Oregon. Anti-MTR and anti-pipeline activists in West Virginia are fighting the destruction of their homes, communities, and the landscape. Meanwhile, the Sierra Club is one of the "Big Green" organizations of mainstream US environmentalism dating from the late nineteenth century and is deeply associated with the preservationist wilderness ideal.[1] Each is concerned with stereotypically white political concerns such as libertarian politics, Appalachia, or Nature. Although not directly tied to real property as were the events of the previous chapter, these cases of social mobilization or protest share the same interior logic as the property bind explored in those cases. A settler logic of individualism, acquisitiveness, and domination that prevents or limits connection or relationship unites these diverse forms of "white" political activism despite their diverse aims and interests.

Since the 1970s' turn to neoliberalism, ideologies of color evasiveness and hyper-individualism have prevailed in white American political culture and have discouraged group and community-based protests. Discussions of class have long been most notable for their absence in American political culture, in which everyone thinks they are middle class, although this has changed in the first decades of the twenty-first century.[2] In the United States, issues of economic inequality are often referenced through a language of race (as in terms like "the ghetto" which racialize poor urban neighborhoods). Expressions like these normalize both white wealth and the poverty of racialized others.[3] Public discourse continues to use biological, genetic, and physical differences to supposedly explain poverty and justify social exclusion.[4] Neoliberalism also relies on references to cultures of poverty and cultural racism to explain economic inequalities in the absence of a critique of the capitalist political economy.[5] Even when inequality is the focus of a political campaign, as it was for Bernie Sanders in 2016, the focus is often on injured "ordinary Americans" who are perceptibly coded as white and male.[6]

In addition to this tendency to racialize political economic conflict, a resurgence of overt racism since the 2016 election has brought with it an increasing weaponization of the specific post-racial or color-evasive claims of neoliberalism.[7] This is exemplified in the Trump administration's attack on Native American sovereignty, which was couched in the language of individual responsibility (specifically regarding state legislation requiring employment to qualify for Medicaid). The Trump administration pushed to end exemptions to Medicaid work requirements for tribes, calling these exemptions "illegal preferential treatment" based on race. Besides eliminating healthcare for tens of thousands, this policy challenged the sovereign status of Indigenous nations. Indigenous nations have treaties with the US government requiring the government to provide healthcare. This attempt to remove their exemptions from the Medicaid work requirement also was an attempt to redefine sovereign tribes as another group of racial minorities in the United States purportedly looking for special treatment.[8] This effort reflects both the entitlement to absorb the territories covered by the treaties, and the alienation, which denies the treaty was ever an agreement between two parties, at the heart of settler colonialism.[9]

The unmarked center of US racial formation, whiteness, depends on a foundational alienation—a rejection of relationship with racialized others—but at the same time it depends on a disavowal of this alienation.[10] Because of this disavowed rejection I argue that white protest is often articulated in the form of race-based injury, which represents a return of the repressed. Injury is expressed as "reverse racism" which grants to white people the status of "real" victim, or it is expressed through a counterfactual claim of shared experience with racialized others, or both. In an example of the first, the Trump administration defined tribal Medicaid employment exemptions as unfair racial preferences for minorities (or reverse discrimination). The second is seen most often in the claim to Native American identity or "blood," especially Cherokee identity, popular among white people.[11]

However, the disavowal at the heart of the settler complex also depends on an assumption of white entitlement, innocence, and agency. This innocent agency is the stuff of white saviorism and white beneficence that has been historically constructed against disempowered others, and which makes coalitional work difficult.[12] This chapter will consider how these complexities shape the collective claims of injury on the part of several "white" groups in the United States.[13] The examples of the Bundy family's protests, the Sierra Club's environmentalism, and grassroots activism in Appalachia will illustrate the settler complex that links these diverse instances of white protest.

From Whiteness to the Settler Complex

White identity in the United States is determined by property and property relations. The desire to appropriate, protect, and conserve white property is at the heart of US racial politics.[14] The acquisitive individualism characteristic of liberal personhood, and exemplified by the white male property owner, has historically been used to separate Indigenous and other communities with different property relations from their land, through the Homestead Act and the Dawes Act, among other practices.[15] Acquisitive individualism has been enshrined in US law and culture as the best, most rational, and advanced form of relationship to place and nature.[16] Native American collective relations to place are not understood as representing either a civil claim to property rights or an "improvement" of land as dictated by Lockean property theory.[17] This doctrine of *terra nullis* was used to justify the expropriation and genocide of Native people across the continent.[18] Policies such as the

Homestead Acts, the Indian Appropriation Act, and the Dawes Act segmented the western United States into tracts of private property, public land, and reservations, many of which were further divided into allotments assigned to individual Native men as heads of households. These allotments were an attempt to rewrite Indigenous land relations on the model of gendered individualism, as well as a method of expropriation of Native land, as the small allotments often ended up in the hands of wealthier and more powerful white owners.[19]

This material and ideological connection between whiteness and property necessitates an understanding of white political and rights-seeking behavior that accounts for the specific ways that white settler culture relates to land and nature. Property is at the center of rights and justice in the US legal system, and rights to property are favored over other forms of rights not related to property ownership.[20] In the context of the United States, this means using the lens of settler colonialism to understand the complexities of the politics of land rights and environmental issues.

Denying Kin

The settler complex is based on a historically derived legal and cultural alienation (or refusal of relationship) from other humans in the form of enslavement of African and African-descended people and expropriation of Native land.[21] Property ownership was already central to European conceptions of self-rule and democratic citizenship dating at least from the late eighteenth century, when Kant declared that only property owners were truly capable of self-governance.[22] This exclusive property- and class-based claim to first-class citizenship and self-determination is very likely behind many settlers' drive to immigrate to the so-called New World, which appeared to offer "a constant supply of new territory with which to satisfy the proprietary aspirations" of the oppressed people of Europe.[23] These aspirations are expressed in stories such as the film *Far and Away*, which traces the progress of Irish immigrant homesteaders in the American West.[24]

A second alienation, or refusal of relationship, occurs when land is transformed to abstract property. As property, land is severed in ways indifferent to place and ecology for the ease of individual ownership and market exchange, or in the name of national territory.[25] The abstraction of land into individual or national property is a refusal of the human relationship with other living things and landforms. For example, the US-Mexico border disrupts the lives of thousands of species struggling to accommodate settler-made obstructions.[26] The border also creates hardships for the Indigenous Peoples such as the Tohono O'odham whose territory it divides.[27] The reduction of people, nonhumans, and landscapes to property breaks the web of relations recognized in many Indigenous worldviews, as exemplified by the Yakama Nation whose community includes sea lions, salmon, and the Columbia River in a not always harmonious web of kinship.[28]

Property is based on an abstract logic of equivalence, which reduces places to natural resources to exploit or to protect, and sees space, landforms, and living beings as generic equivalents that are subjected to sale, exploitation, or conservation, but not as representing a specific set of relationships, responsibilities, or communities. This follows the logic of colonization, which emphasizes the differences and minimizes the interconnections between subjects and objects, and in which agency and will reside entirely in the subject, or master position.[29] The market becomes the lens through which the land is viewed, and the primary subjects of law become those (supposedly) most fully realized humans who control property to exploit or protect, rendering claims to nonproperty rights such as access to clean water, air, or other nonmarket values unintelligible.[30]

Difficulties in the Fight for Justice

The division of land into abstract units of equivalence, and the separation of species into resources to exploit or protect, generate many irrationalities. As mentioned in the introduction, examples of this relatively banal observation proliferate in the many "monsters" that populate the contemporary world.[31] These monsters include climate change, global radiation drift, and persistent organic pollutants in breast milk, fights for rights to hunt or fish traditionally when industrialization has decimated nonhuman populations, and oceans of plastic.[32] The inability to amass the collective will to face these issues is related to the prominence of discourses of privatization, personal responsibility, and especially, acquisitive individualism. While the problems are collective in nature, the proposed solutions are almost always individualist.[33]

The political theory of neoliberalism was first implemented in the "political laboratory" of the reactionary authoritarian economic austerity regimes that crushed burgeoning socialism in Latin America.[34] By the late 1970s in Britain and the United States, economic neoliberalism had combined with a white racial reaction to the collective social movements of the Civil Rights era. Minoritized people claiming their rights to the benefits of the welfare state contributed to a racial reaction of privatization and tax revolt.[35] Neoliberal policies, based on the market as the primary model for all social institutions, and on the individual as the locus of all rights, have performed a massive redistribution of wealth upward since the mid-twentieth century.[36] The racial code words (reverse discrimination, forced busing, personal responsibility, etc.) that helped to dismantle the gains of affirmative action, integration, and the expansion of the welfare state were also effective at dismantling the programs that helped disadvantaged whites.[37] The neoliberal doctrine of individualism and personal responsibility has become so pervasive that even anti-racist groups like Black Lives Matter evoke charges of racism, and gathering to protest injustice is portrayed as equivalent to the activity of organized hate groups.[38]

In the context of neoliberalism, proper citizenship is identified with private, entrepreneurial individualism, homeownership, and a biopolitics of self-care. This norm of privacy, self-care, and individual responsibility enables the eruption of protest to be interpreted as the problem instead of the injustice that inspired the protest.[39] In such instances, the aggrieved person is identified as the source of the trouble.[40] In light of the idealized identification of white people as the winners of the American dream, as successful participants in neoliberalism, and as the "ordinary" American taxpayer to whom American politics are addressed, the experience of real and perceived injustice on the part of "white" people can bring about some complex and contradictory political claims.

This chapter traces the connections between three disparate examples of "white" protest. Once again, the apparent differences in these examples may disguise their underlying structural similarities. In the first example, the sovereign citizen movement of the Bundy Ranch standoff and Malheur Wildlife Refuge occupation articulated settler narratives of the frontier in combination with appropriations from the Civil Rights movement. This surprising articulation was perhaps prompted by the election of a nonwhite president. For the Bundy family and their supporters, public land management was interpreted as infringing on the sovereignty and "civil rights" of the ideal, independent American of Turner's frontier thesis. Next, Big Green environmental organizations such as the Sierra Club promote a politics of green consumption, liberal sentimentality, and the white savior complex that tends to disavow or minimize white victimization, and to frame environmental problems as distinct from social issues. This leads to some shaky coalitions with environmental groups such as the anti-mountaintop removal (MTR) activists in the West Virginia coalfields. The last example considers how in the fight against coal and gas extraction and transport in Appalachia, this environmental damage is perceived as threatening a white version of indigenous inhabitation. Underlying all of these cases is a form of abstracted individualism that denies kinship, interconnection, and history, and views nature in terms of personal property.[41] Each of the following examples illustrate how whiteness and the settler colonial complex impede real progress toward social justice in the United States. Optimistically, the Sierra Club and the Appalachian cases offer a potential for anti-racist white politics.

This Land Is Our Land

The Bundy family are widely known as flag bearers for a particular kind of white sovereign citizen movement. First, family patriarch Cliven Bundy claimed injury in his dealings with the Bureau of Land Management (BLM), which is in charge of all federal public land in the United States. In 2014, the BLM tried to seize Bundy's cattle from land he had been using, without paying the required grazing fees, for decades.[42] Using Lockean logic, Bundy claimed a preemptive right to the resources and denied the right of the US government to own any land. Given the role of the state in establishing the right to private property, it is remarkable that individualism can become so paranoid that it turns on the foundation of its ownership, the state sovereignty that established the western lands as property in the first place.[43] The standoff that arose to defend Bundy's cattle included hundreds of heavily armed militiamen defying the federal government. The armed standoff occurred against the backdrop of President Obama's second term in office and his expansion in several cases of national monument status to BLM land.[44] Cliven Bundy's militancy was a rebellion of sovereign (white) citizens against an overreaching, newly racialized, big government.[45] Bundy's triumphant post-acquittal "press conference," in 2018, delivered to friends with whom he had just shared steak, is a full-throated claim to white settler privilege. Establishing his status as a "maker, not a taker,"[46] Bundy expressed the hope that his guests had enjoyed the steaks he'd provided, exclaiming, "I'd like everybody in the world to enjoy . . . good food. I harvest that with my cattle, [and] my cattle convert that into an edible commodity."[47]

Extolling the American virtue of "freedom for a man to be able to produce and provide and be happy" which he saw as being enshrined in the Constitution, a "blueprint for this type of life," Bundy claimed that "we the people" are the government, and that no central government has any legitimacy over Clarke County, Nevada.[48] Repeating that he had no contract with the federal government or any other government, he blamed his fellow citizens for thinking they must deal with the federal government at all. Borrowing both vocabulary and logic from John Locke, he proclaimed that his "improving" of the land gave him rights to the land, and that this right in fact stemmed from "the pioneers . . . the first one to come in here . . . [and] the first drop of water [his team of horses] drank." His right to the water, and presumably the land, thus stems from the "first pioneers . . . creating a beneficial use of a renewable resource," thus gaining "preemptive rights."[49] The trouble arose when the ranchers hired the federal government to adjudicate among several claimants to these preemptive rights, leading to the government overstepping and claiming ownership.

There was a notable inequality in the delicate treatment the armed ranchers and allies received in their 2014 demonstration and standoff, compared to the treatment of unarmed demonstrators in Ferguson, Missouri, the same year, who were met with tanks, tear gas, and rubber bullets for protesting the murder of Michael Brown.[50] The white privilege granted to the ranchers was underlined by an aggressively claimed whiteness. Bundy shared his views on African Americans with reporters after the standoff, asserting that today "[Black people] have nothing to do." He opined that Black people had been better off in slavery, picking cotton. This opinion makes his defense in the trial all the more ironic. His defense attorney argued that Bundy and his allies had simply been participating in an American tradition of protest harkening back to the Reverend Martin Luther King Jr. and the protests in Selma, Alabama.[51] Following his acquittal on a legal technicality, the Bundy family found their doctrine of preemptive rights (i.e., settler rights) in a less adversarial position with the subsequent federal administration.

With the new and sympathetic federal administration in place, the family might not have pursued their agenda of hyper-individual rights and sovereign citizenship as aggressively in 2018 as they did in 2016. That year Cliven's son Ammon, his brothers, and many of their sympathizers invaded and occupied the Malheur Wildlife Refuge in Oregon.[52] Echoing his father, Ammon Bundy declared, "This land belongs to the people. We must get our government [under] control and back to benefiting the people." This statement made no mention of the Northern Paiute, who have never ceded the land.[53] The occupiers rummaged through Northern Paiute artifacts held in the refuge and used large equipment to dig latrines in the middle of culturally significant sites.[54]

Despite this total disregard for the Northern Paiute, the Bundy family's perception of their own status as oppressed victims of the federal government led family members to offer to join the Sacred Stone Camp at Standing Rock, North Dakota, during the Dakota Access pipeline protest in 2016. This was an apparent attempt to join in coalition with Native Water Protectors on the basis of a shared experience of oppression. However, the Bundys' wealth came at the expense of Indigenous dispossession, and their literal trampling of unceded Native land was a forthright claim to settler entitlement and an enactment of settler violence, as historian, Water Protector, and Standing Rock Camp founder Ladonna Brave Bull Allard (Standing Rock Sioux) explained.[55] Nevertheless, perhaps because their claim to preemptive rights to Native land is so fundamentally immoral, it seems they were compelled to justify their protests through comparisons to histories of racial injustice and Indigenous oppression. Deeply disturbed by the Bundy family's comparison of their protests to Indigenous struggles, Allard wrote that "The Bundy militia were fighting for their right to make money, while we are fighting our children's rights to clean drinking water."[56]

Explore, Enjoy, Protect

No group could be more seemingly opposed to the Bundy family than the Sierra Club. The Sierra Club is one of the largest green organizations in the United States and is generally associated with progressive politics and the embrace of federal environmental regulations. Nonetheless, the same settler complex that defines the Bundy claim to preemptive rights to Nevada and Oregon land underlies the Sierra Club and its white American environmental ethos.[57] The idealized wilderness that the Sierra Club was founded to preserve is a product of nineteenth-century industrialization and the closing of the American frontier.[58] In the mapping of the American landscape into property, specific places were rendered interchangeable as cities, wilderness, farmland, or ranchland, creating a functionally equivalent abstraction divorced from Indigenous communities' relationships to places and specific ecologies. In other words, for settlers, exploitation and preservation are two sides of the same coin.[59] Land should be "returned" to the "people" for its best or highest use as a resource (in the Bundys' worldview) or "saved" from some people for other people, in the name of Nature (in the Sierra Club's view).

John Muir, the founder of the Sierra Club, thought of the spectacular nature of the West as a sacred natural cathedral, capable of sustaining the spirit of the right kind of observer. He saw the Indigenous inhabitants of this so-called wilderness as people not removed enough from nature to properly enjoy it; humans and nature needed to be clearly separated for each to be at their best.[60] The dualism of humanity and nature is instrumental to the objectification of nature, not simply as ranchland to exploit, but also as a pristine collector's object in the hands of wilderness preservationists. Both reflect the commodification of nature, as expressed in the Sierra Club's slogan once displayed on the organization's website: "Explore, enjoy, protect."[61] The current website demonstrates the organization's shift toward a more socially conscious and inclusive environmentalism.

The dualism of human and nature allows for a good and evil perspective that puts the blame for environmental harms on (bad) humans or too many (of the wrong) humans. Sierra Club California's history of struggles with their membership and board regarding questions of immigration and population in the United States reflects this historical tendency to focus on an idealized wilderness and to neglect specific histories of human groups interacting more or less sustainably with places and ecologies.[62] This liberal American environmentalist orientation tends to blame environmental problems on so-called overpopulation, illegal logging and mining, Indigenous hunters and fishers, and other small resource users, instead of on the Global North's massive industrialization, overconsumption, and militarization.[63]

In the early 2000s, the Sierra Club's West Virginia office began to work with grassroots groups fighting MTR coal mining in the state. When I interviewed one of the activists working for the Sierra Club in 2004, we both acknowledged that the organization had not had an active environmental justice platform until that time. At the height of the Sierra Club's Beyond Coal Campaign in West Virginia, celebrity activists Darryl Hannah and Robert Kennedy Jr. joined many others in a highly publicized demonstration in front of Marsh Fork Elementary School, which was located down a hill from an earthen dam holding back billions of tons of toxic coal slurry.[64] Despite these protests, mountaintop removal has continued its massive expansion in West Virginia. Movement members express that they've been abandoned by the celebrities and the Sierra Club, as award-winning coalfield activist Maria Gunnoe put it, "Most of them have left and moved on and are now fighting other issues with more funding. I don't understand why they didn't complete the job and end mountaintop removal."[65] The website for the Sierra Club's Beyond Coal Campaign currently focuses on the retirement of coal-burning power plants as its main objective, while including the general goal of "keeping it in the ground."[66]

There is a sad sense of inevitability to the coalfield activists' feelings of betrayal by the Sierra Club. The presence of humans, many of them miners, dependent on the mining industry in the affected area, complicates mainstream white environmentalism. Rather than being the subject of a story with bad guys (industrial developers) and good guys (nature to protect), the coalfields are a historically complex place with complicated relations between corporations, residents, and the nonhuman environment. Some of the historical baggage includes the devaluation of the area in the national imagination, as a sacrifice zone. As activist Bo Webb put it, "mountaintop removal is not an accident."[67] The economic, cultural, and political marginalization of the southern West Virginia coalfields is instrumental to enabling the continual destruction of the mountains. This devaluation was perceived as being behind the celebrities' abandonment of the local activist groups after the "fashion" of fighting MTR was over. The intensity of local conflict over the issue, combined with the overall economic depression and associated pre-scription drug misuse epidemic, combine to paint a picture far from the Sierra Club's usual pristine wilderness backdrop.[68] A long-term solution for the coalfields will require community-building and sustainable eco-nomic opportunities. This failure of coalition-building reflects some of the challenges of fighting environmental damage from within a "settler colonial complex."[69] The settler colonial complex divides environmental issues from social issues, which has historically left Big Green organiza-tions ill equipped for the nuances of environmentally minded organiz-ing aimed at building community and social justice.[70]

Environmental Justice and "White" People Trying to Get It Right

The coalfield activists fighting mountaintop removal occupy a unique position in America's cultural landscape. Appalachians are sometimes imagined as the "whitest" people in America and simultaneously as rep-resenting a failure of normative standards of whiteness. Having in the past been lauded as "our contemporary ancestors" or "unadulterated" Anglo-Saxons, they are also decried as hillbillies, welfare dependents, and generally ignorant people (with the latest iteration including the imagi-nation of the region as being defined by support for the 2016 and 2020 Republican presidential candidate).[71] This liminal position is reflected in the bad feelings that remained after the Sierra Club moved on.

Poor, disempowered, and generally marginalized white Appalachians are often invoked to deny the existence of white privilege. How can white privilege exist if white people experience such poverty and environmen-tal injustice? The Sierra Club and various celebrities' involvement in the anti-MTR movement was perceived in retrospect by local activists as a form of exploitation for publicity. In light of their subsequent abandon-ment and neglect while the struggle against the environmental disaster of coal continues, the failure of this coalition clearly reflects class- and region-based inequalities. However, the language of privilege or lack thereof can mask the real working of whiteness, or perhaps more precisely the settler complex, in US political culture.

As Patrick Wolfe argues, "in the contradictory tension between desiring and rejecting the Native, ambivalence emerges as a primary settler affect."[72] This ambivalence is clear in the contradictory claims of both whiteness and indigeneity of white Appalachians. White Appalachians often identify with Native Americans in a variety of ways, including identifying with the experience of losing their land though (internal) colonialism, identifying with the land-based lifestyle and place-based identity of Native Americans, and by forming coalitions with Native Americans.[73] As discussed in the introduction, claims to long-term inhabitation and place-based identity often rest on a history of "six generations" in a particular place, a time frame that coincides with the expropriation of Indigenous Peoples. In other words, the claim to indigenous-like inhabitation rests on a history of white settler violence toward the Indigenous Peoples of the region. This identification represents an appropriation of the concept of colonialism as well as a problematic claim of white setter indigeneity in Appalachia.[74] This framing allows white Appalachians to identify simultaneously with Revolutionary War–era American settlers and with the Indigenous people they displaced.

Wolfe identifies settler culture as the appropriation of both land and Indigenous culture, and the denial of this appropriation.[75] At the same time as appropriating Indigenous identity or culture as American heritage, settler culture simultaneously attempts to erase the contemporary and past existence of Indigenous people. This is how Indigenous names and decontextualized symbols of Indigenous cultures can be misappropriated for use as place names, sports mascots, or military equipment with no corresponding relation to the Indigenous people to whom these names or symbols belong.[76] Because of this erasure of the Indigenous present and past in settler culture, white privilege and the ecological calamity of industrial modernity are conceived of not as a product of a messy interactional history between differing human groups, but as an innate property of (white) people and (white) culture in a universal history of development.[77] History becomes a ladder of unidirectional human development, not a varied multiplicity of human possibilities that have been actively erased.[78] Activists in Appalachia are perhaps among the most educated white people in America about issues of environmental injustice, and because their fight is so overwhelming, their energies are often consumed with the crisis that is in their own backyard. Unless there is a recognition of the role of the settler complex in enabling MTR and other forms of hyper-extraction, the environmental justice coalitions they join are necessarily limited in their scope.

An illustration of the limitation comes from the fight against the natural gas fracking and pipeline boom. In a beautiful spot that would be destroyed by a planned pipeline, a property owner showed me a billboard that activists had erected describing the dangers of the new, larger pipelines being rapidly built radiating from West Virginia.[79] These are high-pressure, 42-inch natural gas lines that carve a 150-foot-wide right-of-way through the landscape, with a potential impact radius of a mile in the event of an explosion. Nearby, tiny crosses marked the graves of species that would be impacted by the development. A plot of sacred corn represented the contribution of Indigenous activists from North Dakota. He said that some people from Standing Rock "came . . . had a ceremony and prayed." Although he saw the connection between the struggles, his main appreciation was for the contribution of the tribal members to the protection of his property and the environment in West Virginia. My question about coalitions was answered with a description of a coalition between West Virginia counties all dealing with this pipeline. This may reflect what Kai Bosworth calls partnership with "no real concessions" and a "presumption of allyship" without a serious consideration of Indigenous perspectives.[80] Most likely despite the intentions of the visitors from Standing Rock, this property owner hadn't yet fully articulated the connections between the pipeline impacting his property and the Standing Rock struggle.

However, many Appalachian activists and members of more radical organizations participated in the Standing Rock protests and educated themselves on settler colonialism at the same time. These transformations are happening in real time as the struggle continues. Frequent references to the slogans "Water Is Life," "No Pipelines on Stolen Land," and to Turtle Island, by the most radical Appalachian anti-pipeline activists, the tree sitters and their supporters, demonstrate the leadership of Indigenous activists and an increasing recognition of the interconnectedness of the pipeline struggle with settler colonialism.[81] In the fight for environmental justice, white protesters need to recognize settler colonialism in order to comprehend the reality and roots of our current environmental and political crisis. This comprehension needs to be enacted through acts of reciprocity, not symbolic allyship. These examples represent both the limitations and the potential of environmental justice coalitions among white Appalachians and groups of color and Indigenous groups. These emerging coalitions will need to address the disavowed injustice at the heart of settler culture as well as the current environmental destruction it enables.

Conclusion

The distance between the Bundy ranchers and Appalachians trying to preserve life in the mountains is vast, but they are connected by a belief in the morality of the US settler state and its property structure. Those who seek environmental justice will need to get beyond preserving their own property in order to make effective coalitions with Indigenous people and people of color that do not replicate the settler complex of denial and disavowed relations. This is especially critical given that the Trump administration led a resurgence of the claim of whiteness and settler privilege, by claiming that "our ancestors tamed a continent,"[82] by attempting to reduce sovereign Indigenous nations to racial minorities, and by embracing white nationalism and violence.[83]

At a Water Protectors workshop held in 2018 at an Appalachian university, four speakers discussed how they worked to protect water for their children and future generations. Two were white women from Appalachia, working in organizational capacities to protect water from fossil fuel extraction. Two were Indigenous, one with a tribal identity and a specific landscape at the heart of her organizing, and the other an activist at large working on various causes in the eastern United States. What emerged from their panel discussion was an uncomfortable theme—politics as usual, and the system set up by various environmental protection agencies—is increasingly revealed as a road that only leads to one place: the frack pad, the pipeline, the mine. In other words, the discussion highlighted the fact that the (white settler) legal and political system was *designed* to encourage and enable the exploitation of resources, the extraction of fossil fuels, and the desecration of ecological systems and the natural commons. Institutional channels do not lead to substantive environmental justice, even with a sympathetic administration.[84] The political, economic, and legal structures of settler culture are also responsible for the relative powerlessness of communities in the pathway of fossil fuel extraction and transport.

One member of the mostly white audience raised the question of how to take white supremacism into account in environmental organizing, but the ensuing discussion revealed that power evasiveness was still a major force as several people referred to "our common struggles" which should bring us together across differences. The panelist who had previously identified her tribal affiliation gently took the gathering to task for using Indigenous people as tokens, and the other Indigenous woman pointed out the overwhelming whiteness of the audience itself. Another audience member asked how effective coalitions could be made, considering the issues that were becoming apparent. Panelists called for practical action in material support of Indigenous people, which would build real relationships that increase trust and community—all steps that could help decolonize environmentalism and other social justice work.

Environmentalists interested in environmental justice, and other antiracist white social movements, need to clearly differentiate themselves from the Bundy family, on more than a surface or aesthetic level, which means coming to terms with white supremacist settler histories that underlie property relations to land. It also means questioning the general presumption of innocence of the US government and its legal processes, which are based on the fundamental alienation of the property relation. Organizers must root out white supremacist ideas of acquisitive individualism in favor of solidarity, connection, and relationship. However, as the panelists' discussion subtly made clear, this may require moving beyond the established protest scaffolding the settler state provides. White environmental activists need a fuller recognition of history and of the settler complex that undermines environmental politics. Settler culture makes kin out of people with vastly different goals, like the Sierra Club and the Bundy family, who share a possessive, abstract, frontier orientation to the American landscape, while alienating potential allies for an environmental justice-based coalition that could bring about real substantive change.

3

The End of (Settler) Time

Apocalypse, Environmental Crisis, and Settler Eschatology

We lived in an electric world. We relied on it for everything.
And then the power went out. We weren't prepared. Fear
and confusion led to panic. The lucky ones made it out of the
cities. The government collapsed. Militias took over, controlling the food supply and stockpiling weapons. We still don't
know why the power went out. But we're hopeful that someone will come and light the way.
—Expository voice-over, *Revolution*

Stories construct worlds, those aesthetic orderings on the chaos of biophysical reality that human beings seem to require for survival.[1] The
stories we tell matter for our ecological futures.[2] The settler future
imaginary or *eschatology* is shaped by Christian theology, and dwells
on apocalyptic scenarios of the end times, whether zombies, disease, or
nuclear war are responsible.[3] Eschatology is an area of theological study
that focuses on the end of the world. Such a phrase—the end of the
world—presupposes a linear historical trajectory, aimed toward an end
point, or a destination. Apocalypse, or Revelation, forms a deep structural condition of possibility for the narratives of developmentalism and
linear progress that underlie settler time. Settler time promotes and is
reinforced by chromonormativity, or the expectation embedded in global
capitalism that linear time governs all human activity across the globe.[4]
Rational and empirically based fears for the future, rooted in a growing
awareness of the unsustainability of the present, are expressed in apocalyptic science writing and fiction.[5] The power of apocalyptic scenarios in
the US national imagination resonates with what Rifkin calls settler time.
This linear and end-times-oriented view of history assumes that "the past
is an alien space separated by an unbridgeable gulf from the present."[6]

For Indigenous Peoples experiencing settler colonialism, the apocalypse has already happened, is currently happening, and the post-apocalyptic business of survivance and rebuilding is in progress.[7] Settlers are the recurrent agents of destruction toward Indigenous networks of human and more-than-human relations.[8] In contradiction to these Indigenous temporalities of return and relation in place, for the settler apocalyptic narratives under consideration here, the past is erased by the future, whether by an accumulation of events, or by a singular moment of transition that negates the past. Rifkin explains, "[s]uch a vision of history can be seen at play in the imagining of certain national events, like the Civil War, as moments of transition in which the country breaks away from a degraded past."[9] Thus, much like the imagined spatial negation embodied in sacrifice zones which are written off for a higher purpose, settler time views the past as disposable on the route to an end. Not only places but times can be discarded in the service of temporal progress. In Rikfin's words, "processes of settler temporal recognition and inclusion . . . depend on treating the straightness of time (and the ongoing transcendence of the past) as given."[10] Thus, settler time works according to a politics of disposability.[11]

Euro-American sociology rests on a taken-for-granted doctrine of modernization and developmentalism that has institutionalized it as a colonialist project.[12] Perhaps unconsciously, this end-times-oriented, quasi-theological view presupposes a final destination, or terminus. But modernization theorists tend not to explore this possibility, instead often positing a metaphorical "end of history" and a prevailing steady state of free-market globalization and high mass consumption.[13] The significance of the apocalyptic for US culture is evident, however, in popular narratives that explore both secular and religious versions of these end-of-times imaginaries (for example, the TV series *The Walking Dead* and other zombie stories, and the Christian Evangelical *Left Behind* book series and films). In many of these narratives the US settler state, "western civilization," or a universalized notion of "human society" are subjected to similar processes of elimination as those that are foundational to settler colonialism, in a "move to innocence" that naturalizes those processes.[14] As Tanana Athabaskan scholar Dian Million and sociologist Avery Gordon have argued, fictional worlds represented in stories like the ones under consideration in this chapter provide insight into amorphous social structures of feeling that more positivist forms of analysis can miss.[15] These fictional narratives matter, because they help determine what futures are imaginable in the present and therefore what actions are imaginable. In comparison to these settler narratives underwritten by racist developmentalism and white supremacism, Black futurisms such as the work of Octavia Butler and Indigenous futurisms offer a future imaginary informed by contemporary practices of survivance.[16]

How do the property bind and the settler complex explored in the last two chapters relate to end-times theology? Many contemporary anxieties, whether expressed as fears of so-called overpopulation, or resource wars, or end-of-times catastrophes are related to the linear and developmental trajectory of the Darwinian ladder of competition that is imagined as progress in settler time. The atomized rights-bearing individual of Garrett Hardin's fable populates this imagination, standing in for humankind. To elucidate these connections this chapter examines the threads of settler end-of-times imaginaries in three post-apocalyptic narratives. A short story, a TV series, and a Netflix movie, these diverse narratives are united by their preoccupation with fossil fuels and energy, a preoccupation that marks them as exemplary of late fossil fuel culture. Collected over a period of many years, these stories caught my attention because each has a grounding concern with the material realities of modern industrial society. Each reflects, in short, the sensation of *petromelancholia*, or

> the conditions of grief that *we*[17] experience when hydrocarbon resources start to dwindle, the feeling that *we* are slowly but surely losing access to cheap energy (and all affects that come with that) when it becomes obvious that *our* experienced non-scarcity is largely an ill-conceived illusion.[18]

In these stories, ordinary elements of energy infrastructure play a role in otherwise fantastical visions of mineral extraction, the power grid that electrifies society, and the impact of fracking on the land and people. Perhaps not coincidentally, each of these petromelancholic narratives also takes place within the bounds of a settler colonial society, specifically the United States and Australia. In both places the

contemporary settler state seems to be cracking under convening political, social, economic, cultural, and environmental crises. However,
while these narratives explore these cracks in contemporary fossil fuel
society, they each are to some degree limited by the logic of settler culture that relies on a narrow vision of the human.

In January 2020, while Australia was experiencing unprecedented
wildfires drawing apocalyptic comparisons, the Australian prime minister was busy promoting coal.[19] Throughout its own summer of 2020,
the United States experienced mass protests against the racism of the
justice system and police brutality, all while experiencing a breakdown of the healthcare system due to COVID-19.[20] In the United States
things reached a unprecedented peak, with a mob storming the capital
in January 2021 to protest certifying the votes of Democrats and people of color.[21] Australia and the United States are clearly very distinct
with respect to their particular ecological, political, social, and cultural
formations. However, they both share the deep structure of white supremacist settler societies and share similar settler cultural forms.[22]

"People of Sand and Slag," a short story by American science fiction
writer Paolo Bacigalupi, concerns a post-human and post-biological
"nightmare" future of endless extraction.[23] This story was first published in 2004 and was reprinted in a collection of post-apocalyptic
narratives (*Wastelands*) in 2008. The story's depiction of a completely
mutilated landscape, void of recognizable life, resonates with contemporary post-mining landscapes.[24] The narrative occupies a settler spatiality of a hyper-technological US future (set in the remains
of Montana and Hawai'i) where actual (ecological) place matters very
little. The second narrative, the US TV series *Revolution* which aired
on NBC in 2012–2014, evokes a reconstituted frontier, in the wake of
the mysterious loss of electric power. Much of the series' initial tensions come from historically American efforts to control territory and
struggles over white masculine sovereignty. Finally, the Netflix film
Cargo, made in Australia, is the only one of the three not to participate
in Indigenous erasure. In *Cargo*, natural gas fracking is suggested to be
at fault for a "virus" that turns its victims into ravening zombies. And
despite the containment efforts put forth by the settler government, in
the end, settler civilization is destroyed and the land returns to Indigenous "old ways."[25]

Not So Post-Humanist after All: "People of Sand and Slag"

Unsurprisingly, the people of sand and slag are mine workers. However, rather than actually mining, they provide military-style security for SesCo, which owns the automated mining compound where they work in Montana. The biting satire of this story relates to its post-humanism.[26] Although it is post-humanist in the biological sense (the cyborg characters are augmented with weeviltech in their guts that enables them to digest sand and slag, with auto-regeneration, speed, and strength upgrades for defending the corporation, and with various aesthetic features), it is decidedly settler humanist in its vision of the future devoid of more-than-human life.

In her analysis of "An Ecomodernist Manifesto," Eileen Crist notes that for ecomodernists, we are always already in a situation where there are "only" humans. As she points out, despite the extinction crisis and other signs of ecosystem collapse, the authors of the manifesto see no real evidence of limits to growth because

> humanity [has not yet encountered] some insuperable obstacle to demographic or economic expansion, such as a hard agronomic boundary in food production or the depletion of some indispensable and nonsubstitutable resource. Since no such obstacle has arisen, nor threatens arising in the near future, then it follows that there is remarkably little evidence for humanity having breeched, or soon breeching, limits to growth.[27]

"The Ecomodernist Manifesto" promises a benign Anthropocene achieved through technological development that will allow humanity to live a modern life of convenience and plenty. While nonhuman nature is of course impacted by this global technological modernization, as humanity progresses in wealth, the remaining nonhuman nature can be removed from the primary scene of human life, to be placed, for example, in preserves and be left alone. Human freedom, the Manifesto's highest ideal, as it has been for modernization theory in general, is generated through nonhuman unfreedom. There is only "us."[28]

This vision of humanism nearly perfectly describes the nightmare world of Bacigalupi's story; vastly augmented humans are surrounded by "biojobs" and "centaurs." These creations are worker cyborgs de-signed and used much like the massive, automated mining machinery that grinds into the Montana landscape leaving slag heaps, containment ponds, tailing pits, and an absence of biological life. When a *dog* miracu-lously appears among the slag heaps and poisoned pits, the characters can only relate it to something they once saw in a zoo—uncloistered biological life has become impossible. When the character Jaak tries to feed the dog his arm (because he can simply re-grow another), his aug-mented flesh makes the dog sick.

Bacigalupi's story satirizes the ecological modernization manifesto. Pre-weeviltech life is contained in zoos, as a curiosity with no purpose. The story suggests that human life itself has been reduced to nothing but work, violent virtual games, and hedonistic vacations among the garbage-strewn and petroleum-soaked beaches of Hawai'i and Cancun. The story exaggerates the alienation of settler capitalism to the point of absurdity and tragedy, as the dog (an animal almost guaranteed to make the most ruthless capitalist scratch it behind the ears) struggles to survive the toxic landscape of their beach vacation. The post-human characters live easily on sand, slag, or toxic waste that can be digested by the weevils in their bellies. But the dog needs clean water and food and so in the end they kill and eat him. They get no great pleasure from the rare treat of meat.

The problem of toxic waste is overcome in Bacigalupi's narrative by technology that makes humans able to coexist with the waste. Their lives and relationships only shallowly skim the surface, and the contract to SesCo is apparently the most significant relation in the characters' lives.[29] In this apocalyptic scenario, although the characters are unboth-ered, narrative irony makes the tragedy clear. Before the beach vacation when they kill it, the narrator Chen spends a night sleeping with the dog—the miraculous remainder of the interrelated web of life on Earth, those other forms of life that are like us, but are not us and are not for us—and after the dog is gone, "sometimes, [he misses] it."[30]

The biological posthumanism of the human characters in "People of Sand and Slag" serves to put into relief the ecological humanism of the story; the dog represents the Other, the nonhuman relations, the life-for-itself on Earth that the humanism of modernization and ecomoderniza-tion disregards. The story highlights the truncated nature of a human freedom that relies on others' nonfreedom. Ecological modernization that proposes to use technology to overcome the environmental crisis without sacrificing modern conveniences and wealth implicitly excludes the poorest and most marginalized from the category of the human. For example, by disregarding the rare earth minerals mined by enslaved labor that enable modern technology, ecomodernization writes modernity's casualties out of the human.[31] In this sense it is no different from the liberal possessive individualism of the Enlightenment.[32]

In effect, Bacigalupi shows us an alternative ending for the video "Man" discussed in the introduction.[33] Instead of invoking extraterrestrials who come and stomp Man to death as he sits on his throne of garbage, this story is Earthbound. Human ingenuity (weeviltech) prevents the demise of Man along with his habitat. But it shares with the video the flattening of relations and the vivisectioning of the web of life that erases other lifeways that enable multispecies flourishing. In this narrative, the settler complex not only eliminates Indigenous Peoples, it also steamrolls any alternative to extractive capitalism. Bacigalupi offers an anti-capitalist critique by demonstrating the simplification of life to its bare needs and the end of curiosity, love, or uncertainty. However, what goes unelaborated in the narrative is the fact that the story's vision represents the triumph of settler colonial control over human and nonhuman Others, using technology to maximize the "knowability, capture-ability, map-ability . . . of settler futures, asserting ownership over land and sky."[34] Its naturalized US settler geography—suggested by the characters' vacation travel from Montana to Hawai'i—represents an image of white supremacist settler futurity.

Revolution: Frontier World Revisited

An American television series that aired on NBC from 2012 to 2014, *Revolution* features a mysterious worldwide loss of electrical power, and the subsequent collapse of the United States' social order. The show's world-building was accessible and amenable to folks taking part in the resurgence in American right-wing politics who were reacting to the Obama presidency at that time.[35] This twenty-first-century right-wing perspective maintains indifference to the global ecological crisis except for certain very narrowly defined political implications. Consider this

Tea Party member's comment on climate change that suggests the limits of concern: "The politicians and those people—celebrities. Most of them may or may not believe [in climate change], but it's an opportunity for them to gain power."[36]

Revolution centers questions of "power" in a post-apocalyptic Western package that reflects anxieties about the sustainability and morality of modern US settler society, but without addressing the material or ideological foundations of these anxieties.[37] It raises the question of the sustainability of contemporary society, but rejects a consideration of social justice, collective interest, or the kind of cooperative action that sustainability requires.[38] The series employs a double meaning of power—physical and social—that largely coincides with the dualistic categories of modernity, which divide human experience into quadrants of nature and culture.[39] *Revolution* provides a lens to consider how the settler complex impedes a communal response to the ecological crisis.[40] Far from presenting an opening for transformative politics, *Revolution's* post-apocalyptic settler colonial world responds to the crisis with a retrenchment of key elements of the settler complex: *homo economicus*, heteronormative patriarchy, and the dangerous freedom and charismatic violence of the frontier.

Challenges to one form of (material) power, such as in Obama's so-called war on coal, which threatened the entrenched coal industry in West Virginia, are frequently experienced as a threat to related forms of (cultural) power, or American national identity, especially when that is expressed as patriarchal masculinity, guns, and hyper-individualistic libertarianism.[41] This would help explain the sentiment expressed by a Tea Party member quoted in the *New York Times*, "They're trying to use global warming against the people . . . It takes away our liberty."[42] As discussed above, a *world* is an imagined, aesthetic ordering imposed on an open-ended reality, in the same manner as generic conventions order a narrative.[43] The world of *Revolution* brings us human/nature dualism in the form of a disconnected environmental consciousness reflecting settler alienation, that makes cooperative sustainable transformation nearly impossible to imagine, while bolstering a denial of the human vulnerability revealed by environmental crisis.

When the electricity goes out, combustion engines, aircraft, and batteries also cease functioning. With the power apparently gone for good, society devolves to "fear and confusion," leading to "panic." "Natural" hierarchies emerge to match conservative American worldviews, as expressed in the first season's opening voice-over: *The smart or lucky ones got out of the cities. The others died there.* The story picks up again 15 years after the power went out, when the United States is broken, splintered into the California Commonwealth, the Plains Nation, the Wasteland (the Southwest up to Idaho), a much-expanded Texas, the Georgia Federation in the Southeast, and the scene of most of the action, the Monroe Republic in the Northeast to upper Midwest. In short, although familiar national borders (i.e., with Canada and Mexico) continue to designate the end of territorial significance, the United States itself has reverted to a condition similar to that of the early to mid-nineteenth century. This geopolitical setting, featuring corrupt cities and dangerous frontiers, resonates with a white-settler mythology of US territory.[44] With an implicit reference to Native Americans, the Plains Nation performs the settler ideal of appropriating indigeneity both as heritage and as a white masculine proving ground.[45] *Revolution*'s post-apocalyptic world draws on the conventions of the Western movie genre to represent its version of essential human nature.[46]

The cause of the blackout is a mystery for most of the first season, and there is absolutely no reference in the first season to any actual source of electricity, whether coal, nuclear, or solar, etc. Eventually, a nanotechnology called nanites are discovered to be responsible for the failure of electricity. Nanites can be activated or deactivated by using special amulets (again, there is no reference to a grid or power source). As one Facebook commenter phrased it early in season one, this premise is a "fairy tale."[47] In other words, this framing centers insecurity about current energy systems but avoids a specific critique of those systems. Rather, in its imagined frontier geography and its Western aesthetic, the story is focused on the essential American identity that is revealed by the disaster.

The brutality and psychopathy of bad men provide a foil for heroic masculinity in frontier narratives, illuminating the essential source of sovereignty, which is imaged to stem from purely human control over others.[48] *Revolution* mobilizes libertarian definitions of freedom, post-feminist patriarchal masculinity, and a post-racial, neo-confederate frontier. The loss of electrical power throws the world into chaos and essentially fractures the social contract. Violent crime becomes rampant, social order breaks down, and many people die—especially those in the cities. Vigilantism eventually gives rise to family compounds, republics, and political territories that replace the United States, which has crumbled but is still represented by a group of rebels who secretly venerate the US flag. These American-identified rebels compare favorably to the sadistic psychopaths in Monroe's militia, who ruthlessly torture any dissenters. These stories resonated with 2012 election-year appeals to "real Americans."[49] In the puzzling contradiction between admiring patriotism (the oppressed rebels who secretly venerate the US flag) and deploring the Patriots (the evil US government in exile), the series also reiterates the sovereign citizen discourse of Cliven Bundy, who reveres the American flag while rejecting the authority of the federal government.[50]

In the frontier world of *Revolution*, all security is family security, there is no *res publica*.[51] The blackout initiates an era where protecting the family is paramount and falls (naturally) to patriarchs. In episode after episode, narrative tension is generated by the need to rescue, protect, or locate a family member. Family compounds and medieval-style suburban villages become political players, and political struggles play out in terms of the patriarchal family, not the collective good. Revolution exposes the "natural" (colonial) moral order that operates through patriarchy, biological kinship, and the fight for individual freedom.[52] The chaos that erupted after the blackout is unexplained and unexplored; the series simply assumes the breakdown of society without electricity or cars. But order is reestablished through the agency of white male military folks like General Sebastian Monroe (David Lyons) and Miles Matheson (Billy Burke). Through their ruthless use of force, they restore a semblance of order in less than 15 years. Family is the source of both morality and weakness for the characters, a framing which evokes the libertarian and neoliberal political philosophy that makes the family the only real unit of collectivity, organized by a natural hierarchy of dominance.

Positing the family as the only source of social order against the chaos of crime or corruption of politics is inherently patriarchal and is based on a naturalized value hierarchy of physical strength.[53] It reflects the alienation of the settler from human and more-than-human community, through the imperative of nuclear family independence.[54] Hence, questions of family loyalty, hidden paternity, and failed motherhood are the principal sources of drama, while physical violence is expansively celebrated in Western-style shootouts, torture scenes, and massive displays of weaponry. *Revolution*'s world thus eternalizes the United States even while imagining its demise. Settler futurity emerges here through the show's vision of human nature. This imagined future centers on a paranoid white-savior individualism and a denial of collective social and material relations. This refusal to acknowledge human beings' dependence on community and the materiality of the biosphere shapes not only the affective structures of contemporary settler culture but also its disastrous environmental policy.[55]

Cargo: Man. Woman. Natural Gas

Cargo was based on a short film released in 2013 that featured a striking image, a zombie carrying a baby in a backpack carrier.[56] Hence, it is a zombie film in which fatherhood is a central theme, and with it, patriarchal gender relations. Nevertheless, *Cargo* manages to avoid Indigenous erasure and the complete naturalization of the settler state even if it appears that the involvement of Indigenous people was an afterthought. "It wasn't until we had locked down that we were going to be shooting in South Australia that we then started researching the Adnyamathanha people."[57]

The film opens with a scene of Thoomi (Simone Landers) running through the bush and shows large bonfires burning zombies. Thoomi is hiding her infected father Willie (Bruce R. Carter) from the rest of her community and feeding him with animals she hunts. She's built a muzzle out of twine and sticks to keep him from biting. Despite Thoomi's efforts, Willie escapes from containment. Next, we see Andy (Martin Freeman), a British expat, and his white Australian settler wife Kay (Susie Porter) on a houseboat navigating the Murray River, evidently escaping from the city. Andy fishes out some "containment assistance" kits from the river, which include a syringe for assisted suicide and a map of Australia marked red around the edges where the outbreaks apparently started. The resonances between this map and the images of the 2020 Australian bushfires is remarkable.[58] Soon we see what I presume is the titular cargo, Andy and Kay's baby daughter, Rosie (Marlee Jane and Lily

Ann McPherson-Dobbins), who is crying from hunger as her parents count their dwindling food supplies.

They come upon a wrecked, half-submerged sailboat, and while his family sleeps, Andy goes hunting. He's carefully dressed in protective gear and using an abundance of caution he enters the boat cabin and starts collecting food. A sudden noise stops him, and he sees that the closet door has just opened an inch. He quickly exits the cabin and returns to his own boat. Showing his wife Kay the food, he points to himself and says "Man." He points to her and says "Woman." After making clear his role as a provider, he assures her that his adventure to the boat was safe, not mentioning the closet door. Andy takes a nap with Rosie and, not being forewarned, Kay decides to explore the other boat on her own. Kay's approach lacks the caution of Andy's and her trip brings disaster. When Andy awakens to a fussy Rosie, he finds his wife sitting in the bathroom with an ugly bite on her leg.

The zombies in Cargo are caused by a virus, and the virus takes 48 hours to develop into full-blown zombiehood. The containment assistance packages have watches that keep track of the hours counting down. When forced off the boat after Kay's bite, Andy makes a series of bad decisions that result in him getting bitten by Kay as she turns. At this point, with his own watch on countdown, Andy now is looking for someone to care for Rosie. At a mostly deserted station, where he hoped to find a hospital, Andy meets Etta (Kris McQuade), a white teacher suffering from cancer. She informs him that the Indigenous students she used to teach (including Thoomi) have left the station and are now "living in the old ways." She reports that "mobs [i.e., Indigenous communities] from all over the country are coming together . . . They sensed it, those who stayed connected." In Thoomi's memory, we see the elder Mr. Cleverman (David Gulpilil) warning a group around a fire, "They are poisoning this land you know. This country's changing. It's sick. We all get sick. You get sick too."

Etta tells Andy to seek out the Indigenous people who have gathered in hunting parties to "cleanse the land of the sick ones." Leaving the station, Andy comes upon a natural gas frack pad. Official signs marked "Oil & Gas," and "Caution, Live Well Site" are joined by a hand-painted banner proclaiming "Frack Off" and an Indigenous Australian flag. Immediately after seeing this, we meet a white couple, Vic (Anthony

Hayes), an oil and gas man, and Lorraine (Caren Pistorius). The supposedly safe home of Vic and his "wife" Lorraine turns out to be a horror
when Vic shows Andy how he is keeping an Indigenous child (Thoomi)
in a cage as zombie bait, so that he can shoot the zombies and steal
their valuables. He explains, "You can't catch fish without bait. When
this is over people are going to want things. Whoever controls the market, power, gas, all the shiny shit, will be sitting pretty." Mr. Cleverman is
in another cage, and Vic tells him, "I told you mob. The wells are mine
along with what's in them. Fuck with me and I'll fuck with you." His
condition worsening, Andy tries to sneak off at night and kill himself,
but Lorraine joins him and tells him she is an unwilling captive of Vic.
Vic discovers them and puts Andy in the cage with Thoomi. Later, when
Andy and Thoomi escape, Vic wakes up and shoots at them, killing Lorraine, who uses her body to shield the others. Mr. Cleverman is no longer in his cage when they arrive to release him.

Thoomi finds her dad dead and cradled high in a tree to save him
from being eaten by the other zombies. Despite her grief, she stays with
Andy to help him and Rosie find her people. Along the way they fight
again with Vic, who tries to steal Rosie, in exchange for "his" Lorraine.
Andy says, "Lorraine wasn't yours" and it is not clear if that is a categorical statement or a reference to Vic's lie about her being his wife. In any
case, Rosie is a precious cargo. As the virus progresses Andy devises a
way for Thoomi to use him to get both children to safety.

After Andy's final conversion, we see a group including Mr. Cleverman and Thoomi's mother Josie (Natasha Wanganeen) killing zombies
with spears and burning their corpses. Out of the smoke emerges Andy,
with Rosie and Thoomi on his back. Andy's plan was to construct a lure
of bloody intestines that Thoomi could dangle on a stick in front of Andy's face to steer him to her people. Thoomi and Rosie end up safely in
the Wilpena Pound, a circular basin in the Flinders Mountain Range,
where an Indigenous community welcomes them both. We see "thank
you" written in white paint on Rosie's belly, and Andy is interred in a
tree like Willie, in honor of his efforts at saving Thoomi.

According to Simone Landers (Thoomi), "'Cargo' isn't really a zombie
film. 'The Virals' are symbolic of the Western pollution . . . the film promotes the Indigenous respect for the land, and I am proud to be a part
of that."[59] Vic's greed and rapaciousness represent the capitalistic evil of

Oil & Gas and highlight the distinction of "the old ways" of the Indig-enous peoples in the film. Thoomi starts out by explaining to Andy that the "ghosts" like her father have lost their souls, and that Mr. Cleverman can cure them. While we don't see proof of this, Mr. Cleverman does manage to escape from Vic's cage and rejoin the group, who is effectively "cleansing the land of the sick ones."

Thoomi's efforts to protect her father are the inspiration for Andy's plan in the end. Because she didn't see her father as simply an undead zombie, she learned how to communicate with him, directing him places with the scent of blood, preventing his bite, and enclosing him away from the hunting parties. By doing this, she creates a zombie se-miosis, or relationship of shared meaning, in which the bloody intestine becomes a legible sign for the zombie Andy that enables Thoomi and Rosie to effectively communicate with him even after his conversion.[60] This intersubjective behavior is particularly highlighted with the con-trast of Vic's objectifying cruelty.

However, even in its conclusion with Australia presumably cleansed of settlers, the centrality of a white father to the story undermines the film's critique of settler Australia. The foil of Vic makes it clear that Andy is a good man, husband, and father. Unlike Vic, he understands the new circumstances presented by the disaster and sees Thoomi and Lorraine as human beings, while Vic stupidly remains "the grasping and avari-cious white man."[61] As a Brit, perhaps he (ironically) carries a bit of in-nocence of the Australian settler complex. The white Australian women are likewise innocent, in particular baby Rosie, who survives through the superhuman efforts of her father, Thoomi, and the Indigenous com-munity that will become her new family.[62] These settler "moves to inno-cence" recall the meme that circulated on social media in 2020, in which the climate crisis exemplified by that season's massive fires was said to be represented by the skyline's resemblance to the black, yellow, and red Indigenous Australian flag.[63]

Conclusion

The end-times futurity exemplified by the post-apocalyptic texts dis-cussed in this chapter demonstrates the commitment of settler culture to a transformative event that leaves the past behind. Like the spatial disposability implied by the sacrifice zone, the past is a nuclear landscape "we" must leave behind. The linear and developmental time that characterizes these narratives highlights the importance of the new in settler culture, as "the feeling of futurity as rupture, a disjunction between what was and what will be that retains the continuity of dominant frames of reference while generating the sensation of the unexpected."[64] The petromelancholia of these narratives highlights a general awareness on the part of settler publics of the unsustainable present of settler culture.[65] Mourning for a lost (imagined) control over nature is characteristic of these settler apocalypse stories.

Despite the long-standing underpinning of apocalyptic tropes in many western cultural forms, the end of times has gained a "new lease of life . . . after becoming linked to the Anthropocene."[66] The term "Anthropocene" has become a popular metonym for the current emergency. The ease of its adoption seems related to the fact that it reflects a classical humanism; it either spreads the blame evenly across our species or excludes those who are *not* responsible from the category of the human. Thus, the Anthropocene can ironically be seen as a reclamation of liberal human control (this is *our* fault). Anti-colonial critics have often pointed out that trouble, precarity, and disruption are characteristics of the experience of colonization, and that the experience of this by the global North in the postmodern era should be seen less as a novelty than as representing aftershocks from the brutally violent displacements of European colonization.[67]

In her critique of the concept of "risk society," Mackey notes that "Certainty is often conceptualized as an unequivocally desirable and positive state of affairs," that is nonetheless constantly at risk. She continues, "[m]any theorists assert, as if it is a self-evident universality, that all people require certainty, a sense that our lives and futures are secure and not at risk."[68] With language harkening back to the Enlightenment philosopher Hobbes's war of all against all, Mackey suggests that the concept of ontological security "constructs a particular view of a *normal* world . . . that we all supposedly share, a world that requires constant engagement to *control* the inevitable anxiety of dealing with constant threats and dangers."[69] The idea that the world is a dangerous place that must be above all controlled often leads to a conservative impulse to "return" to "normal."[70] In the context of the settler state, the property rights of settlers are an example of something that (supposedly) has already been settled long ago, but which are disrupted by Indigenous activism. The certainty promised by control is therefore always already normal, but simultaneously always displaced into a hoped-for future of "getting back to normal."

Property law, a "good business climate," and normatively shared expectations of alienability and individualism create settler certainty.[71] This certainty is based on hierarchical sovereignty, individual property ownership, and the assumption of settler state hegemony.[72] Certainty requires control, mastery, and domination. Other forms of community, sovereignty, and temporality are disruptive to this certainty:

> Relations between bodies that have been displaced, that have been sub-jected to escalating forms of geopolitical restriction, that occur within explicit and implicit forms of ritual and collective activity, that are linked by nonnuclear modes of desire and care, that are connected across chron-ologically divided periods, and that are inhabited and animated by the work of prophesy all lie outside "conventional genealogy" and the norma-tive lines" of settler national time.[73]

So, is precarity related to the apocalyptic environmental destruction of the current global hegemony? Or does the sense of a rising tide of pre-carious life reflect the crumbling of the foundations of the settler state? As Mackey argues, in settler colonialism "[t]he risks and uncertainties of settler societies were . . . transferred onto the colonized, resulting in centuries of state-imposed uncertainty, risk and danger to individual and collective selves."[74] In other words, this newly felt uncertainty on the part of settlers is conditioned by an imagined certainty that was always based on the domination of Indigenous Peoples and their relations by settler colonial violence and property.

Imagining a world without such efforts at control, without a binary opposition between security and chaos, calls for challenging the foun-dations of its desirability.[75] Certainty requires control. Interactions between relationally autonomous equals are never certain. On the con-trary, relationships between equals require constant maintenance and good faith action.[76] The tragedy of Bacigalupi's "People of Sand and Slag" is that they have done away with this possibility. The land and biosphere have simply collapsed under the weight of settler capitalist "epistemologies of mastery." Indigenous futurisms like that of Louise Er-drich's (Turtle Mountain Band of Chippewa Indians) novel *The Future Home of the Living God* explore the limitations of such epistemologies. In this story, pregnant women become the object of surveillance and a violent attempt at control by a religious fundamentalist pseudo-state because evolution seems to have reversed itself in a more-than-human rebuke to modernization theory and developmentalism. Meanwhile the Ojibwe reclaim territory and sovereignty as the settler state falls into chaos.[77] The loss of deadly settler certainty provides renewed possibility for Indigenous thrivance.[78]

When the artificial comfort enabled by modern technology disap-pears in a recreation of the American frontier in TV's *Revolution*, the foundation of settler power becomes evident as force. Certainty here is obtained only by physical domination of the Other, in a frontier-like war of all against all. The agency of the possessive individual is enabled by a sense of "entitlement, of always knowing and controlling."[79] Anti-colonial sovereignty, however, is based not on domination and control of the Other, but on relation; relations between relatives and equals, none controlled by the others, none of whom can live without the others.[80] Again, from an Indigenous perspective, Cherie Dimaline's (Georgian Bay Métis) near-future speculative novel *The Marrow Thieves* reflects the mutual interdependence of kinship relations working to preserve Indigenous life and knowledge in the midst of an ongoing settler cam-paign of elimination.[81]

Interestingly regarding *Cargo*, the filmmakers suggest that Andy and Thoomi represent such a relation; "both need each other to survive."[82] The challenge *Cargo* makes to settler culture is constituted in part by the film's simple recognition of the existence of Indigenous people in Aus-tralia. Despite this recognition, the film's narrative focuses on the self-sacrifice of Andy as a white father to a white baby, and thus continues to focus on white Australia. As an apocalyptic struggle that ends with Andy's death, the film identifies human society and its conflicts with the settler state. It projects a more innocent and nondevelopmental future marked by a "paradigmatic Indianness" at the film's end in a space where empire has run its course.[83]

Up to now, I've attempted to use exemplary events and stories to give voice and tangibility to the structures of feeling of settler culture, and the property bind that limits personhood at the same time as it defines it. The final two chapters will take up these affective and economic structures in settler culture as expressed and challenged by the natural gas fracking and pipeline boom in West Virginia. As the settler texts examined here perhaps make clear, the context of the United States as a settler colony is usually unspoken, unnoticed, and unchallenged by the dominant white society. Centering the idea that it is, indeed, a settler colony troubles many of the comforts and touchstones of ordinary white American life. However, as reflected in the increasing urgency of apocalyptic narratives as explored in this chapter, the foundations of settler certainty are perhaps cracking under pressure.

4

Lessons from the "Hellmouth"

The View from Inside a Sacrifice Zone

You have someone that's lived on their family farm for four generations . . . and someone . . . says "Hey, we want to drill; we're going to offer you $2500 dollars." And . . . [they're] looking at the old wells that we have here [that are] not that awful big in the scheme of things. . . . And they think, "Well you seem like a nice boy, and I sure could use $2500 dollars, and so I'm going to sign these papers and let you all drill here." But what they don't realize is first of all, they should have gotten $25,000 maybe. Secondly, he's not a nice boy. And thirdly, the well pad is the size of a small city.
—Cassandra, resident of northern West Virginia

Cassandra's comment, above, summarizes her view of how the selling or leasing of mineral rights in an eastern natural gas play works out in practice. Each individual (surface) property owner has the choice to sell or lease their mineral rights (unless they don't because someone else already made that choice in the past). The contract between surface owners and the gas and oil industry is unbalanced from the beginning, as the individual must negotiate with a large and organized corporate force. Each individual owner's choice affects their human and nonhuman neighbors, but the piecemeal process of property rights and contracts leaves no room for collective reflection. In this chaotic energy frontier, things are lost before they are measured.[1]

In the past decade, the exploitation of the Marcellus Shale natural gas play has exponentially increased the impact of natural gas drilling in West Virginia. The state has a long history with the oil and gas industry. During the last 50 years, however, the industry had made a comparatively smaller impact on the landscape than coal, for example.[2] The oil industry hit its peak in the early twentieth century. Since that time the residents of the historically most important oil- and gas-producing region, including several northwestern counties of the state, have been familiar with the sight of small gas wells and their accompanying storage barrels accumulating the oil extracted at the same time as the gas. These are so-called conventional wells, such as Cassandra describes as "old well pads," above, and the area is dotted with them, along with small pipelines leading to collection facilities and compressor stations.

With the technological advancements of hydro-fracturing and horizontal drilling, massive amounts of natural gas in the Marcellus Shale have become available for production.[3] This means that the residents of north central West Virginia have seen a boom in natural gas well drilling. This boom has come with a proliferation of acres-large deep gravel well pads accompanied by massive compressor stations and waste management facilities. In order to exploit the natural gas reserves most effectively in West Virginia, the industry has sought permission to build multiple large pipelines across the area to export the gas to Canada, to power plants in the southern United States, to cracker plants on the Gulf coast, as well as to liquid natural gas exporting stations on the Atlantic coast. In addition, the area has been flooded with heavy truck traffic servicing the wells, disposal sites, and pipeline construction sites.[4] A proposed Appalachian Storage Hub on the Ohio River would create a petrochemical storage and processing zone that, among other things, would produce plastic pellets using the overabundance of gas from the Marcellus Shale.[5]

After massive, organized resistance and regulatory missteps, the Atlantic Coast Pipeline was cancelled.[6] The Mountain Valley Pipeline, still in the works, is struggling, and the boom in natural gas development seems to have slowed in the absence of a reliable market.[7] However, the rush for natural gas has already transformed the land, economy, and community, possibly irrevocably. Frack pads, compressor stations, and other gas infrastructure remain. To what future does this development lead? What avenues are paved through this activity, and which are foreclosed? The exponential growth of natural gas production, storage, processing, and transportation greatly increased the impact of the industry on the lives of residents and communities of northern, central, and southeastern West Virginia and has violently rerouted the future these communities will experience.

This chapter and the next draw on 24 interviews with West Virginia property owners, activists, and other residents in the natural gas play and areas targeted for pipeline construction, conducted during the summers of 2017 and 2018. All participants were white; 13 were men and 11 women. Identifying details have been altered and pseudonyms are used to maintain participants' confidentiality. Many were property owners affected by drilling or pipelines, but other participants were also activists, or simply concerned about the development happening in the area. In the end, all who agreed to be interviewed were highly generous people affected directly or indirectly by natural gas development. Some were heartbroken and hoping that they could bring attention to the injustices they were experiencing. One was a geologist, employed as a consultant by the industry, who offered a more sanguine opinion on natural gas. Because of my interest in property, I focused most closely on landowners affected by eminent domain or the split estate doctrine, although a few interviewees did not own property. Interviews were open-ended and focused on hearing people's experiences, asking about effects on their property if applicable, and their thoughts on the effects of natural gas development in the region, plus any other topics they wanted to discuss. While not all participants are directly quoted here, these interviews provided me with an insight into how property owners and other residents experience the increasing presence of the natural gas industry in their communities and on the land. In addition to the interviews, I attended several events sponsored by various environmentalist groups fighting fracking or pipeline development in the state.[8] While interviewing and traveling around the state, I got a small taste of what living in a natural gas development zone feels like, as described below.

In this chapter, I explore how this expanding industrial infrastructure reflects the destabilization and precarity of the late-fossil fuel economy. The fracking boom in West Virginia does not represent a specifically Appalachian geographically focused industrial sacrifice and culturally rich tradition such as the extraction of coal does, but instead makes up just part of a widespread national boom of oil and gas extraction and transport that stretches from Texas to Colorado to North Dakota to Pennsylvania with uneven environmental and economic effects on communities.[9] These uneven effects fracture some of the baseline assumptions of US white settler culture about citizenship and property rights, and about the relationship between progress, development, and improvement of property.[10] The gas boom has affected communities all over the country where the market in mineral rights and rights of way leads not to flourishing, but to precarity and sacrifice.

Succinctly describing this precarity, the impacts of the expansion of fracking on people's feelings of security in their property rights, and the implications for the region's future, Cassandra, the activist and blogger quoted above, explained:

> Everyone feels like they're being tricked. And you have the sense that you've got to read the newspaper reflexively every day and look for something [that might be happening] because your life could essentially end. Your farm could be over. I have a friend who lives on the lip of that monstrosity out there [an acres-large compressor station for natural gas] and she can't have a conversation on her porch anymore. And her family has been here for six generations, and her kids don't want to stay here because there's no reason to stay.

Sacrifice Zones and Property

A sacrifice zone is a concept developed in environmental justice literature to designate a geographical area and community that is subjected to toxic waste disposal, industrial development, or resource extraction.[11] Derived from the language of nuclear weaponry and testing, the sacrifice zone is a place considered expendable in the service of a greater good, whether that be national security or economic growth. In being sacrificed, the area is written off (thrown away) for the foreseeable future, leaving behind a toxic waste dump or otherwise poisoned landscape. The coalfields have been the focus of much of the literature on West Virginia as a sacrifice zone.[12] Petroleum and petrochemical processing in the southern United States has created a sacrifice zone known as "Cancer Alley," an epithet that refers to the cumulative and synergistic effects of the high concentration of refining and processing plants on residents' health in Louisiana's St. James Parish.[13] The impacts of fracking were brought to the general public's attention in Josh Fox's documentary *Gasland* (Fox 2010). As discussed in the introduction, the film began at his childhood home in Pennsylvania, a place just beginning to feel the effects of fracking, and moved to the western United States and back through the southern Cancer Alley to see the interconnected system of natural gas extraction, transportation, and processing. *Gasland* provides a large-scale view of the problems experienced by people living near natural gas and related industries and the outsized influence of the industry in politics, leading the filmmaker to suggest that the United States in general is a "gasland" or sacrifice zone.

An analysis of mineral rights and property ownership in Denton, Texas, revealed some of the specifics of the environmental injustices of natural gas exploitation. Tired of the numerous frack pads proliferating around homes and schools, the people of the city of Denton voted to ban fracking within their city limits. After their vote, the Texas state legislature passed legislation forbidding such local bans, in order to protect the property rights of the mineral owners, the majority of whom lived out of state.[14] Like other forms of fossil fuel extraction, natural gas fracking pits mineral owners' or lessees' interests against those of surface residents. The fracking and pipeline boom in West Virginia represents an explosion of extractive activity in the region that doesn't promise significant economic benefits to surface property owners or the area workforce.[15] Because of this gap in foreseeable benefits, this hyper-industrialism may begin to disrupt the political logic (i.e., the costs for some are outweighed by benefits for the many) that has justified unsustainable industrial development.[16]

The natural gas industry distributes the harmful effects of fossil fuel extraction beyond previously existing sacrifice zones. Bringing these effects further into the open raises questions about the settler state's promise of progressive economic development. In settler time, the past is said to be abandoned in favor of the future, through the means of the new and exotic (in this case technology). This addition of new technology like fracking makes a temporal disjunction between "what is and what will be" in the name of inevitable progress; however, such "an impression of change . . . depends on the actual shattering of environments and lifeways for those from whose lands newness is extracted as an exploitable resource."[17] Free-market competition is said to drive the American economy to always seek out the highest and best use for every piece of real property.[18] In combination with the growing awareness of climate change and other environmental disasters, the local effects of natural gas extraction, transport, and processing have perhaps begun to contradict the settler imagination of future economic flourishing on a wide scale.[19]

Alienability, or the quality that makes it possible for individuals to buy and sell "real property," is the linchpin of capitalist economic development and of American national identity. Individuals buying and selling individual parcels of land participate in the market and in the quest for the American Dream. This alienability of land as property is a cultural organization of the human relationship to land that exists in sharp distinction from systems based on shared rights to resources, recognition of interdependencies, and an inseverable relationship between a People and place.[20] Furthering this alienability, the split estate doctrine allows for the horizontal division of surface from mineral rights, each of which can then be owned by different people. Thus, deciding the highest and best use of the land can become a struggle between these two owners. As the Bureau of Land Management (BLM) notes, this usually results in prioritizing the rights of mineral owners over those of the surface owner because the surface owner must allow the mineral owners to access their property; they are literally standing in the way of development.[21]

In what is currently known as the western United States, mineral rights are often held in reserve by the federal government which can issue leases to industry for development.[22] In the East, the federal government owns a smaller percentage of the land; however, many people do not control the mineral rights attached to their surface property.[23] In mineral-rich Appalachia, these mineral rights may have been severed for over a hundred years, but the practice of severing mineral rights has gained new popularity as the financial promise of exploiting mineral resources (especially natural gas) has grown.[24] Even in cases where the surface owner has retained legal ownership of the rights, a preexisting lease can extend control of the mineral resource indefinitely into the future. Conflicts over these increasingly incompatible sets of rights are at the center of the intensification of West Virginia as a sacrifice zone.[25] As Cassandra explained:

I own . . . full [mineral] rights, but it doesn't matter, it's already been leased. So, it's a contract that I'm bound to even though I had no say in it. And [I get] about $8 a year. Now . . . I'm happy that I have gas on my property; we get free gas in my house. But what bothers me is if they decide that they want to put a big city-sized frack pad there, I don't think I have the power to keep that from happening. I find it irritating when they run the drill [on the conventional well on my property], which they do about once a week for about an hour . . . Honestly if I had to trade off "annoying once a week" for "free gas all year" I probably would still make that trade, but to not have any control—it seems anti-constitutional to me, because we have constitutionally protected property rights that are not being respected.

While fracking hinges on the deployment of the split estate doctrine and the buying and leasing of mineral rights, pipeline development, when unsupported by landowners, relies on eminent domain.[26] The Federal Energy Regulatory Commission (FERC) is the regulatory body that authorizes the use of eminent domain to use property for interstate pipeline construction even against the landowners' wishes. In the case of the pipelines in West Virginia, this has been justified by the concept of the public interest, a controversial notion that leads many residents in the pipelines' paths to question whether the headlong rush to extract and export natural gas is in *their* interest.[27]

As Greg, an activist and resident of a southeastern county, explained, the pipeline boom threatens to transform the lives of people living in its path. He told me the story of a retired man who had "looked really hard to find property . . . to retire to. Bought this beautiful piece of property . . . with the old growth forest . . . [his plan for his] retirement years was to . . . walk through the woods, sit on the front porch, and look at his old growth trees." Due to the now cancelled Atlantic Coast Pipeline (ACP), which used eminent domain to claim property along its path, 11 acres of this old growth forest were set to be cut. The man joined the fight to stop the pipeline, but because of the continued threat from the ACP, eventually sold the property and moved away from the area. Greg continued, "There's thousands of stories, people [whose] plans and dreams for their property is now dictated by somebody in Richmond,

Virginia or Pittsburgh. . . . Well, you know, we got to get this gas to the ocean for export because somebody needs a bigger boat."

Fracking the Future

The fracking boom in West Virginia started about a decade ago with the development of horizontal drilling and hydro-fracturing technology that allowed access to the vast Marcellus natural gas play, a much deeper reservoir than could be accessed by conventional wells, and further below that, the Utica formation.[28] When initial well development techniques borrowed from elsewhere encountered difficulty in the terrain of West Virginia, the state legislature passed a bill regulating the emergent industry in the state. These new regulations led to a flourishing of well activity in northern West Virginia. According to my informant Frank, a long-time critic of the industry, initial well drilling technology was ill-suited to the mountainous terrain and caused many landslides and other problems for nearby residents, which generated resistance in the form of protests and lawsuits. Once the law was passed, drilling took off in the state, with a brief decline when natural gas prices fell due to a glut in the market in 2016.[29] Adding to the impression of the whole situation being a pyramid scheme, shale gas wells produce most effectively in the first two years of their existence, which spurs the industry to constant speculation, exploration, and drilling to maintain profit margins.[30]

Echoing the fate of small towns that have gotten in the way of mountaintop removal mining, Mobley, a small community in Wetzel County, was entirely dismantled in the name of natural gas extraction, processing, and transportation.[31] Its residents faced the same choice as those in the coalfields who find their homes have become obstacles to extraction: to sell or be driven out. Fumes from a processing plant and heavy diesel truck traffic had already made the place unsafe when the company bought the remaining houses in order to establish, in Frank's words, "mile marker zero," where the Ohio Valley Connector and Mountain Valley Pipeline will start their journeys in opposite directions. Across the forested valley from this site sits a Mark West plant, a so-called midstream facility for processing, storing, and transporting gas.

These industrial eruptions on the rural landscape can seem small in comparison to the large-scale exploitation of the coalfields.[32] However, these eruptions are interconnected by expanding pipelines and the large numbers of diesel trucks carrying pipeline segments, chemicals, and brine, which create the overall impression of what Frank called a "spider web." This expression echoes the term *asabakeshiinh*, or spider, used by Diné and Hopi people to refer to the Peabody coal mining complex on their lands in the southwest, and emphasizes the sense of expansive strangulation experienced in an extractive sacrifice zone.[33]

Sacrifice is an is apt term for describing the extractive fossil fuel–dominated landscape of West Virginia, in particular the southern coalfields, which have seen thousands of acres of mountains permanently flatted by the practice of mountaintop removal coal mining.[34] Popular slogans like "Coal keeps the lights on" represent the ethos of sacrifice in the name of breadwinning masculinity and national energy security.[35] Ironically, the boom in natural gas threatens the future survival of the coal industry, due to the market logic of maximizing efficiency.[36] But for many residents witnessing the proliferation of frack pads, processing plants, and pipelines, without a significant return in local employment, the logic of economic development as progress rings hollow.

Fracking destabilizes narratives of future flourishing in the area. By putting into question why people would want to stay, it makes clear the ways sacrifice zones represent a wasting of place that exemplifies the "annihilation of space by time." This phrase refers to the overcoming of spatial barriers by capital (or financial investment), which seeks to speed up the process of transforming labor to money.[37] Here, I want to highlight how land (space) is a barrier to accumulation, by holding the gas in place. The network of meters-deep gravel well pads and pipe yards, fracking wells with "legs" extending miles in all directions, high pressure pipelines heading in multiple directions, and processing and cracker plants together work to overcome these spatial barriers. The infrastructural ruin left behind by fossil fuel extraction highlights the sacrifice of the present for profit in the name of an imagined future.[38] For natural gas, the profits are projected, the market is emergent, employment hoped for, but the waste of water and land comes first and is irreversible.

Land

One notable characteristic of natural gas extraction is the way it is simultaneously everywhere and nowhere. Unlike coal, which dominates the landscape visually, especially through surface mining, coal processing, and railroad transportation, the oil and gas industry has, at least at first glance, a lower profile. The smaller conventional wells and their shed-sized storage barrels dot the landscape with industrial referents, but nevertheless remain marginal in a mostly rural setting of farms, forests, and narrow mountain hollows. The new, acres-large well pads with multiple fracked wells concentrate the impact of the industry in one nondescript place, while disguising its long reach underground via the "legs" of the horizontal wells that can reach miles in different directions. Visually, these new well pads resemble large flat gravel parking lots. The compressor stations and waste disposal facilities are more obvious signs of industrial development. The impact of the industry is further expanded through the numerous pipelines, already built or under construction, that are planned to speed the highly pressurized gas away from its origins, and the underground storage fields that keep the gas on reserve for future use. Another seemingly thoughtless impact on the environment are pipe yards, holding pipe segments for pipelines waiting to be constructed, that consist of acres of deep gravel covered in stacks of 36- to 42-inch steel pipes, destined for a wildly sinuous path that crosses streams and mountains, cutting a 150-foot slash through farms and forests and under rivers and roads.

Bill, a retired educator and rancher with a 500-acre farm, was worried about the impact of the proposed pipelines and possible new wells on his property. Bill's language showed his identification with his property. He said there weren't any gas wells "on me" [i.e., on his property], but his farm sits on an underground natural gas storage field where tons of natural gas is stored in anticipation of the greater fuel needs of winter. Bill recounted how one of these storage fields had started to leak:

> The gas began to come up in people's [water] wells, and it was this one fellow . . . who built a house and drilled a [water] well . . . his well blew out and caught on fire and they had a flare there that was 50 to 75 feet

high! And what do you do when your storage field breaks to the surface? What do you do? Well what they did [was], [there] was an old pressure station there; they were decommissioning it, and instead of taking it out they changed it so that it pumps out of that area, so the gas flows into this area, from all around, and they keep pumping it out and pumping it out and pumping it out, and that keeps the pressure low enough so that people don't have too much problems with their wells, you see. Ha ha, isn't that a hoot?

The instability of this storage field echoes the inherent volatility of the natural gas economy in perpetuity, unsettling communities and making residents uneasy in their homes.

Sam, the owner of a smaller farm living near Bill, had pipelines under construction on every side of his property, although as he put it "None of them impact me directly, so I guess you'd say that I have no reason to complain." However, the gas industry was everywhere, and only a reductive view could miss the cumulative effects on the landscape and community. Sam also had a conventional well on his property, thankfully invisible from the bucolic front porch of his small farmhouse which was shaded by flowering vines and surrounded by woods and red-painted out buildings. His relatively small farm of only 100 acres (in his words) was mostly a retreat for him and his wife, who were both retired educators who had farmed as a side-line during their teaching careers and who enjoyed the peace and quiet their property provided. But even the conventional well came with gathering lines (small pipelines leading to a compressor station), and an access road built by the gas company, which was a larger and much more elaborate version of the small gravel driveway that Sam and his wife used to enter the property. This gravel access road designed for heavy truck use was guarded by a locked gate only openable by the company for the sporadic visits from the well and road maintainers.

The rural peace and quiet of Sam's woody acres were not only punctured by this road, the well maintainers, and the occasional visits from oil and gas company representatives asking about leasing a right-of-way for a new pipeline, it was also occupied by the gas itself. As he walked me to my car after our interview, Sam pointed to a depressed area in the grass near his woodshed.

> Right there, there was a leak for a while, from one of the gathering lines. It had rained, and there was a puddle, and I saw it bubbling. So, I got a match and I lit it. It flamed up really big, almost invisible in the daytime, and it just burned there for a while until the wind blew it out.

The underground gas escaping from Sam's yard illustrates the hidden industrialization of a rural landscape. His story brought to my mind the cliché of oil spewing from the ground like black gold. The methane bubbles Sam discovered bubbling up from the puddle didn't signify future riches for him, however, because the mineral rights under his property were owned by a stranger, a man living in Florida, to whom he had spoken only rarely and never met. The gas haunts the landscape, mostly invisibly extending through roads, pipes, and mineral rights to connect diverse places to the industry. When reassuring me of his family's safety, Sam told me he and his wife would be ok, because if necessary, they had access to another piece of land in Pennsylvania where they could go, although that one too had a gas well.

Water

As indicated by the invisible gas bubbling up in puddles and wells, the millions of gallons required for fracking, and the gas traveling in pipelines under rivers and creeks, the industry's most large-scale impact is on water. Fred, a farmer and rancher in northern West Virginia, told me how the wells drilled on his property during the boom's beginning left lasting damage to the water on his property. The gas company had constructed a tailings pond there, where they deposited the sludge produced by drilling. He recounted, "when they were ready to frack; I think they were running out of time; they breached the walls of the pond and just let it ooze all over the place and buried it." Fred enlisted the help of public interest lawyers to get this toxic sludge cleaned up. However, he says the persisting contamination of the water has continued to impact his family, "every time they frack," elaborating that:

> I've had a lot of stillborn calves from drinking that water, because the creek goes entirely though my property. . . . My oldest daughter had a hysterectomy. My . . . daughter in law had a hysterectomy. She's fighting

cancer. My daughter had a big pond with big goldfish in it and, it killed every one of those fish. With the producing.

Currently the industry no longer uses tailings ponds, but uses trucks to move the waste produced from drilling. The inaptly named Clearwater facility, built by the gas company Antero on the border of Doddridge and Ritchie Counties, represents a $300 million investment in concentrating the wastewater generated by the fracking boom in West Virginia. A large industrial complex rising from behind the trees, in the words of Cassandra it was basically "like driving into the lip of hell. If you're a geek, it's the Hellmouth."[39] Because of the proliferation of gas industry activity and well drilling in the region, Antero's regional vice president was able to present this facility as an ecological boon to West Virginia. Fracking uses between 1.5 million and 16 million gallons of water per well.[40] Drawing from wells all over the state, wastewater from wells (called produced water) will be trucked into the facility, the chemical solids from that water will be isolated and trucked to landfills in Oklahoma, and the remaining "salts" will be buried in an adjacent landfill. This concentration of waste and waste treatment should be seen in light of what would happen in its absence, which would be a permanent loss of usable water and the dispersal of toxic sludge around the state. Antero's manager of civil engineering described the work of the facility this way:

> It takes the produced water that has no surface use at this point and separates it essentially in two . . . It takes the 100 percent volume to produce 98 percent clean, surface-discharge-quality water and salt, and then takes those metals or things in the water and makes 2 percent residual solid.[41]

The wastewater the facility is designed to treat is a brine consisting of the (proprietary) chemical mix used to frack the well combined with the (slightly radioactive) produced water that is brought up out of the Marcellus Shale along with the natural gas. To say that it has no surface use is quite an understatement.

After processing, the clean water is recycled for use in another Antero well, the residual solids are headed for a landfill in Oklahoma, and the mineral "salts" that are removed from the water are destined for Clearwater's landfill. The layers of inequality and sacrifice involved in industrial development are highlighted in the shipping of this toxic residue to Oklahoma, the US state with the second highest Indigenous population.[42] This process is designed to reduce the unsustainable quantity of water used in fracking. But as Cassandra pointed out, this landfill sits directly above a creek which drains to the main water intake for the largest town in the county. The Clearwater facility is one institutionalization of a divergent future from the one most likely imagined by residents and enlists the waters of West Virginia in a future of industrial development and sacrifice.[43]

To the south in Summers County, the planned Mountain Valley Pipeline (MVP) route is currently held up by lawsuits, but is projected to cross under the Greenbrier River. Upriver, the Atlantic Coast Pipeline (ACP) had been planned to cross under the Greenbrier at another spot in Pocahontas County. Both pipelines were to send gas to destinations to the south and on the coast.[44] In recognition of its value as a natural resource and significant eco-tourism attraction, the Greenbrier River was designated a protected "Natural Stream" by the West Virginia legislature in 2011; nevertheless the pipeline companies planned to drill into the bedrock under the river in two places, one of which has yet to be halted.[45] The karst topography of southeastern West Virginia provides good farmland and abundant spring water. The former Sweet Springs Hotel was historically one of several resorts in the region capitalizing on the spring water. Today the Sweet Springs Resort Park Foundation is trying to fight the pipeline, restore the old hotel, and promote the spring water as an alternative economic project for the county.[46] These locally imagined futures have been jeopardized by the imperatives of the natural gas boom.

Roads

For Bill, the rancher mentioned above, the oil and gas industry has always been around, and he "took in hatred of the gas company at [his] mother's breast." However, the new horizontal drilling and fracturing, along with the industrial boom in cracker plants and other uses for natural gas, exert new pressures on the community from the industry. One symptom of this was a ramping up of industry presence, in the form of big water trucks, known as "water bottles," carrying water to the frack site and carrying produced wastewater away; enormous flatbed tractor-trailer trucks, each carrying three 50-foot segments of 42-inch steel pipe for the new pipelines; and other related diesel traffic. In Bill's words, these truck drivers "are apt to be . . . very high handed."

The 1–800-See-Trux campaign in the southern coalfields reflects the existence of heightened road danger presented by heavy coal trucks traveling at top speeds on small, winding mountain roads.[47] The water trucks, the enormous trailers bearing three 42-inch steel pipeline segments, and other well traffic increasingly impose the same risk on the oil and gas region of the state.[48] For me, the danger became palpable on a drive I took up to Wetzel County, the heart of the Marcellus gas boom in West Virginia. I used GPS to plot a route over the mountains from Harrison County to Wetzel County for an interview. The route was probably the most direct (thanks, Google Maps), but it took me from the four-lane state Route 50 up to some small gravel county roads with minimal road signage. I was surprised to come upon an EQT gas company truck and several workers standing around on the shoulder while I navigated past on a gravel road through the woods, and they were likely just as surprised to see me. When I finally came out onto a two-lane state road in Wetzel County, I found I had really entered a different world. The road was lined with signs advertising "We Buy Mineral Rights" on telephone poles. Frequent cave-ins or slips in the road led to one-lane passages around crumbling pavement, and speeding guide trucks with flashing lights signaling "outsized load" gave about a second's notice to make way for giant dump trucks, "water bottles," or tractor trailers serving the wells or pipelines.

I was scared. I waited 30 minutes at a pipeline construction site that crossed the road, getting more and more nervous about missing my interview. When I arrived at the meeting point, I was shaken, but the people I was meeting were unsurprised. For both of them the well and pipeline traffic represented a significant difficulty and risk every time they left home. For one, the frequent stops for pipeline construction had disrupted his own health care appointments (traffic delays lead to missing appointments and forced rescheduling) as well as his ability to care for his disabled son. In rural areas, there is often only one direct road in and out of a community, leaving the residents at the mercy of the gas drilling and pipeline construction schedule. Riding in his pickup truck on a tour of the gas and pipeline works in the area, I got a sense of anxiety, helplessness, and frustration from waiting at construction sites and dodging larger vehicles on the twisty, narrow roads. Later, on my way home alone in my Prius, I felt like I'd never have the courage to return to Wetzel County. As it happened, I ended up getting into a relatively ordinary and thankfully minor accident.

I was making a left onto a state two-lane from a one-lane county road, where I had just narrowly avoided several potential head-on collisions with dump trucks and tractor trailers too large for the one-lane road. I had sighed with relief when the two-lane came into view down the hill, but the blind curve to my left hid an approaching car whose driver tried but failed to entirely miss hitting my car as I entered the road. A handful of members of the Wetzel County Volunteer Fire Department showed up seemingly seconds later, before anyone had even called 911. These five or six men quickly pushed both of our cars off the road and out of danger, because they knew that "water bottles," dump trucks, and tractor trailers hauling pipeline segments would be coming around the same blind curve, all at top speed.

The law enforcement officer who drove me to a local restaurant to wait for my ride home explained the situation. The gas and pipeline companies subcontract with truck drivers and shift the risk to the driver. The driver signs a contract assuming the responsibility to take a load from point A to point B, legally and in a timely manner, but the small size of the local roads means that in practical terms, they cannot go around these sharp curves legally, definitely not at top speed, and so they often end up breaking the law and putting their commercial licenses at risk. If the driver breaks the law, they get the citation, they lose their license, and the company finds another driver.

Thus, the gas companies shift the risk to the drivers and the public. Even the guide trucks, which are usually pickups with red flags, flashing lights, and signs warning of an oversized load, put the burden on residents to make way for the larger trucks, rather than ensuring the public safety by slowing down the well traffic. However, the law enforcement officer told me my impression that the trucks were speeding was possibly false because their size makes their speed seem greater than it is. He gave me the overall impression for law enforcement of a major nuisance caused by the boom; people either complained that the gas traffic is too fast or too slow. However, the experience of getting forced off the road was common. A video posted on Facebook in the group Well Traffic Follies is illustrative. The passenger in a personal vehicle following a large tractor-trailer truck filmed the truck as it tried to make a sharp curve going down a two-lane mountain road. The truck was forced by the sharp curve into the left lane and then had to slam on the breaks to avoid a head-on collision with a school bus that was coming up the mountain in that lane from the other direction.[49]

Despite the hope of jobs for the community, many of the jobs related to fracking and pipelines are highly skilled and involve a specially trained workforce, who often follow the work from state to state as they frack the wells or lay the pipelines.[50] These jobs are also temporary, leading to rapid and disruptive short-term population growth, including increased occurrence of sexually transmitted diseases.[51] My informants mentioned traffic control at worksites as an example of the kind of (low-wage) job an unexperienced West Virginian was likely to get. (When I was stopped at one such worksite, the young white man directing traffic told me he was from Ohio.) In any case, a "high-handed" attitude of self-important entitlement from industry workers was often palpable.

Mindy, an activist from northern West Virginia, recounted how friends of hers had the road to their house blocked by construction trucks building a pipeline. Her friend, who was suffering from cancer, had received notice that the pipeline company was using eminent domain to claim the right-of-way for a pipeline through his property, and found the pipeline under construction upon his return from a vacation. The construction trucks frequently blocked access to the house. She recounted, "The night that [he] died? Hospice couldn't get in. . . . His wife had to go out on a four-wheeler . . . to pick up the people from hospice. . . . So, what the hell do you do if they're blocking the road and you need emergency services?"

For Mindy, this cavalier attitude reflected the general disrespect the oil and gas companies and some of their workers had for the people residing in the area. Referring to the one-lane road where this family's house was located, she remarked, "[the workers] park on it . . . their daughter told me, 'We [have to] make them back up.'" Mindy described her own experience with the workers blocking the road with their trucks:

I went up there to visit them. Sure enough, when I was leaving, there was a friggin' dump truck. I just sat there. I got out and took pictures. One guy goes, "What are you doing?" I go, "Checking it out." And . . . I get the third degree: "What's your name? Do you live here?" I go, What's it to you? What's it to you?"And he's like, "Well, I'm going to take a picture of your car." [I said] "Go ahead! I don't give a shit."

The frack boom brought new people into the area and the companies assumed a great entitlement to space and time that angered local residents, as Mindy continued to explain:

If they're in the process of fracking . . . they're bringing in the sand cams and the water trucks and stuff. So, they'll basically take up one whole lane. And that's illegal. They can stop you, their little asinine flagger people who . . . put up their stupid stop thing and keep you sitting there for up to 15 minutes. Ok? They're getting paid to stand there with a stupid sign; I'm not getting paid to sit there. I want to leave [the area], but I can't figure out where to go.

Fire

Mindy's greatest worry, though, was the threat of an explosion. The potential impact radius of a 42-inch highly pressurized natural gas pipeline is about a mile. That means a half mile on either side of the pipeline's path is in what Mindy called "the crispy fry zone." Although the pipeline industry claims the gas lines are extremely safe, the complicated geology of the Appalachian mountains in West Virginia—including impossibly steep slopes for a pipeline route and in places a karst topography that is full of limestone caves and sinkholes—worried many of the people in the pipelines' path.[52] Several people I spoke to also distrusted the stability and quality of construction of these rapidly built and unprecedentedly large pipelines, and this fear was confirmed when a newly installed pipeline on the TransCanada line exploded in Moundsville, West Virginia, in June 2018, leaving a crater and burning up to ten acres.[53] For Mindy, this possibility transformed the way she thought about her home. As she reported telling her daughter, "You might be saving yourself some money here because if that line goes in and it goes [i.e. blows up], you won't have to pay to get me cremated."

Disrespect

The effects of the oil and gas expansion in West Virginia are incremental and synergistic. Small indignities, worries, and inconveniences add up to the overall effect of displacing people within their own communities. Frank recounted that one Wetzel County family had to call the gas company again and again because an older relative's phone line was repeatedly cut. Each "mistaken" excavation by the gas company led to a labyrinthine trip through the disjointed bureaucracy of the company and its subcontractors. Likewise, a pipeline drawing brine away from the frack site damaged her water line, caused her water bill to skyrocket, and eventually led to her water service being temporarily cut off. The cumulative effects of events like the trucks blocking, damaging, and speeding down the one-lane roads, the inconveniences that sometimes rise to the level of endangerment, eventually lead even supporters of the industry to realize, in Frank's words, that they are "just taken advantage of constantly."

These everyday inconveniences are matched, Cassandra argued, by a general disrespect for the people of West Virginia. She described how the low-income status of many area residents enables the oil and gas companies to lowball their compensation for the property. Rather than offering what it is potentially worth, they offer the lowest possible value, often leaving someone who inherited property from family, or whose income is not large enough to purchase a house in a different area, with nothing to replace what they've lost. The companies underestimate the potential worth and thereby contribute to the marginalization of these rural properties. As Cassandra explained:

> Frackers have admitted that they site fracking pads in areas that are impoverished where people don't have the money to fight. . . . They employ scads of high-priced lawyers, to be able to take our [property] rights. [. . .] They're telling you, "Here I'm offering you $2500. If you don't take this, I'm going to drop the price to $2000. If you don't take that I'm going

to take your rights anyway." They can't do that at this point, but a lot of people believe they can and they'll lie to your face and tell you that they can, and so people will sign. Well, once they've signed, it's a contract, and how are you going to prove . . . that you signed under duress? That you were essentially lied to. The stereotypes of West Virginians, that they're dumb, hillbillies, backwards—that works to the advantage of these companies, because they say, "Well, you shouldn't have signed the contract. That was stupid."

The stereotypical poor rural resident, referenced by Cassandra, above, may be unable to afford to present much resistance to the oil and gas industry and their lawyers. And as Cassandra suggests, the gas or pipeline company can use the stereotypes against low-income property owners. However, the fracking and pipeline boom is expanding to affect property owners with more resources and histories of entitlement that offer the potential, at least, of resistance. In the eastern highlands and southeastern part of West Virginia, tourism and agriculture are important economic forces. Bringing pipelines through the forests and rivers of this part of the state disturbs both of these industries as well as the "almost heaven" quality that persists in some places. Sean, a property owner in southeastern West Virginia, recounted with disgust the way he was treated by the pipeline developers:

> They wanted a 150-foot right-of-way [for the pipeline] . . . Now if they put [a pipeline] through here, . . . I [would] have no access to this property over here, and from over here I'd have no access to this property over here. [Gesturing in both directions.] I bought this three years ago with the intention of putting in a primitive campground. . . . they offered me $27,000. For the right-of-way through here, and this property is worth a half a million dollars. It's crazy! . . . I said "My attorney can take it over from here," . . . and I [told her] "Don't call me until it's north of $500,000." Hahahaha. I didn't say anything more to him. And I left.

Sean is a successful real estate developer and had the reasonable expectation that he would be able to continue his business ventures until his property development plans ran into conflict with the pipeline. The laughable offer made by the company was unlikely to be increased, however, because they had the power of eminent domain granted by the FERC to claim their right-of-way through his property. The overbearing and "high-handed" attitude of the extractive industries in West Virginia has the potential to make other forms of economic activity and community impossible. Like "King Coal" in the coalfields, the gas and pipeline companies create a hostile environment from an accumulation of small to large inconveniences, hazards, and disappointments.

The Politics of Herding Jell-o

Disagreements between neighbors or relatives about whether to sell a right-of-way or to sell or lease mineral rights create hard feelings, while joint opposition to the industry can create unlikely alliances. Mineral and surface property owners can hurt their neighbors for their own gain or form new coalitions within and across communities and county lines.

> Well, I think [it's] . . . like herding Jell-O. I mean . . . I would say ninety-five percent of the people were against it until their nephew or their uncle or somebody was able to snap one of these entry-level jobs and make fifteen dollars an hour. . . . [But] I do also know people who have said, "If anybody in my family works for the pipeline, I'll disown them."[54]

The most active gas and pipeline opponents form a network of watershed associations and preservation societies that bridges what often seems to be the great social distance between the coalfields, the southeastern highlands, and the oil and gas fields to the north. At the same time, the historical power of extractive industries in the state makes resistance relatively rare. Sam, the retired educator from central West Virginia mentioned above, gained an (unlikely) local reputation as a dangerous person after a rumor spread that he'd drawn a gun on the gas company representative:

> They promised me they'd have all the reclamation done on the well pad before they started putting in their pipeline to get the gas out and I said, "OK." . . . So, they . . . started showing up here, and I just went out and closed my gate, and I told them "You can't come in." It took them almost no time before they had lawyers out there . . . and they [were] going to

sue us for damages, and for shutting them down for a day or two, and we said, "Well, this is what you promised, and this is what you didn't do and you're not coming in until you keep your promise." . . . But out of that—I got a little bit of a reputation. . . . They were kind of more interested in not causing me harm, or just being more responsible and conciliatory . . . The word got around that I stood them off with a gun. Which is—there is absolutely no way that I would ever do that. Although I do own lots of guns. But just the idea that—that was the rumor that got around which may not have actually hurt me.

The complicated politics of land ownership, divided rights, and ideas of liberty are evident in Sam's experience. He stood up to the company, which drew attention and immediately brought threats of lawsuits for lost income. This reflects the way that the law privileges the mineral owner's right to access their property. However, Sam was also standing on his right as a property owner, which was legally supported by the contract he had managed to negotiate with the company. Interestingly, the community's imagination represented the incident through the lens of a frontier-like armed standoff.

Another sign of increased tension are the accidents and road rage incidents involving "water bottles" and pipeline trucks that make the quotidian experience of driving in their small communities a paranoid business for area residents, as discussed above. Mary, a resident of a rural county to the south, explained, regarding pipeline traffic:

[T]he traffic is terrible and I'm afraid . . . somebody's about to get killed if they come up on their side like that and . . . can't get out the way quick enough. Or maybe there's no room to get out of the way. . . . they're just flying . . . it's becoming dangerous on the roads when they're building it. . . . of course they knew we were fighting the pipeline, but I've had them actually follow me . . . And one of them was taking pictures of me one day. I looked back in the mirror and this guy's got his camera up here [gestures to eye level] and he's taking pictures of me.

The heightened tensions in communities that come along with the natural gas and pipeline boom are of course political, but not down party lines. Conservatives embracing the label "Water Protector" manage to form loose coalitions with the "Back to the land" hippies who led the (so far successful) fight against fracking in one rural county, the more youthful environmental activists, and the tree sitters. A conservative voter concerned about the abundant fresh spring water on her farm, Ellen reported many of her friends who sold the right-of-way to the pipeline company did it because they thought "it's going to happen any-way" and they didn't want to "be associated with . . . hippies." Despite her own concern with the spring water quality on her farm, Ellen main-tained a similar distance in her association with some of the people in her environmentalist group:

> Because [people] think they're nuts. And I don't think they're nuts but I'm not against all fossil fuels, I don't want everything to be run solar. I mean some of them are out there in my opinion. In my opinion I think they're out there, they're just a little too far. I'm pretty mainstream, I'm conserva-tive. So, I don't agree with everything they want—the hippies.

Grace, another resident of this rural county, argued, from the opposite political perspective, "I don't think the pipeline is a party issue. And I don't even think it's a liberal/conservative issue. It's grandpa's land."[55]

Nonetheless, those who spoke out appeared to be the anomaly. When a friend stopped by Ellen's house during our interview and asked what I was doing, Ellen answered in a voice that lowered to a whisper that I was "here to talk about the pipeline," as though afraid to speak the word aloud. This is probably because where one stands on the pipeline issue has become a highly charged moral litmus test. Tracy, another resident of a county projected to be crossed by a pipeline, explained about a few of the older women in her garden club, "Before a couple of little old ladies picked me up they said, 'We want to know what side you're on before you get in the car with us.' And I said, 'Why don't you read my bumper stickers and you'll know.' And they just cracked up; they were flaming liberals."

Even within the activist circles, the general attitude seems to be that the people resisting the industry are troublemakers, and that they require a strong defense in a community mostly used to not making waves. As I sat down to interview Greg, an outspoken anti-pipeline activist, his friend and colleague Sean came in the room and announced, "I defended you yesterday." Greg asked how, and Sean explained,

> You owe me. . . . I was talking to somebody about the pipeline and . . . She said . . . "Why are you all fighting the pipeline?" And [her brother] said . . . "Well Greg's doing that too." And I said, "Don't you bad-mouth Greg." [Laughter] I said, "He is our go-to guy and he keeps us informed." And I said, "If it hadn't been for us, that damned pipeline would have already been done." [Laughter].

Here, the observation by a community member that Greg was fighting the pipeline was represented by a fellow pipeline opponent as "bad-mouthing." But this general impression that protesting is ill-mannered was countered by the activists' resentment against those who sold. Greg explained:

> GREG: "I got a neighbor who sold a big right-of-way. He said, 'I'm against the pipeline but I want my money.' So, he put me and everybody else at risk in the neighborhood. "
> SEAN: "Oh, he would, he would sell God. He would sell God for a nickel."
> GREG: "And I haven't talked to [him] now in about a year."

Conclusion

In November 2017, West Virginia's political leadership announced a memorandum of understanding (MOU) with China's largest energy company, China Energy, for development of a major petrochemical storage and processing hub on the Ohio River, to be known as the Appalachian Storage Hub (ASH).[56] Supporters claimed this development would bring in thousands of jobs and rival Louisiana's petrochemical corridor, "Cancer Alley," mentioned above. This MOU hit some speed bumps in the US federal administration's trade war with China, as well as corruption scandals within the West Virginia state government, but there is still talk of creating the ASH to feed petrochemical plants in Pennsylvania and Ohio.[57] Concerned citizens and environmentalists around the state don't see the billions of investment dollars this deal is to bring to the state as an unqualified boon—rather, they see it as a threat to the area's water and air quality and as an expansion of its status as a sacrifice zone.[58]

The expansion of the sacrifice zone in West Virginia is not a unique event—on the contrary, natural gas fracking and related processing affects areas all over the country, except in places that have successfully banned the practice and now only benefit from others' sacrifice.[59] The effects are widespread, spreading the sacrifice zone to the edge of nowhere and everywhere. Fracking and frack wastewater disposal are responsible for the increasing rate of "man-made earthquakes" in Oklahoma.[60] As explored earlier, even wealthy communities like Porter Ranch, California have suffered the effects of natural gas development.[61] In short, the situation laid out in *Gasland* has only expanded around the country since 2010. This "evacuative despoliation" damages air and water quality and prevents other forms of economic and community development—in other words, it creates sacrifice zones.[62] However, in its spreading, the natural gas boom potentially weakens the deep structure of the sacrifice by decreasing the distance between the winners and losers in fossil fuel society. This narrowing of distance opens up the possibility for questioning the underlying settler logic of progressive economic development toward an ever-brighter future—one based on the highest and best use of private property.[63] Perhaps the increasing pervasiveness of environmental sacrifice in US life manifests the instability of settler temporality, as it suggests there is nowhere safe for this progressive future to unfold. The next chapter explores these cracks in the foundations of settler culture.

5

Fracking Settler Culture

Sacrifice, Property, and Environmental Justice

You know if I was going to do anything, I would make them buy my whole property. I wouldn't sell the right-of-way because, who wants a one hundred twenty-five foot right-of-way through your property that you can't mow over. You can't fence. You can't do anything with it. Pipeline or not, I don't want that right-of-way through the middle of my property. If I was going to sell it, it would be . . . the whole shebang or nothing.
—Sean, resident of a West Virginia county being crossed by a pipeline

The steepest grades on the pipeline route are reinforced with Quikrete and shredded plastic. The hidden danger of a buried high-pressure gas pipe, the deep gravel pipe yards, and the fracking well pads are transforming farm and forest. As discussed in the previous chapter, this sacrifice of place for time (for profit) negates the future progress promised by development discourse and the ideal of free-market competition. The highest and best use of land, according to the market, turns out to be its destruction, in contradiction to the fable of the tragedy of the commons.[1] The alienating legal structure of private property is the bedrock of settler culture in the United States. This alienation (i.e., when the land is treated like a commodity) underpins the destructive extraction that threatens the communities and ecologies in its path.[2] This contradiction, combined with the failure of property rights to protect landowners in the way of gas development, brought me to use fracking as a metaphor as well as a literal term to describe the effect of natural gas on US settler culture.

Because so many of the conflicts over fracking and pipelines are focused on property rights, this chapter is a consideration of how property figures in the injuries residents experience and how these injuries potentially fracture the grounds of settler property culture. Most of the people I interviewed for this project would consider themselves typical Americans: property owners, farmers, workers, taxpayers, and so on. However, the encroaching of the natural gas spider web threatens the foundational assumptions of these identities. As the gas industry expands its operations in the Marcellus Shale, residents often feel their rights are being trampled, and experience insecurity and fear for the places and features of the landscape we hold dear. Interestingly, the words with which people described these experiences with mineral owners, gas companies, FERC, and the pipeline companies often echo the sentiments expressed by white landowners confronted by Native American land claims interviewed by Eva Mackey. As she summarizes, Indigenous land claims "appear to disrupt deep and longstanding feelings [white landowners] have about their rights and entitlements as citizens within nations, particularly with regards to their own property and their rights to fully control that property in the present and the future."[3]

Some of Mackey's interviewees placed their faith in the hegemonic power of settler national identity. As one person put it, "History is history, and as I understand it the white man beat the Indians. There was a war and we won this land."[4] In contrast to this, the white people in the way of the fracking and pipeline boom find their expectations of property rights challenged and dismantled by agencies of the settler state itself. This experience puts into question the privileges some have been able to take for granted and highlights the exploitative underpinnings of the property regimes of settler society. As an Indigenous speaker at a panel on protecting water (discussed in chapter 2 and below) put it, "the chickens are coming home to roost." In other words, the exploitative property logic of settler colonialism turns on its own. This inward-turning moment opens a new window into the cultural politics of property in settler society, as well as making space for the possibility of forging better relations. As Kanien'kehá:ka scholar Taiaiake Alfred argues, settlers should imagine themselves not as citizens with rights descended from colonizers "but as human beings in equal and respectful relation to other human beings and the natural environment. This is what radical imagination could look like."[5]

As Cheryl Harris explains, possessive individualism is at the heart of white supremacist settler identity.[6] It is not surprising then that fracking and pipeline construction through eminent domain has been experienced as a particularly egregious attack on the property rights of surface landowners. This is apparent in the most well-known documentary on the subject, *Gasland*, by Josh Fox, which consists of a kind of performative settler nationalism—a significant part of the film consists of a westward national tour of injured landowners and ranchers. In the United States, property ownership is supposed to be a bedrock of individual freedom, but the split estate doctrine, absentee ownership or control of mineral rights, and eminent domain in the name of an abstract "public good" constrain property rights and pit property owners against each other as they exercise their rights. These asymmetrical struggles in the twenty-first century for financial benefit or safety, for privacy or future expectations are a historical reverberation of the struggles of the nineteenth-century mountain farmer-patriarchs who, at the cusp of industrialization in Appalachia, often found selling their mineral rights was the only way to retain their small subsistence farms, leading to fractured communities, severed mineral rights, and domination by coal.[7] This chapter focuses on how this inward-turning fracturing in the present moment could present the opportunity for taking a new perspective on the structures of extraction, instead of naturalizing them as settler common sense.

In areas affected by fracking or pipeline construction, the claims of mineral owners and pipeline companies backed by eminent domain often challenge landowners' expectations of the future of their property, which has often been in the family "for generations." Newer property owners also feel cheated out of their anticipated future use. Even those with property not directly affected by fracking or pipeline construction find their quality of life diminished through the overbearing presence of well and construction traffic, toxic chemicals, and acres of land converted to gravel lots for well pads, compressor stations, and pipe yards. Companies spray weed killer and drop erosion control pellets from helicopters, threating the status of organic farms and impacting the health of residents near the construction, even if they do not directly touch their property. The experience of being subjected to all of this in the name of a greater good leads people to understand themselves as being in a sacrifice zone and elicits metaphors of colonization and comparisons to Native American dispos-session. A slogan on an anti-pipeline protest sign encapsulates the irony underlying these comparisons: "No eminent domain for private gain," as though eminent domain for private gain didn't very closely describe the history of settler colonial land seizures and urban development projects in what is currently known as America.[8]

The historical echoes between settler colonialism, extractive industry, and the current natural gas rush are expressed visually in a mural dis-played in the Oil and Gas Museum in Parkersburg, West Virginia. The majority of exhibits in the museum celebrate the regional oil boom of the late nineteenth and early twentieth centuries. Yet some attention is also given to the moment, in early US history, when settlers "discovered" oil at a place they called Burning Springs. Oil had of course been used by Indigenous people for various purposes, including as medicine. The mural on display near the door shows stereotypically represented Na-tive Americans dipping oil from the stream, refining it over a fire, and guiding British colonial-era white settlers to the site.[9] *The History of Oil and Gas in West Virginia* notes, "[t]hese 'oil springs' were known and used by the aborigines and Indians of the areas, and were observed and described by some of the first white men to penetrate the western Ap-palachian region."[10] The museum's collection includes models of original wood oil drilling equipment, antique cars and gas pumps, railroad and Civil War memorabilia, and a display of modern hydraulic fracturing technology in the Marcellus Exhibit. A model of the oil boom town of Burning Springs dated from 1865 and a large collection of antique office equipment point to the fact that the heyday of the oil business in West Virginia was over by the early twentieth century.[11] The visual reference in the museum to Indigenous people using the oil and sharing it with settlers renders the oil comprehensible as yet another natural resource "inherited" from Indigenous people, like corn, famously introduced to early settlers by their generous Indigenous neighbors. The painting is located near the entrance of the museum and helps create a visual his-torical narrative in which the oil and gas industry becomes part of the region's natural heritage, along with the many Indigenous-derived place names and histories that punctuate West Virginian geography. The en-folding story of Indians sharing oil with settlers puts the oil and gas industry into a context of settler appropriation of Indigenous heritage.[12]

Appalachian regional identity is another touch point for comparisons to indigeneity. Appalachian identity is often considered to be based on a tradition of reliance on the land through farming, hunting, and gathering, a shared history of resistance to exploitation and extraction, and a multigenerational inheritance of place attachment.[13] Some have diagnosed these claims to place-based identity as "self-indigenizing."[14] But outsiders have also indigenized Appalachian identities, which further naturalizes settler colonial structures. White Appalachians were described by nineteenth-century observers as representing a backward culture, famously destined to disappear in the face of progress like "so many Indians," in a classic expression of the settler logic of replacement.[15] In the twentieth century, Henry Caudill, deploring the excesses of the coal industry in the Cumberland Mountains, described white Appalachians as "indigenous mountaineers" in terms that compare Appalachian identity with the characteristic place attachment of Indigenous peoples and reiterate the oddity of such a place attachment to mainstream America. "The indigenous mountaineer coal miner was so deeply rooted to the country that he felt a powerful attachment to the familiar hills, valleys and institutions surrounding him."[16] These self- and other-indigenizing descriptions also resonate with many white West Virginians' claims of Cherokee ancestry and frequent comparisons between the land-based culture of white Appalachians and that of Indigenous peoples.[17] These gestures of settler appropriation and naturalization end up performing the same function as all such claims do: asserting white settler rights to land.[18]

Interviews with property owners in areas targeted for fracking and pipeline construction revealed a mixed bag of settler entitlement to property rights commingled with the awareness that their experience with losing land to the powerful has deep roots in US economics and history. These interviewees occupy an idealized, if not powerful, position as American citizens: that of rural, white property owners. They also occupy a specific position in American culture as Appalachians, often considered marginal or "backward" within a national progress narrative, but who often also see themselves as holding onto a rare and nonconformist tradition of land- and place-based culture.[19] This lifestyle is seen as being out of step with modern America and at the same time as reflecting more authentic Americana than urban or suburban life. The tension between entitlement and marginalization, and the incongruity between the idealization of property as the root of American freedom and the awareness of its fragility in the face of power, can produce contradictory feelings and cognitive dissonance.

During a discussion about how the modern economy forces people to move around for jobs, specifically referring to the traveling pipeline and fracking crews of the natural gas industry, Mandy, a historical society employee from eastern West Virginia, commented:

> If you have no roots, do you even care whether you're tearing up somebody's homeland? . . . I think in West Virginia we are such a people of place that, no matter what, our land is sacred to us, and when someone comes in and they're tearing up our land, they're tearing up our hearts . . . And I know way down the road our ancestors did it . . . I don't know . . . we are a product of white privilege.

We had been having a lively conversation about how the social ideal of economic growth so often leads to the displacement of people from places they love. Over the course of Mandy's life, her family had been displaced multiple times. First, the state had used eminent domain to claim her family's homeplace as the site for a governmental program, and then her family was displaced again by timber development. At the time of our interview, she was living a few counties away from her homeplace, and we both lamented the modern economic necessity to become rootless in order to survive. We both remarked on how much easier this rootlessness makes environmental destruction. But underlying our recognition of the problematic relationship to land of the dominant culture was our simultaneous awareness of the fundamentally unjust relation of settler property that shaped our own relationship to place.

Mandy's verbalization of this contradiction acknowledges the historical violence of settler colonialism in the United States that displaced the Indigenous Peoples from what is currently called Appalachia. However, she subsequently shifts to a language of white privilege to make sense of it. The shift from dispossession to race talk, through the acknowledgment of white privilege, signals a recognition of historical injustices while remaining within the dominant frame of liberal state multiculturalism.[20] This very common move recognizes the injustice of past land grabs but avoids questioning the legitimacy of the settler state itself. This is an example of the "logic of containment" which "minimize[s] or contain[s] the transformational potential of Indigenous knowledge."[21] This multicultural settler framework conceptualizes the land as always already property and averts attention from how the legal structure of the state and its economic rationality ultimately enable environmental and social destruction.[22]

The expansion of fracking and pipeline development into places previously sheltered from resource extraction potentially troubles the constitution of settler identity. In conversations with property owners, it becomes clear that both the progress of the extractive industry in fracking wells and building pipelines, and the fight against these forms of extraction by activist residents, rest on a settler mindset of private property ownership and the sacredness of property rights. However, these sacred property rights are frequently exposed as illusory for smaller property owners in the face of corporate power. This trouble with property may suggest the possibility of forging better relations in the future. Three fault lines, or contradictions in settler consciousness, became apparent in my interviews with rural residents whose property was targeted by pipeline or frack pad development. Although these fault lines obviously don't lead directly to decolonization or even to a centering of Indigenous perspectives, they signal an emergent potential that is nevertheless critically necessary in the fight for sustainable futures.[23]

Contradiction One: Place Attachment versus Alienable Property

One set of my great-grandparents moved up from the banks of the Greenbrier River in the nineteenth century to settle on a large family farm. Over the years the farm has been whittled down to a few acres, but it still has some of the old outbuildings: the granary, the woodshed, and the cellar. The barn came down in 2017. Such stories of old homeplaces in Appalachia are ubiquitous, and the sight of an abandoned white farmhouse, often more or less falling into decrepitude, is not uncommon. Many people are not as fortunate as my family has been so far, as to be able to hold on to the property.[24] Because we all live in other houses and other places, this property has mostly sentimental value, although I sometimes dream of returning to live there. However, if the tourist industry in the area were to expand further it could raise the monetary value of the property and challenge our sentimental attachment. This example highlights the contradictions between place attachment, modern economic necessity, and property in land.

At the panel discussion I attended, discussed above and in chapter 2, two speakers were white women from Appalachia and two were Indigenous women. The first speaker introduced herself as being "very lucky" because she grew up in a bucolic setting, her family homeplace in Kentucky, a farm where she could be a "wood sprite," and which had been in the family since the 1840s. Her identity as a settler, and the possible connection of this fact to the destruction caused by mining, was left unexamined, despite the presence of Indigenous Water Protectors on the panel. The erasure of the preexisting land theft enables an unspoken and unexamined a priori assumption—that our Appalachian families represent an unusually long inhabitation and relation to place, rather than a relatively short one. A relentless focus on the United States' foreshortened history enables this brief set of relations to take on the appearance of "time immemorial." The constant re-erasure of the time before American settlement resonates with how the "assertion, imposition, and maintenance of settler sovereignty entails the attempted elimination of the conditions of life for countervailing social formations, particularly those of Indigenous peoples."[25]

Greg, who lives in a rural county being impacted by a pipeline taking natural gas to the coast and to power plants in the South, told me his family has owned several hundred acres in the area for 200 years. Again, this timeline puts the acquisition of the land into a historical period of very recent Native dispossession. It may also be worth noting that such references to the value of long-term inhabitation are themselves internally contradictory. First and foremost, the property owners' legal standing (as a property owner) is insufficient under the law to protect them from the pipeline corporations' use of eminent domain. However, by emphasizing our long-term inhabitation as if it adds moral significance to our claim to the place (against unjust extractive industry), we long-term residents put forth a moral principle (i.e., that length of tenure adds significance to ownership) that the colonization, settlement, and commodification of the continent has already rendered illegitimate. It may be that these contradictions are more obvious to some of the residents of the place currently known as Appalachia, precisely because of the local cultural ideal of place attachment. In other words, the desire on the part of some folks to stay in place may make it more obvious how difficult and devalued staying in place can be.

The hollowness of people's hopes of a special non-commodified relation to land in US Appalachia is foreshadowed by George Washington's comments on the property he claimed:

> The tract of which the 123 acres is a Moiety, was taken up by General Andrew Lewis and myself for and on account of a bituminous spring which is contained, of so inflamiable (sic) a nature as to burst forth freely as spirits, and is nearly as difficult to extinguish.[26]

This excerpt from Washington's diary underlines the acquisitive individual behind American independence. As Nichols notes, "Many of the leading figures of the American Revolution made their fortunes in real estate speculation. They specialized in acquiring vast swaths of land from a public entity (originally from the Crown), parceling it out, and selling it to smaller investors at large profits."[27] Accordingly, Thoenen's *History of the Oil and Gas Industry in West Virginia* provides an almost biblical genealogy of landownership passing from rich man to rich man, from speculator to speculator, until the large, important families of the late-nineteenth-century oil boom era were established.

Frequently the land Appalachian people are attached to is owned by absentee landowners, and most subsistence farmers formerly scraped by with a less than iron-clad right to the land.[28] Rather than supporting a blanket claim to a place-based culture, the history of landownership in West Virginia is more aptly described as reflecting a persistent tension between a place-based and a market orientation to land. This tension can sometimes become violent and sometimes can exist between members of a family or even in the heart of an individual. Between a retired couple who had planned to let their children and grandchildren build on their land, and now wish they could sell the whole place to get away from the pipeline, and others who sell the right-of-way to the pipeline in the interest of being able to afford to stay on their multigenerational family property, the tension between alienating property relations and attachment to place is endemic.

As is evident from the general loss of population in the state of West Virginia, market relations generally win out, although with widely divergent outcomes.[29] On one hand, those who stay in place despite massive economic disinvestment are often extremely marginalized, often live with inadequate infrastructure, are sometimes disabled, and may suffer from addiction or other co-morbidities.[30] This extremely marginal property can keep very low-income people in place, in poor-quality housing, without the resources to move.[31] Mandy pointed out that West Virginia doesn't have a big homeless problem, because the very poor often do have access to housing, albeit sometimes in substandard condition. On the other hand, some of those who accommodate the market and move for employment are able to maintain or regain access to family homeplaces or find acceptable substitutes for that property.

Tracy and Steve, a white couple who reside in a southeastern West Virginia county being crossed by a pipeline, told me how they had found their current home, which was located in Steve's home county, after working for some years in a nearby city. They were able to buy a farmhouse that was very similar to the one he'd grown up in. Over the course of his lifetime, then, Steve was able to grow up in one rural homeplace, gain educational and cultural capital by leaving home for school and work, and then return to find a similar version of his childhood home available on the real estate market. The rural county where they lived, however, had changed. Tracy commented, "So many people that this [the pipeline] is happening to here, ran here for that reason [the peace and quiet] and then this happened. I mean [we] know several people that moved here because of our [spring] water, you know." Steve continued, "Yeah . . . growing up here, it's like, 'We're going to stay in the nineteenth century forever.' Then we moved away and came back and it's like, 'What happened?' It changed." Being in the crosshairs of the fracking and pipeline boom reveals the market forces behind the environmental quality or its lack in the community. The market declares itself as the determinant force in shaping the place by pitting property owners against each other and imposing eminent domain. Those who didn't want to cooperate lost control. As Steve commented, "Basically if you have a couple of neighbors that sold rights . . . If your neighbors have done it, you are forced to sell it. So, you don't even have the right to say no."

Despite the privilege of owning property, the fracking and pipeline boom has forced many respondents to fear for their property and the lives they'd imagined having there, as reflected in a conversation with John and Fred, property owners from northern West Virginia in the heart of the gas field. John had had the opportunity to buy a 200-acre farm while working as an educator. He planned to use it for hunting and recreation. He "lost control" of his property, however, when a frack pad was forced on him by the mineral owners. As he recounted, his trouble "started in about [20]07 when I bought the property . . . within a year I was told they were drilling a gas well on it and at that time there weren't any protective laws for the landowners. And [then] they were putting [in the well] and started destruction of the property." Unfortunately for John, he bought the property only a year or two before the fracking boom began. He commented, "[I] had no clue . . . this was coming, or I probably wouldn't have bought it." I asked him if he was considering selling it now. He responded:

> No because—the crazy part [is] now you have to opportunity to make money . . . because of pipelines. They destroy it. It's already destroyed . . . but they're always wanting to put another pipeline. We seem to be in the line of fire where they wanna send pipeline. And so, if, if you choose to you can make a little money.

The meaning or future use of the property has entirely changed due to the gas boom. When I asked about property values, Fred commented, "Would you wanna buy [this piece of property] when you're . . . looking at all those tanks . . . all the time? And it stinks. Producing [gas], oh it never quits. This never quits." He continued, "If you have your mineral rights, [you're] fine with it. If you don't have the mineral rights, you have no rights. We [went] to court with another landowner and the judge told him that . . . it'll always be in the favor of the mineral holders."

Fred had owned his several-hundred-acre farm in the area for 20 years. He recounted his experience with a section of land that "was right in the center, the best piece of ground we had" for making hay. Now, he says, "you can't make nothing there. It's straight up and down, there's nothing." After having the frack pad put in on his property, John was also being approached by "landmen," or contractors working for the gas and pipeline companies seeking rights-of-way for new pipelines or other developments. The landmen try to get landowners to sign a deal for the right to use their property for various reasons. John and Fred both worried about what would happen if they signed. Fred explained what was causing them concern:

> After you sign the paper, then they [think] . . . you signed your rights away. So, they come and do as they please. Like the last pipeline we just signed, we didn't give them no access roads. [We said] "You stay on your pipeline [right-of-way]." Well now they're breaking that agreement because they're trespassing. And I just ain't caught them yet, but they're trespassing.

Landowners in these circumstances are treated as inconveniences to the course of gas development. Fred continued, "my son had a call yesterday from a landman. . . . He wants to give us five thousand dollars to use the road for two years. Which is less than a dollar a foot. [To] have to put up with harassment. So that's not gonna happen." I asked him to explain what he meant by harassment, and he explained:

> Is this not harassment? . . . The noise. And they're running [machines]. . . . You don't know who's on your property. . . . You don't know who's on your property . . . you see somebody come [who has a] Texas license [plate] and you don't know who that is. What's that guy doing on our property?

The gas and pipeline boom has altered the relationship of property owners to their property, leading to feelings of violation, disrespect, and mourning of lost expectations. But because the property is in essence alienable as a commodity, this possibility shapes and limits the relationship that people have with the land. John explained with the experience of a neighbor:

> Back in the seventies, [this man] bought [300 acres] for a . . . getaway. Not knowing anything about minerals . . . we had no clue about it back then. . . . [it] just happened [that the] minerals conveyed . . . [i.e., the mineral rights were sold with the property]. Well, he hadn't leased to the companies yet cause he's anti-gas business. . . . He said, "Me and my wife

just realized even if we lease [the mineral rights] . . . we're never gonna recover the money we should." So, they're working out a deal . . . [they're] gonna get like ten grand an acre to just sell outright. They'll get a huge [payout]. Three, four million. And they said, "To us that's our best deal to go with." . . . And if [the gas company is] paying . . . three or four million for it . . . what's it [really] worth?

Rather than simply reflecting a traditional Appalachian attachment to place, the property regime in West Virginia is characterized by such inequalities of dispossession and privilege. The fracking boom and pipeline bring financial trouble and emotional catastrophe to some who had planned for a peaceful future and put others in a dangerous property bind they cannot get out of. Still others find an unexpected windfall in exchange for their projected future plans.

Contradiction Two: Sacred Land versus Sacred Property

This contradiction was apparent in the situation of Sean, who owned land destined to be crossed by the pipeline. Because the property was visible from the road, Sean had put up a large billboard against the pipeline and had built a chapel for a campground he planned to build there, hoping to use the existence of a religious function against the company's claim of eminent domain. As discussed above, he told me Native Water Protectors from Standing Rock had come to help and had planted some sacred corn on the site while performing a ceremony of blessing. Sean recounted scornfully how the company had offered him much less than his property was worth for the right-of-way for the pipeline. The pipeline construction would effectively ruin the view, destroy the peaceful site, and wreck his hopes of building rental cabins and a primitive campground. Sean was taking part in a lawsuit against the West Virginia Department of Environmental Protection (WVDEP) and FERC for mis-using eminent domain. Much like the large landowner from northern West Virginia John described above, as much as Sean hated the gas industry, he also stated that he would only give up if they bought his entire property. This willingness to sell if necessary indicates the limit to his attachment to those pieces of land, which was after all based on property law. He recognized the sacredness of the land where the pipeline was projected to cross, but the property relation was nevertheless an essential structure of his attachment.

This structured attachment is visible in the mixture of heartbreak over lost expectations (of what the property was supposed to mean to one's life and family) and the loss of its value. Lori, who owned an acre lot in southern West Virginia, was angry at the pipeline company because of its construction's effect on her animals, whose access to a neighboring field was cut off, even though her property was not directly in the pipeline's path. But mostly she worried that her property value had fallen and with it, her retirement plan was destroyed:

> I mean, you know, we're not gonna get enough out of this [property] now. We would be lucky to buy a little piece of land somewhere a whole lot smaller . . . That's not why we bought this. We bought this as our retirement. And, you know, [the pipeline company] just, they took our entire retirement completely away. . . . we're gonna scrounge for the rest of our life now because of it.

Considering how the pipeline had ruined her future, Lori suggested a fair resolution to the pipeline problem that perhaps reflects an idealization of the real estate market:

> But I think anybody that . . . that is within so many feet of that pipeline, . . . if their home is within that distance, then [the pipeline company] should have to buy them out. They've got the money. And then after they put their pipeline through and they get it all re-seeded and all looking pretty again, they can resell it. . . . That's not asking them to give up money. They're determined that they're not hurting [you] to buy [the right-of-way]. So, let them buy everybody out [whose] home is within so many feet of the pipeline.

This suggestion demonstrates how the idea of buying and selling property is at the heart of American conceptions of rights. The extremely wealthy company ought to treat people fairly and simply purchase their property outright if they want to use it. Lori suggests this would be a just and fair thing to do, that would respect people's rights, although not their right to stay.[32] The best we can hope for is compensation. The right not to be displaced is essential to environmental justice but is currently outside of the reach of market-based rights to land.[33]

One person who would probably not agree with Lori's solution was Greg, a resident of a southern county also crossed by a pipeline, who referred to his family's land as sacred. He emphasized that it was sacred to him personally because of long-standing family traditions. While things can be held sacred to an individual or a family, this usage is most likely distinct from the meaning of sacred as used by the Water Protectors of Standing Rock who visited the pipeline's planned route, planted corn, and performed a blessing. Sisseton Wahpeton Oyate scholar Kimberly Tallbear argues against using the word sacred to describe Indigenous relations to nonhuman nature. She argues that communities, places, and other nonhumans should be described as being in relation.[34] This emphasizes the mutual responsibility of Earth's diverse lifeforms to each other's survival. And as settler scholar David Delgado Shorter notes, the concepts of spirituality and sacredness as applied to Indigenous worldviews are tools of colonization. They impose the settler cultural division of spiritual matters from everyday business onto Indigenous worldviews that don't have such a division. He argues that using them to defend the land is "an absurd tactic, as the precedent in American courts has tended toward the capitalistic, and thereby object-orientated, use and production of land for profit."[35] In other words, legal arguments based on the sacredness of a place don't often win in American court. And because settler property ownership severs intersubjective connections between people and nonhuman nature, it reduces land to "a quantifiable good we live *on* rather than a living entity we live *with* and generate knowledge *through*."[36] "Sacredness" thus becomes merely a form of value added to the property.

In fact, the actual sacredness of private property in settler culture normally refers to the sacred rights of the owner to the property far more than anything pertaining to the rights of the nonhuman nature in question. As suggested by Lori's proposal for the mass purchase of land on the pipeline's route, it is the system of rights in property and the market itself which is the most sacred in settler culture. I came face to face with this version of the sacred during a driving tour of the convoluted pathway of the pipeline through Greg's neighborhood. It is nearly impossible to predict when you will cross the pipeline's path, as the mountainous landscape means that the same road will cross it several times, and without an aerial view it is hard to imagine the pathway making any sense. We pulled over off the one-lane county road to observe a pipeline ditch that had been carved into a hillside near a small ranch-style house. I got out of the car to take a picture of the worksite, and a man came out on the porch of the nearby house and yelled at me, "Hey! Do you need something?" I said I was just looking (although I was actually taking pictures). He said, "You're blocking the gate; you've got to move your car." I wondered about this, as I had carefully parked in front of the bright blue port-a-john. I repeated, "Sorry, just looking," and he replied bitterly, "If you weren't interested in this property before, don't be interested in it now, *Missy*."

Surprisingly I found myself in the role of the "stranger with a camera."[37] Feeling clearly in the wrong, I jumped back in my car. Greg, who has been giving people tours of the pipeline construction route since before it broke ground, calmly explained the man's anger. "He sold to the pipeline and doesn't want you taking a picture of it." My embarrassment and nerves were high. I was faced with the discordance between the necessity of Greg's efforts to protect the local environment from the pipeline, and my own discomfort at breaching the social norms that should have told me not to photograph someone else's property.

The man's anger may also provide several insights; on the one hand, I committed an obvious invasion of his privacy by taking pictures of his property, which was a clear-cut violation of courtesy. What's more, I am acutely aware of the cultural politics of photography in the Appalachian context. On the other hand, his anger signals something about what is sacred about private property in settler culture. Greg's behavior, as an activist fighting to protect the environmental quality not just of his own family farm, but of the region in general, necessarily breached community norms about not interfering in other people's business or their property. As discussed above, simply mentioning his involvement in fighting the pipeline was itself referred to as a form of "badmouthing." A primary and essential tenet of private property law is the right to use or enjoy one's property, within legal limits.[38] This man's decision to allow the pipeline to cross his land was a private decision, but as concerned citizens like Greg point out, it was one that affects the entire community. The effects of the pipeline construction potentially encompass the county, the state, and even the globe when water quality and the greenhouse gas emissions from fracking and natural gas processing are considered. The man's anger, then, provides an example of how the sacredness of private property in settler culture enables the reduction of that property to waste.

Contradiction Three: Troubled Coalitions versus Better Relations

Harris quotes Jeremy Bentham: "Property is nothing but the basis of expectation consisting in an established expectation, in the persuasion of being able to draw such and such advantage from the thing possessed."[39] This quote is interesting because it illustrates the control and objectification that is the basis of private property in land. The rights only go in one direction. These expectations underlie the settler colonial complex, as Mackey argues, "Settler fantasies of possession and entitlement . . . are embedded, 'unconscious expectation[s]' of how the world will work to reaffirm the social locations, perceptions, and benefits of privilege."[40] The certainty of these "settled expectations" comes from the state, a form of western sovereignty that relies on the ultimate authority of a "separate ruling entity" in hierarchical relation of domination to society.[41] These "fantasies of entitlement" attempt to erase other forms of sovereignty that stem from caretaking relations between equal beings that need each other to survive.[42]

Despite being naturalized as just the way things are, this state sovereignty is a cultural construction that coexists with the fact of a human capacity to live otherwise. Environmental activism against extraction pushes people's reliance on state mechanisms for justice to its end and reveals the limits of their agency as citizens. Lawsuits, online comments to regulating bodies, and hearings barely constrain the actions of extractive industry. The predominant narrative of the nation features an "ontological expansiveness" that makes it seem as if the settler state is the only way to address these concerns and that all rights come from property ownership and citizenship.[43] If kept within this frame, coalitions are limited to a shallow multicultural inclusiveness that treats settler property relations as inevitable, emphasizes the legitimacy of existing representative democracy, and elides settler colonialism.[44]

U.S. history [is] . . . oriented by a never-ending process of democratic
development . . . Within this frame of reference, Native peoples, histories,
and sovereignties appear not simply as irrelevant but as abereant, . . . because they do not form part of the trajectory through which the present
emerges from the past.[45]

In other words, the challenge is recognizing that the hierarchical settler
state is not the highest, natural, or only possibility for social organization, that other forms of sovereignty exist, and that they involve other
relations. In the absence of this recognition, we settlers act without
respect and in ways that appropriate ideas and resources from other
people and nonhumans without acknowledgment of their value.

During the Q&A after the Water protector's panel discussed above,
an audience member asked about how to incorporate anti-racism into
environmental activism. The first response, from the East Coast Native American speaker, referenced the room itself, its overwhelming
whiteness, and the possible tokenization of the speakers themselves.
When this speaker noted that all issues are connected, another audience member responded with a comment, reinterpreting this to "We
are all fighting the same fight." This move minimized and erased the
connection that had just been raised between white supremacism and
environmental harm. This exchange underlines the tenuous nature of
these coalitions; although "Water is life" brought people together in
Standing Rock and continues to do so, what the phrase means changes
in different contexts. Nick Estes (Lower Brule Sioux Tribe) explains
that Mni Wiconi (water is life) refers to the practice of "being a good
relative . . . to the water, land, and animals, not to mention the human
world."[46] As the phrase travels its different meanings reveal contradictions between understandings of who belongs to community, what
sacredness really designates, and where the limits of these challenges
to extraction lie.

Ellen, whose family farm contained a spring with "pure, fresh water,"
embraced the idea that "water is life" while at the same time expressing
some of these contradictions. She told me that "the land that they're
taking from us is not that big of a deal, my whole fight is about water.
Peoples' water and peoples' safety." The pipeline itself would only cross
the edge of her property. But it would also snake upward into a nearby

ridge where she believed a slip (landslide) or a break in the karst below the surface could easily pollute everyone's spring water. When she described her involvement in the pipeline fight she highlighted her uncertainty, "I'm still pretty active but . . . I don't want to say [I've] lost hope because you [never know until] the gas is going through it." As more and more people started getting hired or wanting to work for the pipeline, she explained, "you could speak up for being against it, a month or two ago and now . . . there are people getting jobs with them and . . . bragging about how much money they're making an hour off of these people and it just, it takes some wind out of my sails." She clearly understood the conflict between wages and water, as she continued:

> They are going to get some money for a while, they're going to get big money, but . . . [they don't] see how it could mess up their water . . . Water is life. If they don't have water, they have nothing. . . . I just pray that it doesn't affect the water. I would rather be wrong than be right about this.

When the Dakota Access Pipeline (DAPL) came up, Ellen's position was more equivocal. FERC (the Federal Energy Regulatory Commission) is the primary overseer of these interstate pipelines. I asked if she thought politicians make any difference in the pipeline fight. Ellen said not really, because "FERC has more power than the president," and referred to "the pipeline situation with Obama," which I interpreted as referring to DAPL and Standing Rock. After confirming with her if that was what she meant, I remarked that Obama had temporarily stopped DAPL but Trump had restarted it. Here, Ellen's Republican party loyalty may have influenced her response: "I don't . . . I'm not against pipelines, at all, but I'm against this pipeline [the one near her home]. There's many reasons and one of them being that this company has never built one, from what I understand, has never built one with this size pipe and length of the pipeline at the same time."

For Ellen, joining the fight against the neighborhood pipeline seemed to be a step away from her political comfort zone. Without going to what she saw as an extreme, of being against all fossil fuel development, Ellen's opposition to the pipeline near her house but non-opposition to others could be seen as NIMBYism. However, protecting water makes NIMBYIsm difficult. It is all connected; her explanation of her concerns was inclusive of everyone's need for clean water as well as her love for the spring on her property.

She continued to explain why she opposed this pipeline in particular, "If it did happen to blow up, between the twenty-one-mile place between cut-off valves in this area, this whole [place], we would all be burned, gone, forever." She went on to say why that mattered to her, in comments demonstrating the shifting and flexible nature of place attachment and identity:

> Which, I'm ready to go if I have to go, but—this is kind of crazy—I was raised in town, I was a town girl . . . when I moved here it was a really weird experience, and I've heard people, mountain people, talk about how they love the mountain and I just thought that was weird. But I can actually say since I've been here, it's hard to explain, but where I look at the mountain, all the time, I truly feel part of the mountain. [laughs] I know that's weird, but I don't know, I just feel . . . it's part of me now. That's all I know. That's all I know how to say it.

Rather than reflecting an essentialized "Appalachian" place-based identity, Ellen's comment reveals the contextual nature of the ability to relate to a particular landform, and, indirectly, the work that it takes to maintain such a connection. This is a relationship that can be cultivated or destroyed.

Despite Ellen's attachment to the mountain, due to the structures implicated in the pipeline fight, our discussion retained its focus on property and property rights. A bit later Ellen's husband Don came in and asked what we'd been discussing. I responded that we'd been discussing eminent domain and the risk to the water. Don said, "Well basically what it boils down to, they take your property and then tell you what you can do with it." And Ellen added, laughing, "And you still pay taxes on it." I said, "Oh yeah, that's the key, that's like, the twist." And Ellen replied, "Yeah, that's the twist. Once you got the knife in your back, that's the twist."

Another example of politically fraught coalitions came up in my interview with Tracy and Steve. Steve reported that he worked in a nearby county in Virginia, which was more politically conservative than the West Virginia county where he lived:

Virginia's putting up more of a fight. And [the county where I work] is an interesting county . . . they're much more right-wing than [this county] in some ways, in a lot of ways. As far as when it comes to fracking and the pipeline [they are] militant against [it]. . . . "Don't tread on me," basically.

In the complicated politics of property rights and pipeline protests, Radical "hippies" like Appalachians Against Pipelines, who Don suggested were from "Massachusetts" with "money behind them," meet the right-wing libertarian protesters Steve described as fighting for "gun rights . . . rebel flags and everything else." Given the pipeline crisis, even the liberals Tracy and Steve could see the logic of this position. Steve argued, "Your rebel [flag] is a stupid thing to fight for. Fight for your rights! I still think armed revolution is not what we need, but if ever you have an excuse to pull those guns, here's a good one." And Tracy clarified, "Property and your rights and your heritage and your land."

The settler entitlement that is unspoken in many of these land claims is more overt when attached to the confederate flag, a symbol of white supremacism. Libertarian property-rights movements can only coalesce with other property owners, despite the coalitions they might desire (such as the Bundy family, who offered support to Standing Rock). If the settler entitlement to stolen land that is currently behind the most common approaches to fighting resource extraction in non-Indigenous contexts is not open for question, there's a limit to how much further than "Not in my backyard" these environmental movements can go. However, the injuries felt by rural landowners who have these pipelines, designated as a public good, forced on their property by FERC, seem to push people to recognize the connections between fossil fuel extraction, economic exploitation, and environmental sacrifice. Don commented, "these [corporations], they live where they want to live and they live how they want to live because that's where they want to live and how they want to live. We want to live here the way we live here because that's what we like. Why should we be punished?" Ellen added, "For living where we want to live, the way we want to live. Just because they're greedy."

Grace, another resident of the same rural county, answered this way when I asked if her community's opposition to the pipeline meant that the people leaned Democratic:

I don't think the pipeline is a party issue. And I don't even think it's a liberal or conservative issue. It's grandpa's land. And I think that's the issue is that you don't have any control over it. They're taking, you know, the land. I mean, you remember the scene in *Gone with the Wind*, when Gerald O'Hara says, "Land, Katie Scarlett, land . . . It's the only thing worth fighting for. It's the only thing worth dying for." They're taking our land—that knows no politics. That's just wrong.

Grace stresses the common humanity of the fight against losing land to extractive industry and suggests the emotional intensity of her and other people's love for the place. However, her comments trouble this shared fight and emotional connection at the same time. The existence of "grandpa's land" suggests a shared inheritance within this community she invokes. Despite Grace's personal belief in anti-racism, the quote she uses reveals a structural assumption of generational property ownership and at least a possible identification with the O'Haras, a fictional family of enslavers. The scene focuses on how Gerald O'Hara, the patriarch of his family, passes on the love of his land to his daughter, but the often-unacknowledged background to the story is that the O'Hara's Georgia plantation was on land taken decades before from its Mvskoke (Muscogee, or Creek) inhabitants who were forced at gunpoint west in the Trail of Tears. The land itself was valued primarily as the means to build a family fortune through enslaved labor. Grace quotes this line in order to show the intensity of people's emotional attachment to land. However, in the context of capitalism and settler colonialism, this love of land is structured by the terms of white supremacist possessive individualism and entitlement that reduce it to a commodity in relation to a single family, representing their fortune at the expense of others.[47]

The love people feel for their homeplaces is not the problem. The legal structures of property limit the ability of people to enact that love by taking care of places, because it limits how we can relate to nonhuman nature and each other. How can we learn to express love for places and landforms without a reiteration of settler entitlement to property? This entitlement to property also carries with it the unspoken and often unrecognized desire for control and the notion of linear human development that underlies the settler complex. The unrecognized settler entitlement and anti-Blackness that underlies activism based on defending property rights needs to be remedied in order for real environmental justice to be imaginable.[48] The love of place and entitlement of mostly white property owners needs to be reconsidered in the context of a responsible recognition of existing settler colonial relations and the violence they entail.

Conclusion

Activist groups like Appalachians Against Pipelines and Third Act Virginia see their fight as part of a common struggle with Indigenous Peoples' including the movements for Land Back and No Pipelines on Stolen Land.[49] However, they are considered radical to many people fighting the pipeline, and I realize that hoping that a significant number of white US citizens will start thinking of themselves as settlers, questioning their attachment to property, or questioning the hegemony of settler state sovereignty is utopian. It is nevertheless by stating the seemingly impossible that we are enabled to reimagine the possible. It is becoming increasingly obvious that Indigenous sovereignty, knowledge, and leadership are indispensable to any optimistic vision of the future.[50] In her discussion of the Onondaga Nation's land title lawsuit in New York, Robin Kimmerer underlines the Nation's unique and specific requests with regard to the Onondaga Lake Superfund site:

> [M]embers of the Onondaga Nation argued that the land title they're seeking is not for possession, not to exclude, but for *the right to participate in the well-being of the land.* Against the backdrop of Euro-American thinking, which treats land as a bundle of property rights, the Onondaga are asking for *freedom to exercise their responsibility to the land.* This is unheard of in American property law.[51]

Attachments to places can be productive of environmental activism. Attachments to privileged places can also contribute to the destruction of places loved by less powerful actors. The double-edged sword of settler attachment is expressed in the struggle of people affected by the fracking and pipeline boom to maintain control over and exclusive use of their property. The limiting framework of property rights to land is also illustrated in the piecemeal work of pipeline companies that break down relations between neighbors who wish to preserve the sanctity of their family's land, and others who "would sell God."

This reductive version of democratic participation that happens primarily through the stakes of individual private property threatens our collective survival, and calls for a revisioning of our self-conception as being party to a treaty.[52] This means acknowledging that there are different ways of relating to nonhuman nature that exist on this continent, recognizing Indigenous sovereignty, and learning from the lessons they offer about caretaking relations and responsibility to other humans and more-than-humans.[53] Most important, perhaps, is to recognize that relationships between equals require a lot of work and lack certainty. This may be the most challenging aspect, as this uncertainty that is inherent in dealings with (human and nonhuman) others who are independent actors with their own agendas is really bad for business. Yet the uncertainty resulting from abandoning white settler "epistemologies of mastery" may one day "be embraced as a key to creativity and imagination."[54] Or, as Tallbear questions, "I consider how things might have been different had more newcomers respected long-established ways of relating already in place. What if settlers hadn't been dead set on cultural evangelizing through governance, religion, and science?"[55]

My goal in pointing out the contradictions that emerge from these interviews about place-based cultures, sacred land, and anti-pipeline politics is to problematize the habits of thought that are propagated by the naturalization of the settler state. In the wake of the expanding natural gas "spider's web," the legitimacy of the fossil fuel extractive complex is called into question by such diverse groups as libertarian proponents of gun rights, conservatives hoping to protect water for their neighbors and children, radical settler environmentalists learning about Indigenous sovereignty, and Indigenous Water Protectors. These coalitions are limited by the alienation of the "frontier mentality" which persists in imagining a natural war of all against all. The primacy of private property as the root of individual rights in the US impedes the realization of how to make and maintain good relations. These habits of thought limit how we can imagine loving the land. The path of settler time as unidirectional progress doesn't leave room for questions about the lessons we can learn from other ways of living. The assumptions of white supremacism that underlie settler colonialism are standing in the way of perceiving the multiplicity of human potential.

Conclusion

"There's No Word Like That in Ojibwe"

The Seventh Fire talks about a new people emerging; people who would retrace their steps and pick up the bundles that were lost. You may have the objects, but you have forgotten what they mean, or perhaps new histories have been written on top of old ones. Picking up your bundle means looking at these things differently.
—Patty Krawec

Stories are never just stories. Respecting the importance of stories as knowledge systems, as frames for perception, and as everyday theories of how the world works is at the heart of this book.[1] Stories of the frontier are essential to the American settler colonial project, including and especially the story of "free land" and the specific type of freedom that it has been perceived to offer. Indigenous, Black, and people of color futurist imaginaries offer counter-stories to the ones white western culture tells.[2] As settler scholars Alissa Macoun and Elizabeth Strakosch argue, citing Veracini, decolonization "needs to be imagined before it is practised, and this has proved especially challenging."[3] They argue that the best role for settler colonial theory is "providing non-Indigenous people in settler states with a better account of ourselves—rather than . . . an account of the entire settler–Indigenous relationship."[4] This book has been an effort to provide an account of how a social structure critical to the story of settler colonialism, private property in land, contributes to the crisis that we currently find ourselves in, but without assuming that this structure is absolute or determinate in human history. On the contrary, the story of private property is only one story out of many that we can tell about ourselves. Accordingly, this conclusion will dwell for a while on a different story.

Anishinaabe writer Waubgeshig Rice's novel *Moon of the Crusted Snow* corresponds well in some ways with the fossil fuel narratives examined in chapter 3.[5] Like NBC's *Revolution*, the drama starts with the failure of electrical power.[6] Just like on the TV show, one of the first impacts of the loss of power concerns the screen habits of children who are suddenly without their favorite form of entertainment.[7] The two narratives could almost be imagined as occurring in the same fictional universe, with *Revolution* encapsulating the events of Rice's book from the perspective of non-Indigenous people in the cities of what is currently known as North America. The book concerns a band of Anishinaabeg who live on a fictional reservation, far from their traditional territory, in what is currently known as northern Ontario. The reservation is largely dependent on food and fuel from the south and is served by a hydroelectric plant that only recently started providing reliable electricity. Other than this shared premise, however, the narrative diverges greatly from non-Indigenous accounts of the fossil fuel apocalypse.

Right on the front dust flap, the framing of the novel is clear: "As one society collapses, another is reborn."[8] As Nick Estes and others have pointed out, settler colonialism is and has been a recurrent disaster for Indigenous Peoples.[9] The characters in Rice's novel, forced out of their traditional lands several generations ago and relocated to the far north, then subjected to boarding schools and the attempted elimination of their language and ceremonies, have already experienced Apocalypse.[10] This is emphasized repeatedly in the book. Noting the easy smile of an Elder, Aileen, after a tense community meeting, the main character, Evan Whitesky, thinks, "She's lived through it all. . . . If she's not worried, then we shouldn't be."[11] Thanks to Elders like Aileen and Evan's parents, the band's Anishinaabe traditions have been continued and revived, including language and stories, subsistence practices like hunting, fishing, and trapping, and ceremonies. I was interested and surprised, therefore, to encounter two widely divergent readings of *Moon of the Crusted Snow* by (apparently) non-Indigenous scholars in academic journals.

The first, "Beginning at the End: Indigenous Survivance in *Moon of the Crusted Snow*," shared my impression of the novel. In Kirsten Bussière's reading, Rice's novel shows how the collapse of settler society "allow[s] for a rekindling of traditional knowledge that is not marred by a western colonial concept of progress."[12] She underlines the optimism inherent in the novel's premise, in that not only does the collapse of settler society provide a "politically mobilizing and agency-creating mechanism" for the resurgence of Indigenous knowledge about how to survive on the land, but it also clearly demonstrates that these skills are present in Indigenous communities already, and that "Indigenous populations already have what they need to endure and prosper in a changing world marked by the threat of anthropogenic climate change."[13] Despite repeated settler colonial efforts to force a "disjointed life" on the community, Elders were able to keep traditional collective ways alive, and despite the terrible hardships of the winter, this enabled the community as a whole to weather the crisis by working together.[14]

Another account of the book, "Petromelancholia and the Energopolitical Violence of Settler Colonialism in Waubgeshig Rice's *Moon of the Crusted Snow*," interprets the book differently. Reuben Martens explains that petromelancholia represents "the conditions of grief that we experience when hydrocarbon resources start to dwindle, the feeling that we are slowly but surely losing access to cheap energy (and all affects that come with that)."[15] Although recognizing the complicated relationship of the fictional reservation in the novel to "cheap energy" and all its affordances, because these have been literally forced on the band by the settler colonial state, Martens sees petromelancholia as a major theme in the book.[16] The materials of fossil fuel–dependent society: plastic, HVAC systems, diesel generators, gas-powered vehicles, etc., are all used and relied upon by the Anishinaabeg on the reservation. The condition of living dependent on all of these, Martens argues, makes it difficult to imagine life otherwise, leading to what he calls "petro-subjectivity."[17]

Rice's book makes clear that this petro-subjectivity or "the fact that the presence and use of oil is ingrained in everything one does" is very much stronger among the non-Indigenous people of Gibson, the fictional northern Ontario city where two young men from the reservation were attending college.[18] Nevertheless, a dependence on fossil fuels is still notable on the reservation. The band has generators that run on diesel, with only half of the fuel they need for the winter in store at the time of the collapse.[19] Evan's younger brother, Cam, is much more interested in playing video games than in hunting or trapping, or otherwise preparing for winter.[20] Evan's own kids are used to watching TV with breakfast every morning.[21] Martens notes that this petro-subjectivity has been "forcibly, unwillingly, and even unconsciously instilled in people through settler-colonial energopolitical violence."[22]

Martens's reading of the book is much less optimistic than Bussière's. He labels it a "trauma narrative" and suggests that the trauma is expressed in "a sense of petromelancholia that persists to the present day and will arguably persist in the Indigenous future."[23] According to Martens, the book "refuses" to allow an optimistic return to balanced life (biskaabiiyang) for Anishinaabeg.[24] Attempting to understand this divergent reading of the novel, I notice that one of the final quotes used in Martens's essay is from Justin Scott, a white Canadian who is the main antagonist of the novel. Martens quotes Scott's derogatory description of the band's resources: "Scott's voice rose and his eyes grew wide. 'Most of them don't even know how to trap! When I took some of those kids out there, they didn't know what the fuck they were doing. If that's your future, then . . . huh.'"[25]

The creeping dread Rice conveys in the novel as TV, internet, and cell phones fail, and then all their hydroelectricity stops working, cutting the community off completely from the outside world just as a crushing winter starts, is nothing compared to the terror inspired by the arrival of Justin Scott. A settler Canadian who follows the trail of the two college students home from Gibson, Justin Scott rides up to the reservation on a black snowmobile carrying stores of guns, ammunition, alcohol, and cigarettes, like the very model of a settler colonizer.[26] Scott receives a generous (if cautious) welcome from the band leadership, a warm place to stay, and is charged with contributing to the community's survival through hunting.[27] He quickly disjoints the community, encourages excessive partying among the young people, and collects his own followers from among the reservation community and other white people seeking refuge. As the winter drags on, Evan's dreams reveal that Scott has become the Windigo, a cannibalistic figure representing the horrors of winter starvation which serves as a warning against greed in Anishinaabe traditions.[28]

The Windigo, according to Kimmerer and Bussière, is a traditional figure in Anishinaabe stories, representing the dangerous hungry times of winter and the perils of individualistic greed.[29] Martens describes its emergence as a symptom of extreme resource depletion, and therefore a result of colonialism.[30] The threat of winter starvation already looms over the community in the book. Scott represents an additional threat to traditional knowledge and community, as he mocks and belittles the community's ceremonies and beliefs.[31] The community is unbalanced by his presence, and his influence leads to the first avoidable deaths in a winter that promises too many deaths.[32] The community leaders establish a careful plan to share the reservation's food and fuel stores fairly with members in order to provide a baseline of nutrition and heat for everyone throughout the winter. This plan requires shared hardship in the interest of mutual survival. As the community's rations get tighter, and believing their survival and comfort justifies any behavior, Scott leads his followers to cannibalism, stealing a body from the band's makeshift mortuary.[33] It is during a scene justifying this behavior to Evan that Scott condemns the band's future chances of survival in the words quoted by Martens above.

However, Scott's point of view represents the avaricious possessive individual of settler colonialism in the book, and therefore he does not have the last word on the community's future. As Elder Aileen reassures Evan:

> They say that this is the end of the world. The power's out and we've run out of gas and no one's come up from down south . . . There's a word they say too. . . . Yes, apocalypse! What a silly word. I can tell you there's no word like that in Ojibwe . . . The world isn't ending . . . Our world isn't ending. It already ended. It ended when the Zhaagnaash [English] came into our original home down south on that bay and took it from us . . . We've seen . . . what's the word again? . . . Yes, apocalypse. We've had that over and over. But we've always survived. We're still here. And we'll still be here even if the power and the radios don't come back on and we never see any white people ever again.[34]

Justin Scott's essential error of valuing his own survival above all else and perceiving the community's members as objects for his own ends is foreshadowed several times in the book. First, when the power goes out, there's a run on the reservation's only grocery store in which people rush to buy as many supplies as they can afford and carry. Neighbors and family members avoid eye contact with those who get less.[35] Then the two returned college students inform the community of how bad things got down in Gibson, where it was every person for themselves and quickly turned to violent chaos.[36] It is only insofar as the band avoids this alienation and shares what they have that half of the community is able to survive the winter. And, contrary to Scott's prediction, the story ends optimistically with the group leaving behind the reservation's infrastructures, because "there was no use for any of it."[37]

With Bussière, I agree that rather than petromelancholia, Indigenous survival is the main theme of *Moon of the Crusted Snow*. And rather than having the last word on the Anishinaabeg's future chances, Scott represents the settler colonial violence and ideologies that they will outlast. His voice does not outweigh the voices of Evan, Aileen, and other characters in the book who repeatedly express faith in the future flourishing of their community. These divergent non-Indigenous readings of the book thus seem to represent on the one hand a listening for the possibility of living otherwise, and on the other a determinist view that we might call petro-fatalism. Although the scars of capitalism, settler colonialism, and fossil fuel extraction are deep and will persist, that does not foreclose future thrivance for this fictional band of Anishinaabeg who are perhaps not so terribly sorry to leave their reservation homes behind.

A reading of the novel based in petro-fatalism appears to rest on an assumption of a binary opposition between modern and traditional ways. It is often recognized among non-Indigenous people that Indigenous Peoples are on the front lines of the global environmental crisis, and that their worldviews diverge greatly from the unsustainable beliefs and practices of global capitalism.[38] The recognition of this fact is not incompatible with settler colonialism, because the binary opposition presented by petro-fatalism supposes that Indigenous people either live isolated in their traditional ways (in which case they are likely to be victims of fossil fuel–driven technology or extraction), or they have been co-opted by modernity and their traditional ways have "faded away" (in which case they experience petromelancholia and are doomed like the rest of us). This point of view reproduces a one-way, linear developmental narrative of history even as it critiques the mainstream western idea of progress that leads to the current crisis. In other words, we may be in trouble, but since we've come this far, there's no "going back." Settler temporality rests on a one-way path for history, and the eternalized future of the settler state makes it difficult to imagine its collapse opening up space for alternative forms of social order and freedom—especially given that the settler state has worked so hard to make those forms appear irrelevant.[39]

Again, this signals the importance of stories. Louise Erdrich (Turtle Mountain Band of Chippewa) also portrays the collapse of settler society as an opportunity for Indigenous freedom in *Future Home of the Living God*, even in the face of frightening new biological conditions.[40] Evolution has reversed itself in this story, leading to unexpected births, and this brings new and unwelcome attention to pregnant women in the transforming settler state. Meanwhile, Anishinaabeg gather strength and autonomy in the new conditions. Another science fiction novel, by Cherie Dimaline (Georgian Bay Métis), *The Marrow Thieves*, centers on a frightening scenario in which the Indigenous people of what is currently known as North America have become a resource for settlers who have lost the ability to dream. "Recruiters" hunt Indigenous people to harvest their bone marrow to provide dreams to the settlers. But this new threat from the failing settler state also offers the chance of freedom and a return to traditional relations for Anishinaabe and other Indigenous people.[41] In each of these stories, hardship and terror are not novelties, and Indigenous survivance in the face of disaster is not a novelty, but it is the collapse of the settler state that opens up new possibilities for alternative futures.[42]

Rice's novel follows this tradition, using the figure of the Windigo as a sign of the "cannibalistic nature of a colonial presence" and perhaps as an allusion to the autosarcophagy of contemporary capitalist and fossil fuel–dependent society and its hyper-individualistic values.[43]

This monster is no bear or howling wolf, no natural beast. Windigos are not born they are made. The Windigo is a human being that has become a cannibal monster. Its bite will transform victims into cannibals too. . . . Born of our fears and our failings, Windigo is the name for that within us which cares more for its own survival than for anything else.[44]

According to Robin Kimmerer, the Windigo didn't originate with settler colonialism, but exists in the conditions of human life through starving times, when the rules for maintaining good relations become hard to follow but even more important. In Rice's book, defeating the Windigo creates the possibility of survival and flourishing. The Windigo serves as a reminder that life is not safe, whether it stands for a rapacious settler colonialism or for the common human danger of social breakdown in hungry times. In Rice's novel, the "Original Instructions" or traditional Anishinaabe knowledges of how to be in good relation provide guardrails to human behavior that enable the community to survive.[45]

Macoun and Strakosch state, "Settler colonialism posits that two political societies cannot exist in one place through time, and that one must necessarily replace the other—either by settlers extinguishing Aboriginal difference or by Aboriginal people expelling settlers (an option rarely countenanced)."[46] Most settler stories assume Indigenous people are part of the past, not the future. The fossil fuel narratives considered in chapter 3 largely follow these patterns: a new (white) frontier society in *Revolution*, and a post-human nightmare of extractive capitalism in "People of Sand and Slag." *Cargo* offers an example of the second choice outlined by Macoun and Strakosch, when the virus results in the excision of the diseased Australian settler society and leaves behind a renewed Indigenous world, albeit one that is not the direct focus of the narrative. Taking the perspective of this Indigenous future, Rice, Erdrich, Dimaline, and others all offer a window to a less deterministic and one-directional world.[47]

In *Moon of the Crusted Snow*, Justin Scott represents the settler mindset of individual self-interest and domination. Although initially he is eager to prove himself as a hunter, he eventually delegates this work to the people who become his dependents. He reassures them that he has "a plan" to deal with the hunger they fear as winter deepens.[48] This isolation from the community, expressed by one of Scott's white "followers" as the growing desire she feels to "hide" from the community, seems to represent in the novel the imposition of acquisitive individualism in defiance of the collective well-being of the reservation.[49] Rice makes it clear that this short-sighted urge for private self-sufficiency is a threat to the community.

Scott not only represents the imposition of the hierarchical private structures of settler colonialism on the reservation, but he also fails to take seriously the Anishinaabe ceremonies and traditions into which he is cautiously welcomed when he arrives. Although he is as much at risk as anyone on the reservation, and as Evan thinks, "*He needs us more than we need him*," Scott disregards the leadership's instructions and only superficially follows ceremonial forms.⁵⁰ His transactional view of sex and other relationships makes clear he discounts the real significance of the Anishinaabe way of life. His limited understanding reduces Anishinaabe ways to hunting, as indicated in his speech quoted above. Here, his behavior resembles the settler logic of containment described by Starblanket and Stark, in which Indigenous knowledge is used as a repository to mine for ideas or clues on how to survive "in a precarious world" but is not centered or seen as world-defining knowledge in its own right.⁵¹ Thus, settler culture continues to reify "divisions between humans and nature, even while considering the Indigenous stories that actively work against this categorization," and as they note, "these tendencies minimize or contain the transformational potential of Indigenous knowledge."⁵²

Scott's character in *Moon of the Crusted Snow* brings the Windigo to the reservation, threatening through his behavior and influence to reproduce the chaos that engulfed the unprepared non-Indigenous people of Gibson. By defeating the Windigo, Evan and the rest of the community are able to leave behind the infrastructure and social structure of settler colonialism—from the reservation houses to the trappings of settler customs like white wedding dresses. This optimistic ending wasn't visible to Scott's character in the novel; white supremacism can only see the one path, and therefore can't perceive hope for the future even when it is offered on a platter. Scott's character represents a settler mindset, so convinced of the unidirectional ladder of development that he trains himself not to see the alternatives that exist in front of him. These alternative ways of life are written off by various means. They are dismissed because of a capitalist view of human nature (all people are naturally greedy and individualistic) and therefore the hope for alternatives is just a romanticization of the past. Or they are written off because of the underlying racial/civilizational progress narrative that says even if other ways of life (once) existed, greed and individualism represent human "progress" and "we can't go back."

The naturalization of private property, the reliance on it as the most rational and hyper-lucid relationship to land possible, draws on the same logic as the civilizational progress narrative. These structures help shape the "colonial unknowing" that limits conceptions of personal agency to property ownership within the legal structures of capitalism in which all roads lead to the frack pad, mine, or toxic waste facility.[53] Settler culture says property empowers, but it only does so for some at the expense of what we get from each other. I hope to have opened up a space with this book for reflection on what property does for us and to us, and what alternative relationships to other humans and nonhumans we are capable of imagining, learning from, and practicing.

The fracking and pipeline boom has heightened the irrationality of the hyper-rational property regime to the point that the harms have become more widely visible across affected communities. The conditions of late fossil fuel society lead not only to petromelancholia, or the anticipatory grief many of us might be experiencing as we foresee a future very different from the present, but also to a growing realization that the risks of fossil fuel extraction will not remain safely "elsewhere" as the chickens come home to roost.[54] In West Virginia the boom in natural gas has demanded only more sacrifice from a state that has already seen too much environmental destruction. The effects of extraction on the landscape, air, water, and future hopes for communities are becoming more tangible to places that don't have histories as sacrifice zones. As extraction intensifies, the laws and structures that are supposed to protect American citizens, through protecting their property, seem only to provide a path for continued extraction.

The property bind reflects a hyper-individualized relation to nonhuman nature and landforms that appears to generate agency, in the form of the American Dream, but actually limits forms of action. Although wealth and property do bring enhanced personal power to some, even those forms of agency are limited in their capacity to protect from environmental harm, as the example of Porter Ranch illustrates. But property is based on a hierarchical covering of dependents by the independent head of household or property owner, and therefore creates hierarchies that disempower more than they empower. Property constrains our relations with nonhuman nature and other humans both practically and in the realm of the imagination. Objectified, nature appears as a screen for the projection of human desires rather than what it is, a complex web of interrelations.

The dichotomy of protection and use is shaped by the settler logic of land as property. This logic of objectification is unidirectional—it leads us to the current environmental crisis. The strategies that derive from the fundamental concern enshrined in the US Constitution for the protection of property are not adequate tools for facing global environmental challenges. These challenges have been brought about by the global hegemony of capital and are the result of these same strategies.[55] This book has focused on the structures of private property and settler culture that characterize the American relationship to nonhuman nature and other humans, highlighting the role of settler property in limiting these relationships and our imaginations. Again, settler colonialism is not the only cause of our current predicament, but rather, it is one that is naturalized and elided in much mainstream social science.[56] The questions we ask and the stories we tell shape the limits of our imaginations.

When those stories include scenarios like the tragedy of the commons or a war of all against all, they project our current alienated and severed subjectivity onto human nature as a whole. The tragedy of the commons uses an imaginary collection of livestock herders to stand in for human nature. Without private property, these livestock herders are represented as having no culture (i.e., no way of collectively organizing their livelihoods). Without property, says this fable, everyone pursues their apparently natural self-interest, which is simply to accumulate more animals than they individually need without regard to the fate of the ecosystems upon which the livestock depend. Since no one owns the fields, no one thinks of their preservation. Eventually everyone's herds will grow so large that the grazing space they share will be destroyed. This is a reductive view of human nature that conflates self-interest with accumulation and culture with private property. The so-called commons in this story is actually a resource frontier.[57]

Like Hobbes's description of the state of nature as a war of all against all, the tragedy of the commons takes modern capitalist acquisitive individualism and projects it over all human history and possibility.[58] These individuals who are at war with each other or busy building their herds without much thought to the consequences are notably undistinguished by culture or location, but their actions present them clearly as individual property owners fighting to protect their property. They generally fit the description from the animated video "Man," discussed in the introduction.[59] This depiction of human nature relies on a unidirectional ladder of development that actively derogates the multiplicity and creativity of human potential. This is the imagination that foresees the loss of electric power leading to chaos, as in *Revolution*, with order only restored by violence. This is the imagination of Justin Scott, in *Moon of the Crusted Snow*, who sees doom ahead for the Anishinaabeg and only more grasping for resources and power for himself. This reductive view of human nature relies on Indigenous erasure. The diversity of human cultures includes many different distributive structures that do not depend on the institution of private property. This diversity is discounted when settler-colonizers chart human progress as a one-way deterministic path toward ourselves.

Robert Nichols notes that western critical theorists persist in the narcissism of looking only at their own antiquity for "alternative normative horizons" when "there are literally hundreds of millions of Indigenous peoples who have long cultivated a deep practice of care as counter dispossession, and unlike Roman law or medieval monasticism, these Indigenous forms of life endure in the present."[60] Although the modern western self-conception that sees itself as the climax of human development persists in portraying Indigenous knowledges as relics of a bygone era, these should rather be seen as representing the ability of communities to persist despite massive efforts to extinguish them.[61]

When talking to young people about their anxieties about the future, I get the feeling that what we (settlers) need now is not more certainty about what we know, but more openness to what we don't know. Too much certainty is often a key mechanism of willful blindness. What Charles Mills calls the epistemology of ignorance perpetuates white unknowing of the consequences of enslavement and colonialism.[62] The certainty of white unknowing facilitates the denial of facts that are literally in front of one's face. Uncertainty and openness to new ideas, on the other hand, allow for the development of cultural humility, or an attitude of being willing to learn. The seemingly automatic lip service in settler culture paid to Indigenous knowledges as representing a distinct (noncapitalist) worldview, and the subsequent discounting of these knowledges as sources of any future possibility reflects too much self-satisfaction, too much certainty, too quick of an assumption about the state of the world. It is as if to say, "I've mastered the knowledge of human possibility, and I know what works and what doesn't." Cultural humility says, "What other paths are there?"[63]

Here at the end, I have a lot more questions than answers. And I don't trust that the answers I've been given will work for whatever my kids encounter in the future. New approaches are required. Similar in form to cultural humility, ecological humility requires decentering human beings and an openness to the unknown, including the nonhuman.[64] Thinking of a place or a person as property leads to dreams of control, the right to exclude, and the ability to take as one pleases. Property is settled, a space of domination. Recognizing a place or a person as representing a value and agency of their own, in a relationship between interdependent entities sharing the biosphere, means accepting uncertainty. Interactions between equals are always unpredictable, remain unsettled, and require effort to maintain in good relation.[65] Relentless critique of "the way things are" is necessary because white supremacism, settler culture, and capitalism repeatedly settle back down into "how it is" and impose their limits on the real as if they were written in stone.[66] The flexibility of human nature means we can't know every possibility for the future. Maybe we (settlers) can't imagine what social, cultural, political, and emotional guardrails will guide us through the difficult metaphorical winter we face. With humility, we can learn to respect others and create relations that are more sustainable.

ACKNOWLEDGMENTS

I would like to thank my interview participants and the many others who helped me understand what was happening on the ground in West Virginia, and who generously shared their worlds and perspectives with me. I give thanks to the many scholars, activists, novelists, artists, and journalists whose work informed this project. I am very grateful that this project was also supported by a grant from the University of Missouri System Research Board. I also received the generous help of Melissa Horner, Barbara Barnes, Becky Martínez, Scott Garson, Mel Constantine-Miseo, Kandice Grossman, Aaron Padgett, Hanna McElduff Harman, and Betsy, Lucy, and David Scott. Thank you all! I appreciate you so much. Thanks to the anonymous readers for New York University Press, who generously shared their time to review my manuscript. Their feedback greatly strengthened this work. Thanks as well to my editor, Ilene Kalish, whose advice was instrumental in finishing this book. Any errors are my own.

METHODOLOGICAL APPENDIX

This book does not follow the typical path of an ethnographic study that focuses on a geographically delimited place, a social group, or the trajectory of a commodity, although it could have done so. Other researchers are working on studies of the effects of natural gas in place, pipeline workers, and natural gas itself.[1] This is not an ethnography of natural gas. Like the substance itself, the effects are dispersed so widely in space and time that I've had trouble grasping the essential form that such an ethnography would take. This book instead reflects my curiosity about the interactions of private property and personhood and how those interactions affect the human relationship with the environment. Fossil fuel extraction reflects this primacy of property through the legal structures of eminent domain and the split estate. My curiosity was redoubled when I interviewed a landowner in the path of natural gas who referred to gas company actions or incursions "on him," meaning on his property. An example of such an utterance would be "I already have one well on me, and now they want to put another." This phrase signified to my ears the deep connections between property and personhood reflected in American culture. While it reflects a privileged position, that of a large landowner, it also reflects something very ordinary.

Treating the land as property is a fundamental structure of objectification and is part of an affective system that shapes the American relationship to the space of the continent currently known as North America. One of the things that particularly struck me was how personal this affective connection was, while at the same time being totally objectifying. This contradiction seemed to me to be born out of the structures of settler colonialism and capitalism that fundamentally shape how land and people are treated in the United States. The election of Donald Trump as president in 2016 sent shock waves through my biological system as well as my familial, social, and professional networks. The return to open declarations of hetero-patriarchal white supremacism in public discourse has been terrifying. But books like *The Broken Heart of America* by Walter Johnson led me to comprehend how unsurprising that election was in the larger context of American history.[2] I was already learning from Indigenous critiques of settler colonialism, and the critical question of how these deep structures shaped our present predicament became impossible to ignore in the context of American sociology. My original interest in property and personhood was impossible to pursue without the inclusion of the structures of settler colonialism in its framing.

The way that landowner imagined the land around him as part of himself seemed a verbal articulation of how property enhances or diminishes the personal agency of individuals. Events kept occurring that seemed to echo the point, and I followed them in different directions for investigations that became part of this book: into the post-industrial, when the bottoming out of the real estate market in Flint, Michigan after the lead crisis only seemed to exacerbate the crisis itself, and into the space of sovereign citizenship, when the Bundy ranching family experienced virtual impunity for taking resources from the federal government and holding an armed standoff. These investigations offered evocative comparisons that highlighted underlying patterns of how property shapes life chances and worldviews. Many of the correspondences I saw were ephemeral, without direct positive connections that could be laid out clearly. In order to trace the connections between property structures in environmental politics and the cultural frameworks that help these events make sense, I looked to fiction for help in discerning the affective structures shaping these entanglements. Stories represent a holistic form of knowledge that enables an expression of truths that positivistic social science prefers not to see.[3] These approaches refuse to discount the deep affective structures that result from the historical entanglements of gender and sexuality, race and family, with property and ideas of developmentalism and progress.

I had already been thinking a lot about the different fantasies of "apocalypse" evidenced by various fictional accounts, including the TV series *Revolution*, which in particular seemed a relic of the Obama administration in its imagination of governmental overreach from a right-wing perspective. Bringing stories further into the project allowed me to follow the echoes between everyday events and their imaginary counterparts in aesthetic representations that attempt to put order on the cosmos. As Daniel Heath Justice puts it, stories can both wound and heal.[4] Stories can also reaffirm harmful conceptual orderings and naturalize power structures, encouraging fear instead of hope.[5] Apocalyptic narratives seem to be accumulating in popular culture, and the ones I chose for this book were notable for their incorporation of fossil fuel or energy themes, which made them unique in a genre that often ignores these as background details. These were chosen as well for their exploration of the social forms that were imagined persisting in these post-apocalyptic scenarios, explorations that highlighted the imagined war of all against all which characterizes property culture. Indigenous and other people of color futurisms offer alternatives to this overdetermined frontier landscape.[6]

Nonetheless, the methodology of the book is largely self-critical, as it takes on these settler capitalist imaginaries and structures in order to see beyond them. The most difficult part of this critical perspective is regarding interviews with folks who may not share my views on these questions. The focus on property leads to a criticism of things that most of my participants take for granted. Property is the most direct and obvious point of leverage in US law to fight for nature, human rights, or environmental quality. Because of this focus, I sought participants who were fighting the pipeline at least partly in the name of property; it is perhaps necessary to emphasize that there are many others doing so without a property connection. At the same time as I was conducting my research, there were many other researchers also interested in fracking in West Virginia. I experienced some difficulty in locating willing interview subjects because of widespread participant fatigue. Many of the region's activists were justifiably tired of helping researchers on projects that provided them little direct benefit.

I found the property focus to be essential because to allow it to remain as an unquestioned backdrop to the problem was to leave the status quo unexamined, which for me seemed to only lead back to where I started. The property connection is personal, as my own attachment to place is tenuously cemented in the terms of private property. Autoethnographic vignettes throughout the text are used to clarify the tensions of navigating my insider/outsider status as a researcher investigating the structures of settler colonialism and the problematic love of place that it can engender. These vignettes allow me to attempt to convey some of the embodied sensations of inhabiting an industrial sacrifice zone that is simultaneously a homeplace, along with the recognition of the fundamental injustice that structures my relationship to place.[7] Autoethnography also allows me to start from an examination of what I know in an effort to move to a new position.[8]

Interviews were very informal and loosely organized about questions regarding people's experiences with the gas industry, how their property was affected, and their feelings about that, and whatever other elements of their experiences they wanted to share with me. The stories, comments, and observations recorded here help make visible the shape of the property structures that underlie the extractive culture of settler colonialism and that work to support that structure. The method of ethnographic interviews allows for reflection on how these structures converge in the context of a particular community and its relationship to land, governmental agencies, and corporate power. Rather than focusing on individuals, the method focuses on the discursive structures these utterances make visible. I recognize that this work may not be what my participants hoped for when they shared their perspectives and experiences with me. Most agreed to be interviewed primarily in order to spread the word about the injustices they were experiencing. Although some are unsure of the ability of the US legal system to help them protect their land and communities, my participants don't necessarily share my view of the role of settler colonialism. However, as part of my responsibility to the world we are making together, this text represents a small challenge to the settler colonial structures that contribute to the current destructive rush to extraction. As powerful world-determining stories and practices, these structures shape our imaginations of what is possible and impossible, despite the intentions or desires of individuals who are far more complex than the limitations of these structures, and who cannot be totally understood within their terms.

My interviews took place over the course of two summers, 2017 and 2018, in part with the support of the University of Missouri Research Board. I traveled all over the state to places that were either in the path of a pipeline or in the heart of the gas field where the frack pads and downstream facilities were being built. The table of participants shows where interviews were conducted, and when, along with a rough dichotomy of whether participants were more affected by the gas production (which mostly happens in the northwest part of the state) or the pipeline construction (which happens over the whole state, but for this project I concentrated on the southeastern part). Interviews were recorded on a digital recorder or on my iPhone and transcribed for coding. Although pipeline construction and downstream gas processing facilities often impact communities of color, in my study all participants were or appeared to be white, reflecting the demographics of rural areas in West Virginia as well as landownership patterns. Participants were assigned a pseudonym according to my socially informed perception of their gender, and identifying details were changed to preserve their anonymity. Participants were not chosen as part of a random sample, but instead were found through my local social networks and snowball sampling. The themes examined here are specific and particular but have relevance for other contexts in which extraction is facilitated by private property. Not every participant is directly quoted in the study, but all contributed to my understanding of the labyrinthine structures of the natural gas industry that I found at first virtually impossible to follow because they don't proceed in any kind of straightforward fashion. Traveling back and forth around the state and getting multiple perspectives from up- and downstream helped me learn to conceptually navigate the natural gas industry. I also attended informational meetings on fracking, pipeline developments, and the proposed Appalachian Storage Hub held by local organizations including the Ohio Valley Environmental Coalition, Appalachian Voices, and others. I recorded fieldnotes in notebooks and verbally on my iPhone for later transcription.

TABLE A.1. Table of participants

Name	Time and location	Estimated age	Position to issue
Frank	2017, Northwestern gas field	70s	Activist
Bill	2017, Northwestern gas field	70s	Landowner
Sam	2017, Northwestern gas field	50s	Landowner
Cassandra	2017, Northwestern gas field	30s	Landowner/activist/blogger
Mindy	2017, Northwestern gas field	50s	Activist
Sean	2017, Southeastern pipeline route	70s, with Greg in 2018	Landowner/entrepreneur
Greg	2018, Southeastern pipeline route	60s	Landowner/activist
John	2018, Northwestern gas field	60s, with Fred	Landowner
Fred	2018, Northwestern gas field	70s	Landowner
Steve	2018, Southeastern pipeline route	40s, with Tracy	Landowner
Tracy	2018, Southeastern pipeline route	40s	Landowner
Grace	2018, Southeastern pipeline route	60s	Landowner
Dale	2018, Southeastern pipeline route	60s, with Grace	Landowner
Tabitha	2018, Southeastern pipeline route	50s	Landowner
Cathy	2018, Northwestern gas field	60s	Landowner
Lori	2018, Southeastern pipeline route	50s	Landowner
Lucy	2018, Northwestern gas field	70s	Landowner/activist
Brad	2018, Northwestern gas field	40s	Industry employee
Mary	2018, Southeastern pipeline route	60s	Landowner/activist
Rose	2018, Southeastern pipeline route	40s	Area resident
Darrell	2018, Southeastern pipeline route	60s	Industry consultant
Philip	2018, Northwestern gas field	30s	Industry employee
Ellen	2018, Southeastern pipeline route	40s	Landowner
Don	2018, Southeastern pipeline route	40s, with Ellen	Landowner

The literature used in this book focuses primarily on the structures of settler colonialism as experienced in the places currently known as the United States and Canada. This reflects personal limitations, historically conditioned opportunities, and historical connections between the legal structures of these two countries. Although Indigenous Peoples in Mexico, and Central and South America also experience and resist settler colonial structures, those structures are distinct in some ways from US and Canadian versions, which derive from British common law and its liberal market structure that has historically centered most fully on individual private property.[9] Primarily due to my limitation to English, works contributing to and drawing from Native and Indigenous studies and critical settler studies in Canada, Australia, and other English-speaking settler states were invaluable to this book. Natural gas fracking and pipeline development also greatly exceed the information related here because they affect lands and people across the United States and around the globe. These happenings are beyond the scope of this book, which retains a relatively narrow focus on fracking in West Virginia due to my desire to focus on a structure of feeling I am implicated within and on a place I feel a sense of responsibility toward.

Because of my goal of centering property as a limiting structure in constructing the human relationship to nonhuman nature, the book doesn't include a thorough conversation on other vitally critical subjects. Among other things, these include further legacies of colonialism and settler colonialism, militarization as environmental disaster, anti-Blackness and other forms of racism as globally significant causes of the climate crisis, neoliberalism's massive transfer of wealth and power to the less than one percent who are responsible for most environmental harm, and how current efforts to push back on the rights of trans- and gender-nonconforming people, LGB people, and women are connected to these issues. The narrow focus of this book is not meant to suggest that the many other contributors to social and environmental damage are not important, but rather to center one that often avoids examination. Centering settler colonialism as a contributor to social and environmental harm and parsing how property works to facilitate this harm has been a very personally motivated goal, as someone who grew up surrounded by the naturalization of these structures and their effects. I also write this as someone who wants this generation to take the necessary steps toward renewed peace and solidarity, rather than toward continued avarice and competition.

NOTES

PROLOGUE

1 Johansen, *Forgotten Founders*; Gunn Allen, "(from) Who Is Your Mother?"

INTRODUCTION

Epigraph: TallBear, "Caretaking Relations."

1 Names and identifying details of interview participants have been changed to preserve their privacy.

2 O'Neill, "Kansas Cleans Up"; DiTirro, "Massive Pipeline Explosion."

3 "What FERC Does," FERC, accessed January 4, 2023. www.ferc.gov.

4 Dalton, "A History of Eminent Domain"; Melton, "Eminent Domain."

5 Bosworth, "'They're Treating Us like Indians!'"

6 Coulthard, *Red Skin, White*, 57.

7 Nichols, *Theft Is Property!*

8 Harris, "Whiteness as Property" ; Whyte, "Our Ancestors' Dystopia Now."

9 TallBear, *Native American DNA*.

10 Byrd, *The Transit of Empire*; Carlson-Manathara and Rowe, *Living in Indigenous Sovereignty*.

11 Bruyneel, *Settler Memory*; Manu Vimalassery et al., "On Colonial Unknowing."

12 Justice, *Why Indigenous Literatures Matter*, 6.

13 Kauanui, "'A Structure, Not an Event'"; Wolfe, "Settler Colonialism"; Carlson-Manathara and Rowe, *Living in Indigenous Sovereignty*.

14 Quoted in Bruyneel, *Settler Memory*, 156–57.

15 Starblanket and Stark, "Towards a Relational Paradigm"; Stark, "Criminal Empire."

16 Williams, *Marxism and Literature*, 132.

17 Kauanui, "'A Structure, Not an Event'"; see also Wolfe, "Settler Colonialism"; Carey and Silverstein, "Thinking With and Beyond Settler Colonial Studies"; Rifkin, *Settler Common Sense*.

18 Bruyneel, "The American Liberal Colonial Tradition," 312.

19 Chapman, "America Claims to Have 'Tamed the West.'"

20 Rifkin, *Beyond Settler Time*, 116; Voyles, *Wastelanding*; Giroux, *Stormy Weather*.

21 Mackey, *Unsettled Expectations*, 167.

22 TallBear, "Making Love."

23 O'Brien, *Firsting and Lasting*.

24 Vimalassery et al., "On Colonial Unknowing."

25 Bruyneel, *Settler Memory*, 181.

26 Bruyneel, *Settler Memory*, 177–78.

27 Alfred, "Cultural Strength"; Starblanket and Stark, "Towards a Relational Paradigm"; Mackey, *Unsettled Expectations.*

28 Simpson, *As We Have Always Done*, 43.

29 Simpson, *As We Have Always Done*, 73.

30 Gina Starblanket, "Numbered Treaties"; TallBear, "Caretaking Relations"; Starblanket and Stark, "Towards a Relational Paradigm."

31 Bruyneel, *Settler Memory*; Gunn Allen, "Who Is Your Mother?"

32 Carlson-Manathara and Rowe, *Living in Indigenous Sovereignty*, 52.

33 Fiola, *Rekindling the Sacred Fire*, 2; Simpson, *Lighting the Eighth Fire.*

34 Estes, *Our History Is the Future*, 1.

35 More-than-human is a term used in Indigenous studies, materialist feminisms, and science studies to stress the importance and agency of the nonhuman life and landforms of the biosphere, and to reverse the implicit cultural hierarchy in western culture of humans above nonhumans.

36 Konishi, "First Nations Scholars," 293; Moreton-Robinson, *The White Possessive*; Mitchell and Chaudhury, "Worlding."

37 TallBear, "Caretaking Relations"; Blomley, "The Ties That Blind."

38 Nichols, *Theft Is Property!*, 31.

39 TallBear, "Caretaking Relations," 32.

40 Blomley, "Property, Pluralism," 191.

41 TallBear, "Caretaking Relations"; Mackey, *Unsettled Expectations*; Willey, *Undoing Monogamy*; Harris, "Whiteness as Property"; Moreton-Robinson, *The White Possessive.*

42 Burns, *Bringing Down the Mountains*; Huseman and Short, "'A Slow Industrial Genocide'"; Zwick, "Comparison."

43 Ladd, *Fractured Communities*; Schneider-Mayerson, *Peak Oil*; Rifkin, *Beyond Settler Time.*

44 TallBear, "Caretaking Relations," 34–35.

45 Nichols, *Theft Is Property!*, 83.

46 Anker, *Ugly Freedoms.*

47 Morrone et al., "A Community Divided."

48 Kennedy, *Environmental Justice.*

49 Jones et al., "Split Estates."

50 Bosworth, "'They're Treating Us like Indians!'"; Nichols, *Theft Is Property!*

51 Moreton-Robinson, *The White Possessive*; Wolfe, *Traces of History*; Williams, *The Alchemy of Race and Rights*; Gordon, *Ghostly Matters*; Archibald, *Indigenous Storywork*; Sandoval, *Methodology*; Stewart, *Ordinary Affects.*

52 "Our home on native land," Native Land Digital, accessed June 7, 2019, https://native-land.ca/.

53 Now I live in Missouri on unceded land inhabited, hunted, and travelled by the Peouaroua (Peoria), Ni-u-koʼn-ska (Osage), and other Očeti Šakówiŋ peoples (Native Land Digital). https://native-land.ca/.

54 Borchard, "From Apalache to Apalachee."

55 Stoll, *Ramp Hollow*.

56 S Pearson, "'The Last Bastion of Colonialism.'"

57 "James Burnes (Burns)—Facts," Ancestry.com, accessed February 20, 2020, www.ancestry.com; Renick, "Attack on Fort Donnally."

58 Hass, *History of the Early Settlement*; Halsey, "Part 3. Land Titles and Pioneers."

59 Hass, *History of the Early Settlement*.

60 Simpson, *As We Have Always Done*.

61 Starblanket and Stark, "Towards a Relational Paradigm"; Starblanket, "Numbered Treaties"; O'Brien, *Firsting and Lasting*.

62 Stark, "Criminal Empire."

63 Rifkin, *Beyond Settler Time*.

64 Gunn Allen, "Who Is Your Mother."

65 Whyte, "Our Ancestors' Dystopia Now," 3.

66 See for example Thoenen, *History of the Oil and Gas Industry*.

67 TallBear, "Making Love."

68 The term "stakeholder," while often used in community empowerment projects, conveys colonizing implications because of its use to refer to those settlers granted land by the settler state (i.e., by staking a claim). Ministry of Citizens' Services, "Terminology in Indigenous Content."

69 Bhandar, *Colonial Lives of Property*; Mishkin, "The Appalachian Storage Hub."

70 Mackey, *Unsettled Expectations*; Tuck and Yang, "Decolonization Is Not a Metaphor."

71 McClean, *Saudi America*.

72 Harris, "Whiteness as Property," 1993, 1721; Daggett, *The Birth of Energy*; Goldstein, "Terra Economica."

73 Polanyi, *The Great Transformation*; O'Connor, "The Second Contradiction of Capitalism"; Tully, "Reconciliation Here on Earth"; Malin, "There's No Real Choice but to Sign."

74 Mitchell, *Carbon Democracy*.

75 Rifkin, *Beyond Settler Time*.

76 Mackey, *Unsettled Expectations*; Rifkin, *Beyond Settler Time*, 169.

77 Daggett, *The Birth of Energy*; Dalley, "The Deaths of Settler Colonialism."

78 Kuletz, *The Tainted Desert*.

79 Taylor, *Toxic Communities*.

80 Giroux, *Stormy Weather*.

81 Rifkin, *Beyond Settler Time*, 169; Mbembe, "Necropolitics"; Bhandar, *Colonial Lives of Property*.

82 Rifkin, *Beyond Settler Time*, 170.

83 Pasternak, *Grounded Authority*, 6; Kimmerer, "The Rights of the Land"; Shorter, "Spirituality"; Starblanket and Stark, "Towards a Relational Paradigm"; Simpson, *Lighting the Eighth Fire*.

84 Rifkin, *Beyond Settler Time*, 170; Freeman cited in Rifkin, *Beyond Settler Time*, 27.

85 Whyte, "Our Ancestors' Dystopia Now"; Estes, *Our History Is the Future*.

86 Denzin, *Interpretive Autoethnography*.

87 Stewart, *Ordinary Affects*, 1.

88 Simpson, *Lighting the Eighth Fire*, 201.

89 Finney, *Black Faces, White Spaces*; Moskowitz, *Standard of Living*.

90 Goldstein, "Terra Economica."

91 Blomley, "The Ties That Blind," 170.

92 Famously at issue in Jane Austen's *Pride and Prejudice*, entailment refers to property that cannot be freely sold or inherited outside of a designated line of male descent.

93 Blomley, "The Ties That Blind."

94 Harris, *Little White Houses*.

95 Jacobs, "Whose Citizenship?"

96 Marx, "The German Ideology: Part 1," 150.

97 LaDuke, *Recovering the Sacred*; Mackey, *Unsettled Expectations*, 153.

98 Estes, *Our History Is the Future*.

99 Bhandar, *Colonial Lives of Property*.

100 Szasz, *Ecopopulism*.

101 Taylor, *Toxic Communities*.

102 McIntyre and Nast, "Bio(Necro)Polis."

103 Parry et al., "Polybrominated Diphenyl Ethers (PBDEs) ."

104 Steinberg, *Slide Mountain*.

105 Blomley, "The Ties That Blind."

106 Burnett, "The Accommodation Doctrine."

107 Yagelski, "Federal or FERC Pipeline Condemnation."

108 Natural gas fracking is not limited to the territory currently known as the United States. However, the causes and consequences of mineral extraction in other parts of the world are beyond the scope of this book. I am focusing closely on a structure of feeling that I personally know well, and for which I feel a relationship of responsibility. It is undoubtedly ironic that in so doing I recenter the United States as an area of study.

109 "Storage Hub?" Appalachian Storage Hub Conference IV, November 5, 2020, www.appastorage.com.

110 Singer, "Down Cancer Alley"; Taylor, *Toxic Communities*.

111 "Can the Marcellus/Utica Build Too Many Cracker Plants?"

112 Gould et al., "Interrogating the Treadmill of Production"; Cunningham, "Bloodbath."

113 Daggett, *The Birth of Energy*, 111.

114 Ward, "China Gas Deal"; Schneider, "Virginia Regulators ."

115 Penn, "Atlantic Coast Pipeline"; Daly, "Unexpected Deal"; Solum, "2022.".

116 Vaidyanathan, "How Bad of a Greenhouse Gas Is Methane?"

117 Monroe, "Natural Methane 'Time Bomb.'"

118 "Making the Plastics Found Everywhere."

119 Clean Energy Fuels, "Clean Energy Natural Gas."

120 "Ethane Cracker Plants: What Are They?" *Climate Reality*, October 23, 2018, www.climaterealityproject.org/blog/ethane-cracker-plants-what-are-they.

121 Scott, *Removing Mountains*; Burns, *Bringing Down the Mountains*; McNeil, *Combating Mountaintop Removal*; Barry, *Standing Our Ground*.

122 CNN Newsource, "Coal Mines Closing."

123 Ward, "WV's Largest Coal Operator."

124 *Gasland*, directed by Josh Fox (International WOW Company, 2010).

125 Khan, "Porter Ranch Leak."

126 Hamilton, "Coping"; Scott, "The Sociology of Coal Hollow."

127 Kolbert, *The Sixth Extinction*; Carrington, "Earth's Sixth Mass Extinction Event."

128 Ortiz, "'Trouble in Paradise'"; IPCC, "Global Warming of 1.5 °C—," October 2018, www.ipcc.ch/sr15/; Gorman, "U.S. Lists a Bumble Bee Species"; Masson-Delmotte et al., *Climate Change 2021*.

129 Mitchell and Chaudhury, "Worlding," 315; Tsing, *The Mushroom at the End of the World*, 19; Mitman, "Donna Haraway."

130 Mitchell and Chaudhury, "Worlding," 319.

131 Gibson-Graham, *The End of Capitalism*, 114.

132 Mitchell and Chaudhury, "Worlding," 321.

133 Brown, *Emergent Strategy*.

134 Mitchell and Chaudhury, "Worlding"; Brown, *Emergent Strategy*.

135 Justice, *Why Indigenous Literatures Matter*, 31.

136 Cutts, "*MAN*."

137 Ahmed, *The Cultural Politics of Emotion*.

138 Tuck and Yang, "Decolonization Is Not a Metaphor."

139 Kite, "'What's on the Earth Is in the Stars,'" 139.

140 Blomley, "The Ties That Blind."

141 Perry, *Vexy Thing*, 28; MacPherson, *Political Theory*.

142 Locke, *Second Treatise of Government*, 20.

143 "Coverture Law," *Britannica*, accessed July 28, 2022, www.britannica.com.

144 See Pachirat, *Every Twelve Seconds*; Perry, *Vexy Thing*.

145 Maynard et al., *Rehearsals*, 18.

146 Mitchell and Chaudhury, "Worlding."

147 Estes, *Our History Is the Future*; Moreton-Robinson, *The White Possessive*; Federici, *Caliban and the Witch*; Haraway, *Staying with the Trouble*.

148 *Béatriz at Dinner*, directed by Miguel Arteta (Bron Studios, Killer Films, 2017).

149 Million, "Felt Theory."

150 Plumwood, *Feminism*.

151 Goldberg, *The Racial State*; Harris, "Whiteness as Property"; Perry, *Vexy Thing*.

152 Million, "Felt Theory."

153 Gaard, "Toward a Queer Ecofeminism"; Federici, *Caliban and the Witch*.

154 Goldstein, "Terra Economica."

155 Mackey, *Unsettled Expectations*, 176; Byrd, *The Transit of Empire*, 54.

156 Byrd, *The Transit of Empire*.

157 Plumwood, *Feminism*, 71; Million, "Felt Theory," 64.

158 Deloria , *Spirit and Reason*, 330; LaDuke, *Recovering the Sacred*, 13.

159 Deloria, *Custer Died for Your Sins*.

160 Shorter, "Spirituality," 442.

161 TallBear, "Caretaking Relations," 38.

162 Steinberg, *Slide Mountain*.

163 Marx, *Capital*.

164 Shorter, "Spirituality."

165 Harris, *Little White Houses*.

166 Willey, *Undoing Monogamy*; TallBear, "Making Love."

167 Huber, *Lifeblood*.

168 Parsons, "The Kinship System"; Rostow, "The Stages of Economic Growth."

169 Huber, *Lifeblood*; Mitchell, *Carbon Democracy*.

170 Mackey, *Unsettled Expectations*.

171 Latour and Porter, *We Have Never Been Modern*.

172 Latour, "Love Your Monsters."

173 Latour and Porter, *We Have Never Been Modern*.

174 Mackey, *Unsettled Expectations*.

175 Tsing, *The Mushroom at the End of the World*, 20.

176 Merchant, *The Death of Nature*.

177 LaDuke, *All Our Relations*.

178 TallBear, "Caretaking Relations"; Tsing, *The Mushroom at the End of the World*.

179 TallBear, "Beyond the Life/Not Life Binary"; Kimmerer, *Braiding Sweetgrass*; Fiola, *Rekindling the Sacred Fire*.

180 Altamirano-Jiménez and Kermoal, "Introduction," 7.

181 TallBear, "Caretaking Relations"; Starblanket and Stark, "Towards a Relational Paradigm."

182 Sullivan quoted in Mackey, *Unsettled Expectations*, 183.

183 Shorter, "Spirituality."

184 Mitchell and Chaudhury, "Worlding."

185 Haraway, *When Species Meet*; Barad, "Posthumanist Performativity."

186 Norgaard, *Salmon and Acorns Feed Our People*, 224.

187 Johansen, *Forgotten Founders*; Ibrahim, "'We Know How to Keep the Balance of Nature.'"

188 Coulthard, *Red Skin, White Masks*, 156; Starblanket and Stark, "Towards a Relational Paradigm."

189 Coulthard, *Red Skin, White Masks*, 13.

190 Rainforth, "How Aborigines Invented the Idea"; Todd, "An Indigenous Feminist's Take."

191 Coulthard, *Red Skin, White Masks*, 157.
192 Adichie, "The Danger of a Single Story."
193 Justice, *Why Indigenous Literatures Matter*, 34.
194 Morton, *Hyperobjects*.
195 Million, "Felt Theory"; Gordon, *Ghostly Matters*.
196 Larsen and Johnson, "The Agency of Place."
197 Daggett, *The Birth of Energy*, 120.
198 Moreton-Robinson, *The White Possessive*; Bhandar, *Colonial Lives of Property*; Mackey, *Unsettled Expectations*.
199 LaDuke, *Recovering the Sacred*, 170–71; Gaard, "Toward a Queer Ecofeminism."
200 Million, "Felt Theory"; Gordon, *Ghostly Matters*.
201 For more information about methodology, please see the methodological appendix.
202 Temin, "Remapping the World"; Rifkin, *Beyond Settler Time*.
203 Rifkin, *Settler Common Sense*; Johnson, "From the Tomahawk Chop to the Road Block."
204 Brown, "Continental Land Back"; Pieratos et al., "Land Back."
205 Tuck and Yang, "Decolonization Is Not a Metaphor."
206 Deloria Jr., *Custer Died for Your Sins*, 180.
207 Walters et al., "Growing from Our Roots."
208 Daggett, *The Birth of Energy*, 202.
209 Perry, *Vexy Thing*; Mbembe, "Necropolitics."
210 Omi and Winant, *Racial Formation*.
211 Not In My Back Yard, discussed further in chapter 1.
212 "Appalachian Storage Hub/Petrochemical Complex."
213 Rice, *Moon of the Crusted Snow*.
214 Kimmerer, *Braiding Sweetgrass*; Walters et al., "Growing from Our Roots."

CHAPTER 1. KEYSTONE, FLINT, AND PORTER RANCH

Epigraph: Radin, "Property and Personhood," 968.
1 This chapter has been adapted from Scott, "Structures of Environmental Inequality." Coulthard, *Red Skin, White Masks*, 65.
2 Reid and Taylor, *Recovering the Commons*, 30–31. Note that the "small r" republicanism Reid and Taylor discuss refers to the "res publica" or public thing, that represents the common good of a political body. Here, liberalism refers to classical liberal economics, or free-market ideology.
3 Mink, "The Lady and the Tramp"; Reid and Taylor, *Recovering the Commons*, 32; Williams, *The Alchemy of Race and Rights*.
4 Kazanjian, *The Colonizing Trick*.
5 Harris, *Little White Houses*.
6 Harvey, *A Brief History of Neoliberalism*.
7 Goldberg, *The Racial State*.
8 Harris, "Whiteness as Property"; Perry, *Vexy Thing*.

9 Crenshaw, *On Intersectionality*; Hill Collins, *Black Feminist Thought*; Stein, *New Perspectives*.
10 Seawright, "Settler Traditions."
11 Crenshaw, *On Intersectionality*; Perry, *Vexy Thing*.
12 Williams, *The Alchemy of Race and Rights*; Gordon, *Ghostly Matters*.
13 Hill Collins, *Black Feminist Thought*; Crenshaw, *On Intersectionality*.
14 United Church of Christ, "Toxic Wastes and Race and Toxic Wastes and Race at Twenty."
15 Been, "Locally Undesirable Land Uses."
16 Pulido, "Rethinking Environmental Racism"; Pulido, "Geographies of Race and Ethnicity I"; Taylor, *Toxic Communities*.
17 Zimring, *Clean and White*; Sze, *Noxious New York*.
18 Nardella, "Identity Politics and Resistance."
19 Senier et al., "The Socio-Exposome."
20 Hill Collins, *Black Feminist Thought*, 84.
21 Williams, *The Alchemy of Race and Rights*.
22 Dian Million, "Felt Theory."
23 Vimalassery et al., "On Colonial Unknowing."
24 Scott, *Seeing Like a State*; Nichols, *Theft Is Property!*; Moreton-Robinson, *The White Possessive*.
25 Harris, "Whiteness as Property"; Meinzen-Dick and Prahdan, "Legal Pluralism"; CAPRi, "Resources, Rights and Cooperation."
26 Mackey, *Unsettled Expectations*, 76–77.
27 Gilbert et al., "Who Owns the Land?"; Food and Agriculture Database of the United Nations, "Gender and Land Rights Database."
28 Stroud, "Good Guys With Guns."
29 Bruyneel, *Settler Memory*, 41.
30 Benz, "Black Femininity"; Lopez, "The Minnesota Police Officer."
31 Garlick, *The Nature of Masculinity*, 6.
32 Cronon, "The Trouble with Wilderness"; Taylor, *The Rise of the American Conservation Movement*.
33 Taylor, *The Rise of the American Conservation Movement*; Finney, *Black Faces, White Spaces*.
34 Cronon, "The Trouble with Wilderness" Hamilton, "Coping"; Taylor, *The Rise of the American Conservation Movement*.
35 Thoenen, *History of the Oil and Gas Industry*; Cronon, *Nature's Metropolis*; Carmody, "How the Flint River Got So Toxic"; O'Neil, "In 1800s, De Celis Owned Most of the Valley."
36 Carson, *Silent Spring*.
37 McIntyre and Nast, "Bio(Necro)Polis"; Mbembe, "Necropolitics."
38 Baptist, *The Half Has Never Been Told*; Wolfe, *Traces of History*.
39 McIntyre and Nast, "Bio(Necro)Polis," 1467.

40 Harvey, *A Brief History of Neoliberalism*; Guthman, *Weighing In*; Omi and Winant, *Racial Formation*.

41 Gilmore, *Golden Gulag*; McIntyre and Nast, "Bio(Necro)Polis," 1472.

42 Taylor, *Toxic Communities*.

43 Szasz, *Shopping Our Way to Safety*.

44 Zimring, *Clean and White*.

45 Gilio-Whitaker, *As Long as Grass Grows*.

46 Bullard, *Confronting Environmental Racism*.

47 Taylor, *Toxic Communities*; Gilio-Whitaker, *As Long as Grass Grows*.

48 Kuletz, *The Tainted Desert*.

49 Kuletz, "Invisible Spaces, Violent Places," 237.

50 Bruyneel, "Race, Colonialism."

51 Sandoval, *Methodology*.

52 Million, "Felt Theory"; Gibson-Graham, *The End of Capitalism*; Hill Collins, *Black Feminist Thought*.

53 Gibson-Graham, *The End of Capitalism*.

54 TallBear, "Feminist, Queer, and Indigenous Thinking"; Morgensen, *Spaces between Us*; Mortimer-Sandilands and Erickson, *Queer Ecologies*; Bennett, *Vibrant Matter*; Stein, *New Perspectives*.

55 Gibson-Graham, *The End of Capitalism*.

56 Buford, "'Rare Discrimination Finding."

57 NIMBY, or Not in My Backyard, refers to an individualistic approach to avoiding environmental hazards.

58 Szasz, *Ecopopulism*.

59 Williams, *The Alchemy of Race and Rights*.

60 Beck, *Risk Society*.

61 Stein, *New Perspectives*, 1.

62 Pearson, "'The Last Bastion of Colonialism'"; Tuck and Yang, "Decolonization Is Not a Metaphor."

63 Weise, *Grasping at Independence*.

64 Lewis, *Transforming the Appalachian Countryside*; Trotter, *Coal, Class, and Color*; Trotter, *African American Workers*.

65 "U.S. Census Bureau QuickFacts: West Virginia."

66 Caudill, *Night Comes to the Cumberlands*, 263.

67 Scott, *Removing Mountains*, 175.

68 Scott, *Removing Mountains*, 175.

69 Coyne, "'That's Just How Things Go in Keystone'"; Lilly, "Trauma in Coal Town."

70 "U.S. Census Bureau QuickFacts: West Virginia."

71 "U.S. Census Bureau QuickFacts: United States."

72 Economic Development Greater East (EDGE), "Mountain Farm Community Grocery."

73 "U.S. Census Bureau QuickFacts: United States."

74 Taylor, *Toxic Communities*; Schwartzman, "Anti-Blackness."

75 Trip, "50 Years into the War on Poverty."

76 Scott, "The Sociology of Coal Hollow."

77 See Vance, *Hillbilly Elegy.*

78 Coyne, "'That's Just How Things Go in Keystone.'"

79 Hendryx and Ahem, "Relations."

80 Sherman, *Those Who Work.*

81 Burns, *Bringing Down the Mountains*; Scott, *Removing Mountains*; McNeil, *Combating Mountaintop Removal.*

82 Scott, "Dependent Masculinity."

83 Bruyneel, "Race, Colonialism," 16.

84 Miner, "Tikibiing Booskikamigaag"; Michigan Family History, "THE TREATY OF SAGINAW, 1819."

85 Taylor, *The Rise of the American Conservation Movement*; Miner, "Tikibiing Booskikamigaag."

86 Miner, "Tikibiing Booskikamigaag," 10.

87 Stockton House Museum, "Stockton House Museum."

88 Carmody, "How the Flint River Got So Toxic."

89 Sadler and Highsmith, "Rethinking Tiebout."

90 Sadler and Highsmith, "Rethinking Tiebout," 146.

91 Sadler and Highsmith, "Rethinking Tiebout," 148–49.

92 Smith, "Flint Water Crisis"; Bellware and Dennis, "Flint Water Crisis"; White, "Court Hears Challenge"; Chariton and LeDuff, "Revealed."

93 Hanna-Attisha et al., "Elevated Blood Lead Levels"; Edwards and Roy, "Flint Water Study Updates."

94 Merrit Kennedy, "Flint Activist Wins Major Environmental Prize," *NPR*, April 23, 2018, www.npr.org; Suggs, "Mari Copeny."

95 Laitner and Zaniewski, "Michigan Ending Discounts."

96 Bosman, "Many Flint Residents Are Desperate to Leave."

97 Melissa Mays quoted in Guarino, "New Crisis for Flint Residents."

98 Joyce Cruz quoted in Bosman, "Many Flint Residents Are Desperate to Leave."

99 Vasel, "You Can Buy a House in Flint for $14,000."

100 Native Land Digital, "Our Home on Native Land"; O'Neil, "In 1800s, De Celis Owned Most of the Valley."

101 O'Neil, "In 1800s, De Celis Owned Most of the Valley."

102 Chatsworth Porter Ranch Chamber of Commerce, "Porter Ranch Then and Now."

103 SoCalGas, "Aliso Canyon Natural Gas Storage Facility."

104 Parvani and Barboza, "SoCal Gas."

105 Yee et al., "SoCalGas."

106 St. John, "Regulators"; SoCalGas, "Aliso Canyon Natural Gas Storage Facility."

107 Chappell, "After Nearly 4 Months"; McNary, "After Aliso."

108 "U.S. Census Bureau QuickFacts: United States"; Energy Justice, "Justice Map."

109 Stevens, "After Prodding from City."

110 Stevens, "After Prodding from City."
111 Ellen Oppenberg quoted in Maddaus, "What Went Wrong at Porter Ranch?"
112 Brandon Ly quoted in Maddaus, "What Went Wrong at Porter Ranch?"
113 SoCalGas, "Return Home Information."
114 Yee et al., "SoCalGas."
115 "Save Porter Ranch."
116 David Balen quoted in Kourhi, "Gas Leak."
117 US Census Bureau, "Table B25077."
118 Kourhi, "Gas Leak."
119 Nazaryan, "Methane Gas Crisis."
120 Bullard, *Confronting Environmental Racism*; Taylor, *Toxic Communities*.
121 Yee et al., "SoCalGas."
122 Egan, "Amid Denials."
123 Oostling, "Study."
124 Stelloh, "Judge Approves $626 Million Settlement."
125 Black in Appalachia, "The Podcast."
126 Lilly, "Trauma in Coal Town."
127 Coontz, *The Way We Never Were*; Scott, *Removing Mountains*, 100–101.
128 Omi and Winant, *Racial Formation*; Guthman, *Weighing In*.
129 In Maddaus, "What Went Wrong at Porter Ranch?"
130 Hardin, "The Tragedy of the Commons."
131 Byrd, *The Transit of Empire*, 54.

CHAPTER 2. THE CONTRADICTIONS OF "WHITE" PROTEST
Epigraph: Allard, "Why Do We Punish Dakota Pipeline Protesters?"
1 This chapter has been adapted from "Settler Culture, Property, and the Contradictions of White Protest," in *Protecting Whiteness: Whitelash and the Rejection of Racial Equality*, Cameron D. Lippard, J. Scott Carter, and David G. Embrick, eds. University of Washington Press, 2020. Republished by permission of the copyright holder, the University of Washington Press. Cronon, "The Trouble with Wilderness."
2 Edwards, "Alexandria Ocasio-Cortez's Tweet."
3 Bettie, *Women without Class*.
4 Wray, *Not Quite White*.
5 Omi and Winant, *Racial Formation*; DuBois, *Black Reconstruction*.
6 Branigin, "Why Some Black and Brown People Can't Trust Bernie Sanders."
7 Omi and Winant, *Racial Formation*; Takei, "How Police Can Stop Being Weaponized."
8 Diamond, "Trump"; McKay et al., "Theorizing Race."
9 Bruyneel, "The American Liberal Colonial Tradition."
10 Dyer, *White*.
11 Sturm, *Becoming Indian*; TallBear, *Native American DNA*.
12 Cole, "The White-Savior Industrial Complex"; Wolfe, "The Settler Complex"; Mackey, *Unsettled Expectations*.

13 Here, I put white in quotation marks to emphasize that the whiteness of these groups is not necessarily based on their membership all belonging to the white racial category. Rather, it represents the fact that these groups' issues are not racially marked in themselves, and in general, are promoted by people in the "white" position in society.

14 Lipsitz, *The Possessive Investment in Whiteness*.

15 Nichols, *Theft Is Property!*, 41.

16 Hardin, "The Tragedy of the Commons"; Harris, "Whiteness as Property."

17 Kazanjian, *The Colonizing Trick*; Shiva, *Earth Democracy*.

18 Moreton-Robinson, *The White Possessive*.

19 Miner, "Tikibiing Booskikamigaag"; Taylor, *The Rise of the American Conservation Movement*; Roberts, "Who Belongs in Indian Territory?"

20 LaDuke, *All Our Relations*; Fry, "Fracking and Environmental (In)Justice"; Radin, "Property and Personhood."

21 Kauanui, "'A Structure'"; Wolfe, *Traces of History*; King, *The Black Shoals*.

22 Goldberg, *The Racial State*.

23 Wolfe, "The Settler Complex."

24 Finney, *Black Faces, White Spaces*; *Far and Away*, directed by Ron Howard (Imagine Entertainment, 1992).

25 Schneider, "'There's Something in the Water'"; Scott, *Seeing Like a State*.

26 Carswell, "Trump's Wall."

27 Náñez, "A Border Tribe." .

28 LaDuke, *All Our Relations*; Schneider, "There's Something in the Water"; Norgaard, *Salmon and Acorns*.

29 Plumwood, *Feminism*.

30 LaDuke, *Recovering the Sacred*; Lucas, "No Remedy for the Inuit."

31 Latour, "Love Your Monsters."

32 Alaimo, *Exposed*; Schneider, "There's Something in the Water"; Lucas, "No Remedy for the Inuit."

33 Cuomo, "Climate Change."

34 Barder, "American Hegemony Comes Home."

35 Omi and Winant, *Racial Formation*.

36 Harvey, *A Brief History of Neoliberalism*.

37 Omi and Winant, *Racial Formation*; Edsall and Edsall, *Chain Reaction*.

38 Bennett, "Republican Senator"; Merica, "Trump."

39 Guthman, *Weighing In*; Huber, *Lifeblood*.

40 Ahmed, *The Cultural Politics of Emotion*.

41 TallBear, "Caretaking Relations."

42 Levin, "Stunning Victory."

43 Deleuze and Guattari, *Anti-Oedipus*.

44 Varinsky, "Here's Every Piece of Land."

45 Reeve, "Just How Racist Is the 'Obama Phone' Video?"

46 Klein, "Romney's Theory."

47 Redoubt News, "Video: Cliven Bundy."

48 Redoubt News, "Video: Cliven Bundy."

49 Redoubt News, "Video: Cliven Bundy."

50 Swaine and Holpuch, "Ferguson Police."

51 Mencimer, "Cliven Bundy's Lawyer."

52 Inwood and Bonds, "Property and Whiteness."

53 Keeler, "'It's So Disgusting.'"

54 Keeler, "'It's So Disgusting'"; Killgrove, "Bundy Militia."

55 Allard, "Why Do We Punish Dakota Pipeline Protesters?"

56 Allard, "Why Do We Punish Dakota Pipeline Protesters?"

57 Wolfe, "The Settler Complex."

58 Cronon, "The Trouble with Wilderness."

59 Schneider, "There's Something in the Water."

60 Merchant, "Shades of Darkness."

61 Sierra Club, "Sierra Club Home Page."

62 Cone, "Sierra Club to Remain Neutral."

63 Rutherford, *Governing the Wild*; Guha, "Radical American Environmentalism."

64 Nilles and Hitt, "From the Senate to the WV Coalfields."

65 Quoted in Biggers, "Mountaintop Removal Never Ended."

66 Sierra Club, "Beyond Coal."

67 Quoted in Biggers, "Mountaintop Removal Never Ended."

68 Bell, *Fighting King Coal.*

69 Wolfe, "The Settler Complex."

70 Taylor, *The Rise of the American Conservation Movement.*

71 Frost, "Our Contemporary Ancestors"; Semple, "The Ango-Saxons of the Kentucky Mountains"; MacFarquhar, "In the Heart of Trump Country."

72 Wolfe, "The Settler Complex," 8.

73 Scott, *Removing Mountains.*

74 Pearson, "'The Last Bastion of Colonialism.'"

75 Wolfe, "The Settler Complex," 12.

76 Bruyneel, "Codename Geronimo."

77 Wolfe, "The Settler Complex," 12; Deloria, *Custer Died for Your Sins.*

78 Mitchell and Chaudhury, "Worlding"; Gibson-Graham, *The End of Capitalism.*

79 These events will be discussed in more detail in chapters 4 and 5.

80 Bosworth, "'They're Treating Us like Indians!'"

81 Appalachians Against Pipelines, "Work Site Disruption"; Lopez, "MVP Tree-Sitters."

82 Le Miere, "Donald Trump."

83 Merica, "Trump"; Gessen, "Elizabeth Warren."

84 Kohl et al., "From 'Marginal to Marginal."

CHAPTER 3. THE END OF (SETTLER) TIME

Epigraph: Expository voice-over, first half season of *Revolution* (NBC 2012–2014).

1 Morton, *Hyperobjects.*

2 Archibald, *Indigenous Storywork.*

3 Williams, *Combined and Uneven Apocalypse*; Kite, "'What's on the Earth Is in the Stars.'"

4 Rifkin, *Beyond Settler Time*, 37; Zylinska, *The End of Man*.

5 Mitchell and Chaudhury, "Worlding"; Dalley, "The Deaths of Settler Colonialism."

6 Rifkin, *Beyond Settler Time*, 39.

7 Justice, *Why Indigenous Literatures Matter*, 168; Estes, *Our History Is the Future*.

8 Awasis, "'Anishinaabe Time.'"

9 Rifkin, *Beyond Settler Time*, 39.

10 Rifkin, *Beyond Settler Time*, 39.

11 Giroux, *Stormy Weather*.

12 Go, *Postcolonial Thought*.

13 Fukuyama, *The End of History*; Rostow, "The Stages of Economic Growth"; Asafu-Asjaye et al., "An Ecomodernist Manifesto."

14 Dalley, "The Deaths of Settler Colonialism"; Kite, "'What's on the Earth Is in the Stars'"; Tuck and Yang, "Decolonization Is Not a Metaphor."

15 Million, "Felt Theory"; Gordon, *Ghostly Matters*.

16 Brown, *Emergent Strategy*; Mitchell and Chaudhury, "Worlding."

17 The "we" in this quote appears to refer to "modern humans" in its original context. The universality of this "we" will be explored in the book's conclusion.

18 Martens, "Petromelancholia," 195, my emphasis.

19 Noak, "Why Australia's Prime Minister Just Defended Coal"; McCleery, "Bushfire Smoke."

20 Aleem, "From Coast to Coast"; Farr, "The Pandemic."

21 Washington Post Staff, "Woman Dies."

22 Moreton-Robinson, *The White Possessive*; Wolfe, "The Settler Complex"; Bhandar, *Colonial Lives of Property*.

23 Bacigalupi, "People of Sand and Slag."

24 Palmer, *In the Aura of a Hole*.

25 *Cargo*, directed by Ben Howling and Yolanda Ramke (Netflix, 2017).

26 Tidwell, "The Problem of Materiality"; Wolfe, *What Is Posthumanism?*

27 Crist, "The Reaches of Freedom."

28 Crist, "The Reaches of Freedom"; Asafu-Asjaye et al., "An Ecomodernist Manifesto."

29 Tidwell, "The Problem of Materiality."

30 Bacigalupi, "People of Sand and Slag," 54.

31 Bales, *Blood and Earth*.

32 MacPherson, *Political Theory*.

33 Cutts, "*MAN*."

34 Kite, "'What's on the Earth Is in the Stars,'" 143.

35 Frankel, "The Traumatic Basis."

36 Greenberg et al., *Inside the GOP*.

37 Keeler, "A Postapocalyptic Return"; Barad, "Posthumanist Performativity."

38 Klein, *This Changes Everything*.

39 Deloria, *Spirit and Reason*.

40 Wolfe, "The Settler Complex."
41 Schneider-Mayerson, *Peak Oil*; Formisano, *The Tea Party*.
42 Broder, "Climate Change Doubt."
43 Morton, *Hyperobjects*.
44 Braun, "'On the Raggedy Edge of Risk.'"
45 Bruyneel, "Race, Colonialism."
46 Keeler, "A Postapocalyptic Return."
47 "Revolution."
48 Kite, "'What's on the Earth Is in the Stars,'" 143.
49 Moore, "Can Red State and Blue State America Coexist?"
50 Redoubt News, "Video: Cliven Bundy."
51 Kharkhordin, "Things as Res Publicae."
52 Perry, *Vexy Thing*.
53 Haraway, *Staying with the Trouble*.
54 Huber, *Lifeblood*.
55 Dalley, "The Deaths of Settler Colonialism"; Mitchell and Chaudhury, "Worlding."
56 IMDb, "Cargo (2017) Trivia."
57 IMDb, "Cargo (2017) Trivia."
58 Waterfield, "Out of Control Australian Wildfires."
59 IMDb, "Cargo (2017) Trivia."
60 Kohn, *How Forests Think*.
61 Rifkin, *Beyond Settler Time*, 80.
62 Cargo is largely a story about saving a white baby; the white baby is joyfully welcomed by the Indigenous community at the end of the story. This narrative reverses the intent of the policy of the Australian government that for decades forced Aboriginal children into white families, schools, and domestic servitude; a practice that falls under the United Nations' definition of genocide. The escape of three girls from such a training program for domestic servants inspired the movie *Rabbit-Proof Fence* (directed by P. Noyce, Rumbarala Films, 2002). It is unclear whether this reversal was intentional on the part of the filmmakers, but it may have been noticed by actor Natasha Wanganeen, who acted in both films.
63 McCleery, "Bushfire Smoke"; Tuck and Yang, "Decolonization Is Not a Metaphor."
64 Rifkin, *Beyond Settler Time*, 169.
65 Martens, "Petromelancholia."
66 Zylinska, *The End of Man*, 4.
67 Sandoval, *Methodology*; Smith, *Decolonizing Methodologies*; Estes, *Our History Is the Future*.
68 Mackey, *Unsettled Expectations*, 29.
69 Mackey, *Unsettled Expectations*, 29.
70 Mackey, *Unsettled Expectations*, 30.
71 Mackey, *Unsettled Expectations*, 53–54.
72 Mackey, *Unsettled Expectations*, 57.
73 Rifkin, *Beyond Settler Time*, 191.

74 Mackey, *Unsettled Expectations*, 33.
75 Tsing, *The Mushroom at the End of the World*.
76 Mackey, *Unsettled Expectations*, 130–40.
77 Erdrich, *Future Home of the Living God*.
78 Walters et al., "Growing from Our Roots."
79 Mackey, *Unsettled Expectations*, 176.
80 LaDuke, *All Our Relations*; TallBear, "Caretaking Relations"; Mackey, *Unsettled Expectations: Uncertainty, Land and Settler Decolonization*, 175.
81 Dimaline, *The Marrow Thieves* (Toronto, Canada: DCB, 2017); Horner et al., "Ni Keehtwawmi Mooshahkinitounawn."
82 IMDb, "Cargo (2017) Trivia."
83 Dalley, "The Deaths of Settler Colonialism"; Byrd, *The Transit of Empire*, 54.

CHAPTER 4. LESSONS FROM THE "HELLMOUTH"

 1 Tsing, *Friction*.
 2 Thoenen, *History of the Oil and Gas Industry*; Ohio Valley Environmental Coalition, "Deep Shale Oil & Gas."
 3 "Marcellus Shale Fact Sheet."
 4 O'Leary, "A Win-Win Marcellus Shale Tax Incentive"; O'Leary, "Impacts of Gas Drilling in Wetzel County"; Ohio Valley Environmental Coalition, "Deep Shale Oil & Gas."
 5 Corkery, "A Giant Factory Rises"; Mishkin, "The Appalachian Storage Hub."
 6 Penn, "Atlantic Coast Pipeline"; Atlantic Coast Pipeline, "Home."
 7 Limpert, "Investors Are Reevaluating."
 8 For additional information about methodology, see the methodological appendix.
 9 Zwick, "Comparison"; Ladd, *Fractured Communities*.
10 MacPherson, *Political Theory*.
11 Kuletz, *The Tainted Desert*; Fox, "Mountaintop Removal in West Virginia."
12 McNeil, *Combating Mountaintop Removal*; Morrone et al., *Mountains of Injustice*; Bell, *Fighting King Coal*.
13 Blodgett, "An Analysis."
14 Fry, "Fracking and Environmental (In)Justice"; Malewitz, "Abbott Signs 'Denton Fracking Bill.'"
15 Ward, "West Virginia Is Grappling."
16 Hamilton, "Coping with Industrial Exploitation."
17 Rifkin, *Beyond Settler Time*, 169.
18 Sullivan, *Manufactured Insecurity*.
19 NBC News and Greta Thunberg, "Read Greta Thunberg's Full Speech."
20 Harris, "Whiteness as Property," 1993.
21 Bureau of Land Management, "Programs."
22 Paterson, "Could Drilling Rigs Pop Up?"
23 Ballotpedia, "Federal Land Ownership by State."
24 Weise, *Grasping at Independence*; Conlin and Grow, "Special Report."

25 Ballesteros, "West Virginia Woman Dragged Out of Capitol."

26 Guillon, *Fracking the Neighborhood*.

27 Andrews, "How Would You Improve the Natural Gas Pipeline Process?"

28 U.S. Geological Survey, "USGS Estimates 214 Trillion Cubic Feet."

29 Grattan, "Natural Gas Production."

30 McClean, *Saudi America*.

31 See Scott, "Dependent Masculinity."

32 Zwick, "Comparison."

33 LaDuke, *Recovering the Sacred*, 35.

34 Scott, *Removing Mountains*; Burns, *Bringing down the Mountains*.

35 Habeeb, "Coal Keeps the Lights On"; Roberts, "Why Coal Has a Hit on 'America's Got Talent.'"

36 Fox, "Natural Gas Now Beats Coal"; Silverstein, "Bloomberg."

37 Harvey, *The Condition of Postmodernity*.

38 Watts, "Petro-Violence."

39 This is a reference to the television show *Buffy the Vampire Slayer* in which the hero defends humans from demons in Sunnydale, California, the location of the "Hellmouth" (Warner Brothers 1997–2001, UPN 2001–2003).

40 US Geological Survey, "How Much Water?"

41 Quoted in Young, "Antero's Clearwater Facility."

42 Rezal, "The States Where the Most Native Americans Live."

43 US EPA National Center for Environmental Assessment, "Hydraulic Fracturing for Oil and Gas."

44 Mishkin, "4th Circuit"; Mishkin and Ward, "What Happens."

45 West Virginia State Legislature, "WV Code Chapter 22."

46 "Sweet Springs Resort Park."

47 West Virginia Public Service Commission, "Coal Transportation FAQ."

48 Harvey, "Lawman"; Weaver, "Passenger Killed."

49 Tankersley, "Meanwhile in West Virginia."

50 "Skill Shortages Hamper Fracking Operations."

51 Nuzum et al., "Man Camps"; Komarek and Cseh, "Fracking and Public Health."

52 McCullough, "Landowners."

53 DiTirro, "Massive Pipeline Explosion"; Litvak and Kane, "Officials."

54 Grace, resident of a rural county crossed by the pipeline.

55 The notion of "grandpa's land" is discussed further in chapter 5.

56 Ward, "China Gas Deal."

57 Ward, "West Virginia Paid"; Appalachian Storage Hub Conference IV, "Storage Hub?"

58 Ohio Valley Environmental Coalition, "Appalachian Storage Hub/Petrochemical Complex."

59 Hurdle, "With Governor's Signature"; Healy et al., "Embodied Energy Injustices."

60 Galchen, "The Arrival of Man-Made Earthquakes."

61 Khan, "Porter Ranch Leak."

62 Watts, "Petro-Violence," 205.

63 Rifkin, *Beyond Settler Time*; Sullivan, *Manufactured Insecurity*.

CHAPTER 5. FRACKING SETTLER CULTURE

1 Sullivan, *Manufactured Insecurity*; Hardin, "The Tragedy of the Commons."

2 O'Connor, "Capitalism, Nature, Socialism"; O'Connor, "The Second Contradiction of Capitalism."

3 Mackey, *Unsettled Expectations*, 28.

4 Mackey, *Unsettled Expectations*, 115.

5 Alfred, "What Is Radical Imagination?"; Mackey, *Unsettled Expectations*, 15–16.

6 Harris, "Whiteness as Property."

7 Weise, *Grasping at Independence*.

8 Dunbar-Ortiz, *An Indigenous Peoples' History*; Taylor, *Toxic Communities*.

9 The Indigenous people in this mural are depicted with a feathered headdress belonging to nations farther West.

10 Thoenen, *History of the Oil and Gas Industry*, 3.

11 Thoenen, *History of the Oil and Gas Industry*.

12 Bruyneel, "Codename Geronimo."

13 Smith et al., "Appalachian Identity."

14 Pearson, "'The Last Bastion of Colonialism'"; Leroux, *Distorted Descent*.

15 William Goodell Frost, "Our Contemporary Ancestors," 105.

16 Caudill, *Night Comes to the Cumberlands*, 177.

17 Scott, *Removing Mountains*, 212–14.

18 Reardon and TallBear, "'Your DNA Is Our History.'"

19 Stewart, *A Space on the Side of the Road*.

20 Bruyneel, "The American Liberal Colonial Tradition."

21 Starblanket and Stark, "Towards a Relational Paradigm."

22 Starblanket and Stark, "Towards a Relational Paradigm," 183.

23 Brown, *Emergent Strategy*.

24 Stoll, *Ramp Hollow*.

25 Rifkin, *Beyond Settler Time*, 170.

26 George Washington quoted in Thoenen, *History of the Oil and Gas Industry*, 4. General Andrew Lewis later lent his name to Lewisburg, the county seat of Greenbrier County.

27 Nichols, *Theft Is Property!*, 35.

28 Stoll, *Ramp Hollow*; Weise, *Grasping at Independence*; WV Center on Budget and Policy, "Who Owns West Virginia in the 21st Century?"

29 Stoll, *Ramp Hollow*.

30 Dasgupta et al., "Opioid Crisis."

31 See discussion in chapter 1.

32 Blomley, "The Right to Not Be Excluded."

33 Kern and Kovesi, "Environmental Justice."

34 TallBear, "Caretaking Relations."

35 Shorter, "Spirituality," 444.
36 Starblanket and Stark, "Towards a Relational Paradigm," 182.
37 Trillin, "U.S. Journal."
38 Harris, "Whiteness as Property," 1731.
39 Quoted in Harris, "Whiteness as Property," 1729.
40 Bell, in Mackey, *Unsettled Expectations*, 10.
41 Mackey, *Unsettled Expectations*, 10, 15.
42 Mackey, *Unsettled Expectations*, 9; TallBear, "Caretaking Relations."
43 Sullivan quoted in Mackey, *Unsettled Expectations*, 183.
44 Arvin et al., "Decolonizing Feminism."
45 Rifkin, *Beyond Settler Time*, 52.
46 Estes, *Our History Is the Future*, 21.
47 Moreton-Robinson, *The White Possessive*.
48 Byrnes, "Climate Justice."
49 Appalachians Against Pipelines, "Old and Bold."
50 Estes, *Our History Is the Future*, 22; Norgaard, *Salmon and Acorns*, 226.
51 Kimmerer, "The Rights of the Land."
52 Starblanket and Stark, "Towards a Relational Paradigm"; Mackey, *Unsettled Expectations*, 191.
53 Simpson, *As We Have Always Done*.
54 Mackey, *Unsettled Expectations*, 167.
55 TallBear, "Caretaking Relations," 38.

CONCLUSION
Epigraph: Krawec, *Becoming Kin*, 22–23.
1 Archibald, *Indigenous Storywork*.
2 Mitchell and Chaudhury, "Worlding."
3 Veracini in Macoun and Strakosch, "The Ethical Demands of Settler Colonial Theory," 438.
4 Veracini in Macoun and Strakosch, "The Ethical Demands of Settler Colonial Theory," 438.
5 Rice, *Moon of the Crusted Snow*.
6 *Revolution* aired on NBC from 2012–2014.
7 Rice, *Moon of the Crusted Snow*, 13.
8 Rice, *Moon of the Crusted Snow*, front dust flap.
9 Estes, *Our History Is the Future*.
10 Whyte, "Our Ancestors' Dystopia Now"; Rice, *Moon of the Crusted Snow*.
11 Rice, *Moon of the Crusted Snow*, 57.
12 Bussière, "Beginning at the End," 56.
13 Bussière, "Beginning at the End," 57.
14 Bussière, "Beginning at the End," 50.
15 Martens, "Petromelancholia," 195.
16 Martens, "Petromelancholia," 197.

17 Martens, "Petromelancholia," 198.
18 Martens, "Petromelancholia," 200.
19 Rice, *Moon of the Crusted Snow*, 56.
20 Rice, *Moon of the Crusted Snow*, 33.
21 Rice, *Moon of the Crusted Snow*, 13.
22 Martens, "Petromelancholia," 201.
23 Martens, "Petromelancholia," 207.
24 Martens, "Petromelancholia," 207.
25 Rice, *Moon of the Crusted Snow*, 202; Martens, "Petromelancholia," 208.
26 Rice, *Moon of the Crusted Snow*, 99–100, 125, 131.
27 Rice, *Moon of the Crusted Snow*, 116.
28 Kimmerer, *Braiding Sweetgrass*, 304.
29 Kimmerer, *Braiding Sweetgrass*; Bussière, "Beginning at the End."
30 Martens, "Petromelancholia," 205.
31 Rice, *Moon of the Crusted Snow*, 115–16, 125.
32 Rice, *Moon of the Crusted Snow*, 135.
33 Rice, *Moon of the Crusted Snow*, 201–2.
34 Rice, *Moon of the Crusted Snow*, 149–50.
35 Rice, *Moon of the Crusted Snow*, 60.
36 Rice, *Moon of the Crusted Snow*, 82.
37 Rice, *Moon of the Crusted Snow*, 211.
38 This token recognition of Indigenous difference is present in many instances of environmentalist literature (e.g., *The Overstory*, by Richard Powers, W.W. Norton, 2018) and philosophical literature (e.g., *The Tao of Pooh*, by Benjamin Hoff, Penguin, 1983) and other popular representations (e.g., *Avatar*, film, directed by James Cameron, 2009).
39 Rifkin, *Beyond Settler Time*.
40 Erdrich, *Future Home of the Living God*.
41 Dimaline, *The Marrow Thieves*.
42 Justice, *Why Indigenous Literatures Matter*, 136–37; Horner et al., "Ni Keehtwawmi Mooshahkinitounawn."
43 Bussière, "Beginning at the End," 54; Kimmerer, *Braiding Sweetgrass*.
44 Kimmerer, *Braiding Sweetgrass*, 304–5.
45 Kimmerer, *Braiding Sweetgrass*; Starblanket and Stark, "Towards a Relational Paradigm," 175–207.
46 Macoun and Strakosch, "The Ethical Demands of Settler Colonial Theory," 438.
47 Dillon, *Walking the Clouds*.
48 Rice, *Moon of the Crusted Snow*, 162.
49 Rice, *Moon of the Crusted Snow*, 160.
50 Rice, *Moon of the Crusted Snow*, 116.
51 Starblanket and Stark, "Towards a Relational Paradigm," 181.
52 Starblanket and Stark, "Towards a Relational Paradigm," 182.
53 Vimalassery et al., "On Colonial Unknowing."

54 Martens, "Petromelancholia."

55 Krawec, *Becoming Kin.*

56 Norgaard, *Salmon and Acorns*, 81.

57 Tsing, *Friction.*

58 MacPherson, *Political Theory.*

59 Cutts, "*MAN.*"

60 Nichols, *Theft Is Property!*, 157.

61 Altamirano-Jiménez and Kermoal, "Introduction," 7–8.

62 Mills, *The Racial Contract.*

63 Fisher-Borne et al., "From Mastery to Accountability."

64 Penniman, "The Gift of Ecological Humility."

65 Mackey, *Unsettled Expectations.*

66 hooks and Mesa-Bains, *Homegrown*, 61.

METHODOLOGICAL APPENDIX

1 Ladd, *Fractured Communities*; Guillon, *Fracking the Neighborhood*; Theodori, "Paradoxical Perceptions"; Maslen and Hayes, "'It's the Seeing and Feeling'"; Zwick, "Comparison."

2 Johnson, *The Broken Heart of America.*

3 Gordon, *Ghostly Matters*; Million, "Felt Theory"; Justice, *Why Indigenous Literatures Matter.*

4 Justice, *Why Indigenous Literatures Matter*, 1.

5 Kaminski, "The Neo-Frontier."

6 Dillon, *Walking the Clouds*; Brown, *Emergent Strategy.*

7 Denzin, *Interpretive Autoethnography.*

8 Chin, *My Life with Things.*

9 Saldaña-Portillo, *Indian Given.*

REFERENCES

Adichie, Chimamanda Ngozi. "The Danger of a Single Story." A TED talk posted in 2009. www.ted.com.

Ahmed, Sara. *The Cultural Politics of Emotion*. Edinburgh: Edinburgh University Press, 2005.

Alaimo, Stacy. *Exposed: Environmental Politics and Pleasures in Posthuman Times*. Minneapolis: University of Minnesota Press, 2016.

Aleem, Zeeshan. "From Coast to Coast, Protests against Police Brutality and Racism Are Still Going Strong." *Vox*, June 14, 2020. www.vox.com.

Alfred, Taiaiaka. "Cultural Strength: Restoring the Place of Indigenous Knowledge in Practice and Policy." *Australian Aboriginal Studies (Canberra) 2015*, no. 1 (2015): 3–11.

———. "What Is Radical Imagination? Indigenous Struggles in Canada." *Affinities: A Journal of Radical Theory, Culture, and Action* 4, no. 2 (2010): 5–8.

Allard, Ladonna Bravebull. "Why Do We Punish Dakota Pipeline Protesters but Exonerate the Bundys?" *The Guardian*, November 2, 2016. www.theguardian.com.

Altamirano-Jiménez, Isabel, and Nathalie Kermoal. "Introduction: Indigenous Women and Knowledge." In *Living on the Land: Indigenous Women's Understanding of Place*, edited by Isabel Altamirano-Jiménez and Natalie Kermoal, 3–17. Edmonton, AB: Athabasca University Press, 2016.

Ancestry.com. "James Burnes (Burns)—Facts." Accessed February 20, 2020. www.ancestry.com.

Andrews, Nancy. "How Would You Improve the Natural Gas Pipeline Process?," *West Virginia Public Broadcasting*, July 18, 2018. https://wvpublic.org.

Anker, Elizabeth R. *Ugly Freedoms*. Durham, NC: Duke University Press, 2022.

Appalachian Storage Hub Conference IV website. "Storage Hub?" November 5, 2020. www.appastorage.com.

Appalachians Against Pipelines. 2022. "'Old and Bold' Climate Activists Pressure Blacksburg Wells Fargo Branch. Press Release from Third Act Virginia." Facebook, May 4, 2022. www.facebook.com.

———. 2019. "Work Site Disruption in Greenbrier County, WV. Cherri, Mama Julz, and Jim Blocked Mountain Valley Pipeline Work for 3+ Hours." Facebook, September 10, 2019. www.facebook.com.

Archibald, Jo-ann. *Indigenous Storywork: Educating the Heart, Mind, Body, and Spirit*. Vancouver, Canada: University of British Columbia Press, 2008.

Arteta, Miguel, dir. *Beatriz at Dinner*, June 9, 2017. United States. Bron Studios, Killer Films.

Arvin, Maile, Eve Tuck, and Angie Morrill. "Decolonizing Feminism: Challenging Connections between Settler Colonialism and Heteropatriarchy." *Feminist Formations* 25, no. 1 (2013): 8–34.

Asafu-Asjaye, John, Linus Blomqvist, Stewart Brand, Barry Brook, Ruth DeFries, Erle Ellis, Christopher Foreman, et al. "An Ecomodernist Manifesto." Ecomodernism. org, April 2015. Published online only. www.ecomodernism.org.

Atlantic Coast Pipeline. "Home." Accessed June 10, 2022. https://atlanticcoastpipeline. com.

Awasis, Sakihitowin. "'Anishinaabe Time': Temporalities and Impact Assessment in Pipeline Reviews." *Journal of Political Ecology* 27, no. 1 (January 20, 2020): 830–52.

Bacigalupi, Paolo. "People of Sand and Slag." In *Wastelands: Stories of the Apocalypse*, edited by John Joseph Adams, 39–54. San Francisco: Night Shade, 2008.

Bales, Kevin. *Blood and Earth: Modern Slavery, Ecocide, and the Secret to Saving the World*. New York: Spiegel & Grau, 2016.

Ballesteros, Carlos. "West Virginia Woman Dragged Out of Capitol for Reading State Reps Political Donations." *Newsweek*, February 11, 2018. www.newsweek.com.

Ballotpedia. "Federal Land Ownership by State." Accessed February 16, 2018. https:// ballotpedia.org.

Baptist, Edward E. *The Half Has Never Been Told: Slavery and the Making of American Capitalism*. New York: Basic Books, 2014.

Barad, Karen. "Posthumanist Performativity: Toward an Understanding of How Matter Comes to Matter." *Signs: Journal of Women in Culture and Society* 28, no. 3 (2003): 801–31.

Barder, Alexander D. "American Hegemony Comes Home: The Chilean Laboratory and the Neoliberalization of the United States." *Alternatives: Global, Local, Political* 38, no. 2 (2013): 103–21.

Barry, Joyce M. *Standing Our Ground: Women, Environmental Justice, and the Fight to End Mountaintop Removal*. Athens: Ohio University Press, 2012.

Beck, Ulrich. *Risk Society*. New York: Sage, 1992.

Been, Vicki. "Locally Undesirable Land Uses in Minority Neighborhoods: Disproportionate Siting or Market Dynamics?" *Yale Law Journal* 10, no. 6 (1994): 1383–1422.

Bell, Shannon Elizabeth. *Fighting King Coal: The Challenges to Micromobilization in Central Appalachia*. Urban and Industrial Environments. Cambridge, MA: MIT Press, 2016.

Bellware, Kim, and Brady Dennis. "Flint Water Crisis: Former Gov. Rick Snyder to Face Criminal Charges." *Washington Post,* January 12, 2021. www.washingtonpost.com.

Bennett, Abbie. "Republican Senator Dan Bishop Compares Black Lives Matter, Supremacists." *The News & Observer*, August 14, 2017. www.newsobserver.com.

Bennett, Jane. *Vibrant Matter: A Political Ecology of Things*. Durham, NC: Duke University Press, 2010.

Benz, Terressa A. "Black Femininity and Stand Your Ground: Controlling Images and the Elusive Defense of Self-Defense." *Critical Sociology* 46, nos. 7–8 (November 1, 2020): 1093–1107.

Bettie, Julie. *Women without Class: Girls, Race and Identity*. Oakland: University of California Press, 2014.

Bhandar, Brenna. *Colonial Lives of Property: Law, Land, and Racial Regimes of Ownership*. Durham, NC: Duke University Press, 2018.

Biggers, Jeff. "Mountaintop Removal Never Ended: Coal River Mountaineers Fight On." *Common Dreams*, October 19, 2016. www.commondreams.org.

Black in Appalachia. "The Podcast." Accessed July 15, 2022. www.blackinappalachia.org.

Blodgett, Abigail D. "An Analysis of Pollution and Community Advocacy in 'Cancer Alley': Setting an Example for the Environmental Justice Movement in St James Parish, Louisiana." *Local Environment* 11, no. 6 (2006): 647–61.

Blomley, Nicholas. "Property, Pluralism and the Gentrification Frontier." *Canadian Journal of Law and Society / La Revue Canadienne Droit et Société* 12, no. 2 (1997): 187–218.

———. "The Right to Not Be Excluded: Common Property and the Right to Stay Put." In *Releasing the Commons: Rethinking the Futures of the Commons*, edited by Ash Amin and Philip Howell, 89–106. New York London: Routledge, 2016.

———. "The Ties That Blind: Making Fee Simple in the British Columbia Treaty Process." *Transactions of the Institute of British Geographers* 40, no. 2 (January 1, 2015): 168–79.

Borchard, Kimberly C. "From Apalache to Apalachee: The Making of Early Modern Appalachia." Presented at the Goldsmiths History Society, Online webinar, February 23, 2022.

Bosman, Julie. "Many Flint Residents Are Desperate to Leave, but See No Escape." *New York Times*, February 4, 2016. www.nytimes.com.

Bosworth, Kai. "'They're Treating Us Like Indians!': Political Ecologies of Property and Race in North American Pipeline Populism." *Antipode* 53, no. 3 (2018), 665–85.

Branigin, Anne. "Why Some Black and Brown People Can't Trust Bernie Sanders, in 1 Quote." *The Root*, October 31, 2017. www.theroot.com.

Braun, Bruce. "'On the Raggedy Edge of Risk': Articulations of Race and Nature after Biology." In *Race, Nature and the Politics of Difference*, edited by Donald S. Moore, Jake Kosek, and Anand Pandian, 175–203. Durham, NC: Duke University Press, 2003.

Britannica. "Coverture Law." Accessed July 28, 2022. www.britannica.com.

Broder, John M. "Climate Change Doubt Is Tea Party Article of Faith." *New York Times*, October 20, 2010. www.nytimes.com.

Brown, Adrienne Maree. *Emergent Strategy: Shaping Change, Changing Worlds*. Chico, CA: AK Press, 2017.

Brown, Nicholas Anthony. "Continental Land Back: Managing Mobilities and Enacting Relationalities in Indigenous Landscapes." *Mobilities* 17, no. 2 (March 4, 2022): 252–68.

Bruyneel, Kevin. "The American Liberal Colonial Tradition." *Settler Colonial Studies* 3, no. 3–04 (November 1, 2013): 311–21.

———. "Codename Geronimo: Settler Memory and the Production of American Statism." *Settler Colonial Studies* 6, no. 4 (October 2016): 349.

———. "Race, Colonialism, and the Politics of Indian Sports Names and Mascots: The Washington Football Team Case." *NAIS: Journal of the Native American and Indigenous Studies Association* 3, no. 2 (2016): 1–24.

———. *Settler Memory: The Disavowal of Indigeneity and the Politics of Race.* Chapel Hill: University of North Carolina Press, 2021.

Buford, Talia. "'Rare Discrimination Finding by EPA Civil Rights Office." Center for Public Integrity, 2017. www.publicintegrity.org.

Bullard, Robert D., ed. *Confronting Environmental Racism: Voices from the Grassroots.* Boston: South End Press, 1993.

Bureau of Land Management. "Programs: Energy and Minerals: Oil and Gas: Leasing: Split Estate." October 16, 2016. www.blm.gov.

Burnett, Robert J. "The Accommodation Doctrine: Balancing the Interests of the Surface Owner and the Mineral Owner." *Houston Harbaugh, P.C., Attorneys at Law,* 2019. www.hh-law.com.

Burns, Shirley Stewart. *Bringing Down the Mountains: The Impact of Mountaintop Removal Surface Coal Mining on Southern West Virginia Communities, 1970–2004.* Morgantown: West Virginia University Press, 2007.

Bussière, Kirsten. "Beginning at the End: Indigenous Survivance in Moon of the Crusted Snow." *Foundation: The International Review of Science Fiction* 49, no. 136 (2020): 47–58.

Byrd, Jodi. *The Transit of Empire: Indigenous Critiques of Colonialism.* Minneapolis: University of Minnesota Press, 2011.

Byrnes, W. Malcolm. "Climate Justice, Hurricane Katrina, and African American Environmentalism." *Journal of African American Studies* 18, no. 3 (September 1, 2014): 305–14.

"Can the Marcellus/Utica Build Too Many Cracker Plants?" *Marcellus Drilling News,* July 23, 2018. https://marcellusdrilling.com.

CAPRi (CGIAR Systemwide Program on Collective Action and Property Rights). "Resources, Rights and Cooperation: A Sourcebook on Property Rights and Collective Action for Sustainabile Development." International Food Policy Research Institute, 2010. https://capri.cgiar.org.

Carey, Jane, and Ben Silverstein. "Thinking With and Beyond Settler Colonial Studies: New Histories after the Postcolonial." *Postcolonial Studies* 23, no. 1 (2020): 1–20.

Carlson-Manathara, Elizabeth, and Gladys Rowe. *Living in Indigenous Sovereignty.* Halifax, Canada: Fernwood Publishing, 2021.

Carmody, Tim. "How the Flint River Got So Toxic." *The Verge,* February 26, 2016. www.theverge.com.

Carrington, Damian. "Earth's Sixth Mass Extinction Event under Way, Scientists Warn." *The Guardian,* July 10, 2017. www.theguardian.com.

Carson, Rachel. *Silent Spring.* New York: Houghton Mifflin, 1962.

Carswell, Cally. "Trump's Wall May Threaten Thousands of Plant and Animal Species on the U.S.–Mexico Border." *Scientific American,* May 10, 2017. www.scientificamerican.com.

Caudill, Henry. *Night Comes to the Cumberlands*. Boston: Little, Brown and Co., 1962.

Chapman, Brett. (@brettachapman). "America Claims to Have 'Tamed the West' in 1890 and It Only Took 30 Years for Their Greed to Transform a Delicate, Ancient Ecosystem That Sustained Vast Herds of Buffalo for Centuries into a Barren Desert in the Worst Man-Made Environmental Disaster in U.S. History—the Dust Bowl." June 6, 2019. Tweet.

Chappell, Bill. "After Nearly 4 Months, Porter Ranch Gas Leak Is Temporarily Plugged." *NPR*, February 12, 2016. www.npr.org.

Chariton, Jordan, and Charlie LeDuff. "Revealed: The Flint Water Poisoning Charges That Never Came to Light." *The Guardian*, January 17, 2022. www.theguardian.com.

Chatsworth Porter Ranch Chamber of Commerce. "Porter Ranch Then and Now." Accessed April 5, 2023. www.chatsworthchamber.com.

Chin, Elizabeth. *My Life with Things: The Consumer Diaries*. Durham, NC: Duke University Press, 2016.

Clean Energy Fuels. "Clean Energy Natural Gas." www.cleanenergyfuels.com.

Climate Reality. "Ethane Cracker Plants: What Are They?" October 23, 2018. www.climaterealityproject.org.

CNN Newsource. "Coal Mines Closing at a Faster Rate under Pres. Trump than Obama." WOWK, January 8, 2019. www.wowktv.com.

Cole, Teju. "The White-Savior Industrial Complex." *The Atlantic*, March 21, 2012. www.theatlantic.com.

Cone, Marla. "Sierra Club to Remain Neutral on Immigration." *Los Angeles Times*, April 26, 1998. www.latimes.com.

Conlin, Michelle, and Brian Grow. "Special Report: U.S. Builders Hoard Mineral Rights under New Homes." *Reuters*, October 9, 2013. www.reuters.com.

Coontz, Stephanie. *The Way We Never Were: American Families and the Nostalgia Trap*. New York: Basic Books, 2016.

Corkery, Michael. "A Giant Factory Rises to Make a Product Filling Up the World: Plastic." *New York Times*, August 12, 2019. www.nytimes.com.

Coulthard, Glen Sean. *Red Skin, White Masks: Rejecting the Colonial Politics of Recognition*. Minneapolis: University of Minnesota Press, 2014.

Coyne, Caity. "'That's Just How Things Go in Keystone': Water Woes Indicative of Town's Troubles." *Charleston Gazette-Mail*, June 1, 2019. www.wvgazettemail.com.

Crenshaw, Kimberlé. *On Intersectionality: Essential Writings*. New York: New Press, 2020.

Crist, Eileen. "The Reaches of Freedom: A Response to an Ecomodernist Manifesto." *Environmental Humanities* 7, no. 1 (May 1, 2016): 245–54.

Cronon, William. *Nature's Metropolis: Chicago and the Great West*. New York: W. W. Norton, 1992.

———. "The Trouble with Wilderness; or, Getting Back to the Wrong Nature." In *Uncommon Ground: Rethinking the Human Place in Nature*. New York: W. W. Norton, 1995.

Cunningham, Nick. "Bloodbath In Oil & Gas Stocks Could Continue." OilPrice. com, January 3, 2019. https://oilprice.com.

Cuomo, Chris J. "Climate Change, Vulnerability, and Responsibility." *Hypatia* 26, no. 4 (November 1, 2011): 690–714.

Cutts, Steve. "MAN." YouTube Video, December 21, 2012, www.youtube.com.

Daggett, Cara New. *The Birth of Energy: Fossil Fuels, Thermodynamics, and the Politics of Work*. Durham, NC: Duke University Press, 2019.

Dalley, Hamish. "The Deaths of Settler Colonialism: Extinction as a Metaphor of Decolonization in Contemporary Settler Literature." *Settler Colonial Studies* 8, no. 1 (January 2, 2018): 30–46.

Dalton, Daniel P. "A History of Eminent Domain." *Public Corporation Law Quarterly* 3 (2006): 1–5.

Daly, Matthew. "Unexpected Deal Would Boost Biden Pledge on Climate Change." AP News, July 28, 2022. https://apnews.com.

Dasgupta, Nabarun, Leo Beletsky, and Daniel Ciccarone. "Opioid Crisis: No Easy Fix to Its Social and Economic Determinants." *American Journal of Public Health* 108, no. 2 (December 21, 2017): 182–86.

Deleuze, Gilles, and Felix Guattari. *Anti-Oedipus: Capitalism and Schizophrenia*. New York: Penguin Classics, 2009.

Deloria Jr., Vine. *Custer Died for Your Sins: An Indian Manifesto*. Norman: University of Oklahoma Press, 1988.

———. *Spirit and Reason: The Vine Deloria, Jr. Reader*, edited by Sam Scinta and Kristen Foehner. Golden, CO: Fulcrum, 1999.

Denzin, Norman K. *Interpretive Autoethnography*. Thousand Oaks, CA: SAGE Publications, 2014.

Diamond, Dan. "Trump Challenges Native Americans' Historical Standing." *POLITICO*, April 22, 2018. https://politi.co.

Dillon, Grace L., ed. *Walking the Clouds: An Anthology of Indigenous Science Fiction*. Tucson: University of Arizona Press, 2012.

Dimaline, Cherie. *The Marrow Thieves*. Toronto, Canada: DCB, 2017.

DiTirro, Tessa. "Massive Pipeline Explosion Seen across State Lines." WBOY, June 8, 2018. www.wboy.com.

DuBois, W. E. Burghardt. *Black Reconstruction in America, 1860–1880*. New York: Free Press, 1998.

Dunbar-Ortiz, Roxanne. *An Indigenous Peoples' History of the United States*. Boston: Beacon Press, 2014.

Dyer, Richard. *White: Essays on Race and Culture*. New York: Routledge, 1997.

Economic Development Greater East (EDGE). "Mountain Farm Community Grocery." Accessed January 5, 2023. www.edge-us.org.

Edsall, Thomas Byrne, and Mary D. Edsall. *Chain Reaction: The Impact of Race, Rights, and Taxes on American Politics*. New York: W. W. Norton, 1992.

Edwards, Jim. "Alexandria Ocasio-Cortez's Tweet about Workers Being Paid 'Less than the Value They Create' Is Essentially a Restatement of Marx's

Labour Theory of Value—Here's Why That's Interesting." *Business Insider*, March 10, 2019. www.businessinsider.com.

Edwards, Marc, and Sid Roy. "Flint Water Study Updates." Flint Water Study website, 2019. http://flintwaterstudy.org/.

Egan, Paul. "Amid Denials, State Workers in Flint Got Clean Water." *Detroit Free Press*, January 28, 2016. www.freep.com.

Energy Justice. Justice Map—Visualize Race and Income Data for Your Community. Accessed February 21, 2020. www.energyjustice.net.

Erdrich, Louise. *Future Home of the Living God*. New York: Harper Perennial, 2018.

Estes, Nick. *Our History Is the Future*. New York: Verso, 2019.

Farr, Christina. "The Pandemic Has Exposed Gaping Problems with the U.S. Health Care System." CNBC, October 30, 2020. www.cnbc.com.

Federal Energy Commission. "What FERC Does." How to Partipate. Accessed January 4, 2023. www.ferc.gov.

Federici, Silvia. *Caliban and the Witch: Women, the Body and Primitive Accumulation*. New York: Autonomedia, 2004.

Finney, Carolyn. *Black Faces, White Spaces: Reimagining the Relationship of African Americans to the Great Outdoors*. Chapel Hill: University of North Carolina Press, 2014.

Fiola, Chantal. *Rekindling the Sacred Fire: Métis Ancestry and Anishinaabe Spirituality*. Winnipeg, Canada: University of Manitoba Press, 2015.

Fisher-Borne, Marcie, Jessie Montana Cain, and Suzanne L. Martin. "From Mastery to Accountability: Cultural Humility as an Alternative to Cultural Competence." *Social Work Education* 34, no. 2 (February 17, 2015): 165–81.

Food and Agriculture Database of the United Nations. "Gender and Land Rights Database: Gender and Land Statistics. Table 1F. Distribution of Land Holders by Sex (Females)." 2017. www.fao.org.

Formisano, Ronald P. *The Tea Party: A Brief History*. Baltimore, MD: Johns Hopkins University Press, 2012.

Fox, Josh. *Gasland*. January 24, 2010. United States. International WOW Company. Film.

Fox, Julia. "Mountaintop Removal in West Virginia: An Environmental Sacrifice Zone." *Organization & Environment*, no. 2 (1999): 163.

Fox, Justin. "Natural Gas Now Beats Coal, Even in West Virginia." Bloomberg. Com, May 24, 2019. www.bloomberg.com.

Frankel, Jay. "The Traumatic Basis for the Resurgence of Right-Wing Politics among Working Americans." *Psychoanalysis, Culture & Society* 20, no. 4 (December 1, 2015): 359–78.

Frost, William Goodell. "Our Contemporary Ancestors in the Southern Mountains" (first published 1899). In *Appalachian Images in Folk and Popular Culture*, edited by W. K. McNeil, 91–106. Knoxville: University of Tennessee Press, 1995.

Fry, Matthew. "Fracking and Environmental (In)Justice in a Texas City." *Ecological Economics* 117 (September 1, 2015): 97–107.

Fukuyama, Francis. *The End of History and the Last Man.* New York: Free Press, 2006.

Gaard, Greta. "Toward a Queer Ecofeminism." In *New Perspectives on Environmental Justice: Gender, Sexuality, and Activism*, edited by Rachel Stein, 21–44. New Brunswick, NJ: Rutgers University Press, 2004.

Galchen, Rivka. "The Arrival of Man-Made Earthquakes," *The New Yorker*, April 15, 2015. www.newyorker.com.

Garlick, Steve. *The Nature of Masculinity: Critical Theory, New Materialisms, and Technologies of Embodiment.* Vancouver, Canada: University of British Columbia Press, 2016.

Gessen, Masha. "Elizabeth Warren Falls for Trump's Trap—and Promotes Insidious Ideas About Race and DNA." *The New Yorker*, October 16, 2018.

Gibson-Graham, J. K. *The End of Capitalism (As We Knew It): A Feminist Critique of Political Economy.* Minneapolis: University of Minnesota Press, 2006.

Gilbert, Jess, Spencer D. Wood, and Gwen Sharp. "Who Owns the Land? Agricultural Land Ownership by Race/Ethnicity." *Rural America* 17, no. 4 (2001): 55–62.

Gilio-Whitaker, Dina. *As Long as Grass Grows: The Indigenous Fight for Environmental Justice, from Colonization to Standing Rock.* Boston MA: Beacon Press, 2019.

Gilmore, Ruth Wilson. *Golden Gulag: Prisons, Surplus, Crisis, and Opposition in Globalizing California.* Berkeley: University of California Press, 2007.

Giroux, Henry A. *Stormy Weather: Katrina and the Politics of Disposability.* Boulder, CO: Routledge, 2006.

"Global Warming of 1.5 °C," Intergovernmental Panel on Climate Change. October 2018. www.ipcc.ch/sr15/.

Go, Julian. *Postcolonial Thought and Social Theory.* New York: Oxford University Press, 2016.

Goldberg, David Theo. *The Racial State.* Malden, MA: Wiley-Blackwell, 2001.

Goldstein, Jesse. "Terra Economica: Waste and the Production of Enclosed Nature." *Antipode* 45, no. 2 (2013): 357–75.

Gordon, Avery F. *Ghostly Matters: Haunting and the Sociological Imagination.* Minneapolis: University Of Minnesota Press, 2008.

Gorman, Steve. "U.S. Lists a Bumble Bee Species as Endangered for First Time." *Scientific American*, January 11, 2017. www.scientificamerican.com.

Gould, Kenneth A., David N. Pellow, and Allan Schnaiberg. "Interrogating the Treadmill of Production Everything You Wanted to Know About the Treadmill but Were Afraid to Ask." *Organization & Environment*, no. 3 (2004): 296.

Grattan, Robert. "Natural Gas Production Set for Decline in 2016." *San Antonio Express-News*, January 1, 2016. www.expressnews.com.

Greenberg, S., J. Carville, and E. Seifert. *Inside the GOP: Report on Focus Groups with Evangelical, Tea Party, and Moderate Republicans.* Washington, DC: Greenberg Quinlan Rosner Research, October 3, 2013. www.democracycorps.com.

Guarino, Mark. "New Crisis for Flint Residents: Cost of Home Damage Caused by City Water." *Washington Post*, January 22, 2016. www.washingtonpost.com.

Guha, Ramachandra. "Radical American Environmentalism and Wilderness Preservation: A Third World Critique." In *The Great New Wilderness Debate: An Expansive Collection of Writings Defining Wilderness from John Muir to Gary Synder*, edited by J. Baird Callicott and Michael P. Nelson, 231–45. Athens: University of Georgia Press, 1998.

Guillon, Jessica Smartt. *Fracking the Neighborhood: Reluctant Activists and Natural Gas Drilling.* Cambridge, MA: MIT Press, 2015.

Gunn Allen, Paula. "(from) Who Is Your Mother? Red Roots of White Feminism." In *Women's Liberation! Feminist Writings that Inspired a Revolution and Still Can*, edited by Alix Kates Shulman and Honor Moore, 577–82. New York: Library of America, 2021.

Guthman, Julie. *Weighing In: Obesity, Food Justice, and the Limits of Capitalism.* Berkeley: University of California Press, 2011.

Habeeb, Lee. "Coal Keeps the Lights On: The Story of an Unlikely Singer-Activist." *LifeZette*, March 10, 2017. www.lifezette.com.

Halsey, Francis Whiting. "Part 3. Land Titles and Pioneers (1679–1774), Chapter 2. The Fort Stanwix Deed, and Patents That Followed It (1768–1770)." In *The Old New York Frontier*, 99–105, n.d. Accessed April 5, 2023. https://en.wikisource.org.

Hamilton, Cynthia. "Coping with Industrial Exploitation." In *Confronting Environmental Racism: Voices from the Grassroots*, 63–75. Boston, MA: South End Press, 1993.

Hanna-Attisha, Mona, Jenny LaChance, Richard Casey Sadler, and Allison Champney Schnepp. "Elevated Blood Lead Levels in Children Associated with the Flint Drinking Water Crisis: A Spatial Analysis of Risk and Public Health Response." *American Journal of Public Health* 106, no. 2 (2016): 283–90.

Haraway, Donna Jeanne. *Staying with the Trouble: Making Kin in the Chthulucene.* Durham, NC: Duke University Press, 2016.

———. *When Species Meet.* Minneapolis: University of Minnesota Press, 2008.

Hardin, Garrett. "The Tragedy of the Commons." The Garrett Hardin Society. 1968. www.garretthardinsociety.org.

Harris, Cheryl I. "Whiteness as Property." *Harvard Law Review* no. 8 (1993): 1707–91.

Harris, Dianne Suzette. *Little White Houses: How the Postwar Home Constructed Race in America.* Minneapolis: University of Minnesota Press, 2013.

Harvey, David. *A Brief History of Neoliberalism.* New York: Oxford University Press, 2007.

———. *The Condition of Postmodernity: An Enquiry into the Origins of Cultural Change.* Cambridge, MA: Wiley-Blackwell, 1991.

Harvey, Matt. "Lawman: 2 Individuals Killed in Multi-Vehicle Crash Were Relatives from Shinnston." *WV News*, June 20, 2018. www.wvnews.com.

Hass, Wills De. *History of the Early Settlement and Indian Wars of West Virginia* (first published 1851). Lanner Books, 2019. E-book edition.

Healy, Noel, Jennie C. Stephens, and Stephanie A. Malin. "Embodied Energy Injustices: Unveiling and Politicizing the Transboundary Harms of Fossil Fuel Extractivism and Fossil Fuel Supply Chains." *Energy Research & Social Science* 48 (February 1, 2019): 219–34.

Hendryx, Michael, and Melissa M. Ahem. "Relations between Health Indicators and Residential Proximity to Coal Mining in West Virginia." *American Journal of Public Health* 98, no. 4 (2008): 669–71.

Hill Collins, Patricia. *Black Feminist Thought: Knowledge, Consciousness, and the Politics of Empowerment*. New York: Routledge, 2000.

hooks, bell, and Amalia Mesa-Bains. *Homegrown: Engaged Cultural Criticism*. New York: Routledge, 2017.

Horner, Melissa, Joaquin Munoz, and Robert Petrone. "Ni Keehtwawmi Mooshah-kinitounawn: Lifting Up Representations of Indigenous Education and Futures in The Marrow Thieves." *Research on Diversity in Youth Literature* 4, no. 1 (2021), article 7.

Howard, Ron. *Far and Away*. May 22, 1992. United States. Imagine Entertainment. Film.

Howling, Ben, and Yolanda Ramke, dirs. *Cargo*. October 6, 2017. Australia. Netflix. Film.

Huber, Matthew. *Lifeblood: Oil, Freedom, and the Forces of Capital*. Minneapolis: University of Minnesota Press, 2013.

Hurdle, Jon. "With Governor's Signature, Maryland Becomes Third State to Ban Fracking." *State Impact Pennsylvania*, April 5, 2017. https://stateimpact.npr.org.

Huseman, Jennifer, and Damien Short. "'A Slow Industrial Genocide': Tar Sands and the Indigenous Peoples of Northern Alberta." *The International Journal of Human Rights* 16, no. 1 (January 1, 2012): 216–37.

Ibrahim, Hindou Oumarou. "'We Know How to Keep the Balance of Nature.' Why Including Indigenous People Is Vital to Solving Climate Change." *Time*, September 30, 2019. https://time.com.

IMDb. "Cargo (2017) Trivia." www.imdb.com.

Inwood, Joshua F. J., and Anne Bonds. "Property and Whiteness: The Oregon Standoff and the Contradictions of the U.S. Settler State." *Space and Polity* 21, no. 3 (December 2017): 253–68.

Jacobs, Harvey M. "Whose Citizenship? Social Conflict over Property in the United States." *Social Policy and Society* 19, no. 2 (April 2020): 343–55.

Johansen, Bruce E. *Forgotten Founders: How the American Indian Helped Shape Democracy*. Boston, MA: Harvard Common Press, 1982.

Johnson, Daniel Morley. "From the Tomahawk Chop to the Road Block: Discourses of Savagism in Whitestream Media." *American Indian Quarterly* 35, no. 1 (2011): 104–34.

Johnson, Walter. *The Broken Heart of America*. New York: Basic Books, 2021.

Jones, Kendor P., John J. Welborn, and Chelsey J. Russell. "Split Estates and Surface Access Issues." In *Landman's Legal Handbook*, 181–96. Westminster, CO: Rocky Mountain Mineral Law Foundation, 2013.

Justice, Daniel Heath. *Why Indigenous Literatures Matter*. Waterloo, Canada: Wilfrid Laurier University Press, 2018.

Kaminski, Johannes. "The Neo-Frontier in Contemporary Preparedness Novels." *Journal of American Studies* 55, no. 4 (October 2021): 910–38.

Kauanui, J. Kēhaulani. "'A Structure, Not an Event': Settler Colonialism and Enduring Indigeneity." *Lateral* 5, no. 1 (2016).

Kazanjian, David. *The Colonizing Trick*. Minneapolis: University of Minnesota Press, 2003.

Keeler, Amanda. "A Postapocalyptic Return to the Frontier: The Walking Dead as Post-Western." *Critical Studies in Television* 13, no. 4 (December 1, 2018): 422–37.

Keeler, Jacqueline. "'It's So Disgusting' Malheur Militia Dug Latrine Trenches Among Sacred Artifacts." *Indian Country Media Network*, February 17, 2016. https://indian-countrymedianetwork.com.

Kennedy, Amanda. *Environmental Justice and Land Use Conflict: The Governance of Mineral and Gas Resource Development*. New York: Routledge, 2017.

Kern, Leslie, and Caroline Kovesi. "Environmental Justice Meets the Right to Stay Put: Mobilising against Environmental Racism, Gentrification, and Xenophobia in Chicago's Little Village." *Local Environment* 23, no. 9 (September 2, 2018): 952–66.

Khan, Amina. "Porter Ranch Leak Declared Largest Methane Leak in U.S. History." *Los Angeles Times*, February 25, 2016. www.latimes.com.

Kharkhordin, Oleg. "Things as Res Publicae: Making Things Public." In *In Making Things Public: Atmospheres of Democracy*, edited by Bruno Latour and Peter Weibel, 280–89. Cambridge, MA: MIT Press, 2005.

Killgrove, Kristina. "Bundy Militia Compared to ISIS for Pawing Through Native American Artifacts, Destroying Sites." *Forbes*, January 21, 2016. www.forbes.com.

Kimmerer, Robin Wall. *Braiding Sweetgrass: Indigenous Wisdom, Scientific Knowledge and the Teachings of Plants*. Minneapolis, MN: Milkweed Editions, 2015.

———. "The Rights of the Land: The Onandaga Nation of Central New York Proposes a Radical New Vision of Property Rights." *Orion Magazine*, November/December 2008 edition.

King, Tiffany Lethabo. *The Black Shoals: Offshore Formations of Black and Native Studies*. Durham, NC: Duke University Press, 2019.

Kite, Suzanne. "'What's on the Earth Is in the Stars; and What's in the Stars Is on the Earth': Lakota Relationships with the Stars and American Relationships with the Apocalypse." *American Indian Culture and Research Journal* 45, no. 1 (December 27, 2021): 137–56.

Klein, Ezra. "Romney's Theory of the 'Taker Class,' and Why It Matters." *Washington Post*, September 17, 2012. www.washingtonpost.com.

Klein, Naomi. *This Changes Everything: Capitalism Versus the Climate*. New York: Simon & Schuster, 2014.

Kohl, Ellen, Marianne Sullivan, Mark Milton Chambers, Alissa Cordner, Chris Sellers, Leif Fredrickson, and Jennifer Liss Ohayon. "From 'Marginal to Marginal': Environmental Justice under the Trump Administration." *Environmental Sociology* 8, no. 2 (2022): 242–53.

Kohn, Eduardo. *How Forests Think: Toward an Anthropology Beyond the Human.* Berkeley: University of California Press, 2013.

Kolbert, Elizabeth. *The Sixth Extinction: An Unnatural History.* New York: Henry Holt and Company, 2014.

Komarek, Tim, and Attila Cseh. "Fracking and Public Health: Evidence from Gonorrhea Incidence in the Marcellus Shale Region." *Journal of Public Health* 38 (2017): 464–81.

Konishi, Shino. "First Nations Scholars, Settler Colonial Studies, and Indigenous History." *Australian Historical Studies* 50, no. 3 (August 2019): 285–304.

Kourhi, Andrew. "Gas Leak Disrupts Porter Ranch Housing Market." *Los Angeles Times*, April 16, 2016. www.latimes.com.

Krawec, Patty. *Becoming Kin: An Indigenous Call to Unforgetting the Past and Reimagining Our Future.* Minneapolis, MN: Broadleaf Books, 2022.

Kuletz, Valerie. "Invisible Spaces, Violent Places: Cold War Nuclear and Militarized Landscapes." In *Violent Environments,* edited by Nancy Lee Peluso and Michael Watts, 237–60. Ithaca, NY: Cornell University Press, 2001.

———. *The Tainted Desert: Environmental Ruin in the American West.* New York: Routledge, 1998.

Ladd, Anthony E., ed. *Fractured Communities: Risks, Impacts, and Protest against Hydraulic Fracking in U.S. Shale Regions.* New Brunswick, NJ: Rutgers University Press, 2017.

LaDuke, Winona. *All Our Relations: Native Struggles for Land and Life.* Cambridge, MA: Minneapolis, MN: South End Press, 1999.

———. *Recovering the Sacred: The Power of Naming and Claiming.* Minneapolis, MN: South End Press, 2005.

Laitner, Bill, and Ann Zaniewski. "Michigan Ending Discounts for Flint Water Bills." *Detroit Free Press*, February 9, 2017. www.freep.com.

Larsen, Soren, and Jay Johnson. "The Agency of Place: Toward a More-Than-Human Geographical Self." *GeoHumanities* 2, no. 1 (2016): 149–66.

Latour, Bruno. "Love Your Monsters." *The Architectural League of New York*, March 17, 2014. https://archleague.org.

Latour, Bruno, and Catherine Porter. *We Have Never Been Modern.* Cambridge, MA: Harvard University Press, 1993.

Le Miere, Jason. "Donald Trump Says 'Our Ancestors Tamed a Continent' and 'We Are Not Going to Apologize for America.'" *Newsweek*, April 25, 2018. www.newsweek.com.

Leroux, Darryl. *Distorted Descent: White Claims to Indigenous Identity.* Winnipeg, Canada: University of Manitoba Press, 2019.

Levin, Sam. "Stunning Victory for Bundy Family as All Charges Dismissed in 2014 Standoff Case." *The Guardian*, January 8, 2018. www.theguardian.com.

Lewis, Ronald L. *Transforming the Appalachian Countryside: Railroads, Deforestation, and Social Change in West Virginia, 1880–1920*. Chapel Hill: University of North Carolina Press, 1998.

Lilly, Jessica. "Trauma in Coal Town Remains Raw After Decade on Boil Water Advisory." *West Virginia Public Broadcasting*, June 7, 2022. www.wvpublic.org.

Limpert, William. "Investors Are Reevaluating Mountain Valley Pipeline. Let's Cancel It for Good." *Truthout*, March 9, 2022. https://truthout.org.

Lipsitz, George. *The Possessive Investment in Whiteness: How White People Profit from Identity Politics*. Philadelphia, PA: Temple University Press, 1998.

Litvak, Anna, and Karen Kane. "Officials: W.Va. Explosion Was along Newly Installed Natural Gas Line." *Pittsburgh Post Gazette*, June 7, 2018. www.post-gazette.com.

Locke, John. *Second Treatise of Government*. Edited by C. B. Macpherson. Indianapolis, IN: Hackett Publishing, 1980.

Lopez, German. "The Minnesota Police Officer Who Shot Philando Castile Was Cleared of Manslaughter." *Vox*, July 7, 2016. www.vox.com.

Lopez, Tommy. "MVP Tree-Sitters Allowed to Stay in Pipeline's Path, Judge Rules." *WSLS*, August 2, 2019. www.wsls.com.

Lucas, Anne E. "No Remedy for the Inuit: Accountability for Environmental Harms under U.S. and International Law." In *New Perspectives on Environmental Justice: Gender, Sexuality, and Activism*, edited by Rachel Stein, 191–208. New Brunswick, NJ: Rutgers University Press, 2004.

MacFarquhar, Larissa. "In the Heart of Trump Country." *The New Yorker*, October 3, 2016. www.newyorker.com.

Mackey, Eva. *Unsettled Expectations: Uncertainty, Land and Settler Decolonization*. Black Point, Canada: Fernwood Publishing, 2016.

Macoun, Alissa, and Elizabeth Strakosch. "The Ethical Demands of Settler Colonial Theory." *Settler Colonial Studies* 3, no. 3–04 (November 1, 2013): 426–43.

MacPherson, C. B. *The Political Theory of Possessive Individualism: Hobbes to Locke*. Oxford: Oxford University Press, 1964.

Maddaus, Gene. "What Went Wrong at Porter Ranch?" *LA Weekly*, December 22, 2015. www.laweekly.com.

"Making the Plastics Found Everywhere in Modern Life Comes with a Cost: More Pollution." *Public Radio International*, December 18, 2016. www.pri.org/stories.

Malewitz, Jim. "Abbott Signs 'Denton Fracking Bill.'" *The Texas Tribune*, May 18, 2015. www.texastribune.org.

Malin, Stephanie. "There's No Real Choice but to Sign: Neoliberalization and Normalization of Hydraulic Fracturing on Pennsylvania Farmland." *Journal of Environmental Studies and Sciences* 4, no. 1 (March 1, 2014): 17–27.

"Marcellus Shale Fact Sheet." Institute for Energy Research. Accessed November 14, 2018. http://instituteforenergyresearch.org.

Martens, Reuben. "Petromelancholia and the Energopolitical Violence of Settler Colonialism in Waubgeshig Rice's Moon of the Crusted Snow." *American Imago: Psychoanalysis and the Human Sciences* 77, no. 1 (2020 Spring 2020): 193–211.

Marx, Karl. *Capital: A Critique of Political Economy*. Chicago: C.H. Kerr & Company, 1906.

———. "The German Ideology: Part 1." In *The Marx-Engels Reader*, edited by Robert C. Tucker, 146–200. New York: W.W. Norton, 1978.

Maslen, Sarah, and Jan Hayes. "'It's the Seeing and Feeling': How Embodied and Conceptual Knowledges Relate in Pipeline Engineering Work." *Qualitative Sociology* 45, no. 4 (December 1, 2022): 593–616.

Masson-Delmotte, Valérie, Panmao Zhai, Anna Pirani, Sarah L. Connors, C. Péan, Sophie Berger, Nada Caud et al., eds. *Climate Change 2021: The Physical Science Basis. Contribution of Working Group I to the Sixth Assessment Report of the Intergovernmental Panel on Climate Change*. Cambridge, UK: Cambridge University Press, 2021.

Maynard, Robyn, Leanne Betasamosake Simpson, Robin D. G. Kelley, and Ruth Wilson Gilmore. *Rehearsals for Living*. Chicago: Haymarket Books, 2022.

Mbembe, Achille. "Necropolitics." *Public Culture* 15, no. 1 (2003): 11–40.

McClean, Bethany. *Saudi America: The Truth About Fracking and How It's Changing the World*. New York: Columbia Global Reports, 2018.

McCleery, Adam. "Bushfire Smoke Turns the Australian Sky into a Re-Creation of the Aboriginal Flag." *Daily Mail*, January 4, 2020. www.dailymail.co.uk.

McCullough, Mike. "Landowners Continue to Fight Mountain Valley Pipeline." *WV Metro News*, April 8, 2018. http://wvmetronews.com.

McIntyre, Michael, and Heidi J. Nast. "Bio(Necro)Polis: Marx, Surplus Populations, and the Spatial Dialectics of Reproduction and 'Race.'" *Antipode* 43, no. 5 (2011): 1465–88.

McKay, Dwanna L., Kirsten Vinyeta, and Kari Marie Norgaard. "Theorizing Race and Settler Colonialism within U.S. Sociology." *Sociology Compass* 14, no. 9 (2020): e12821.

McNary, Sharon. "After Aliso: How the Worst Gas Leak in US History Forced Angelenos to Rethink Their Energy Supply." LAist.com, October 23, 2019. https://projects.laist.com.

McNeil, Bryan T. *Combating Mountaintop Removal: New Directions in the Fight against Big Coal*. Urbana-Champaign: University of Illinois Press, 2013.

Meinzen-Dick, Ruth, and Rajendra Prahdan. "Legal Pluralism and Dynamic Property Rights. CAPRI Working Paper." International Food Policy Research Institute, 2002. www.ifpri.org.

Melton, Jr., Buckner F. "Eminent Domain, 'Public Use,' and the Conundrum of Original Intent." *Natural Resources Journal*, no. 36 (1996): 59–85.

Mencimer, Stephanie. "Cliven Bundy's Lawyer Compares His Armed Resistance to the Selma Marchers." *Mother Jones*, September 29, 2017. www.motherjones.com.

Merchant, Carolyn. *The Death of Nature: Women, Ecology, and the Scientific Revolution*. New York: HarperOne, 1990.

———. "Shades of Darkness: Race and Environmental History." *Environmental History* 8, no. 3 (July 1, 2003): 380–94.

Merica, Dan. "Trump: 'Both Sides' to Blame for Charlottesville." *CNN*, August 16, 2017. www.cnn.com.

Michigan Family History. n.d. "THE TREATY OF SAGINAW, 1819." Accessed June 7, 2022. www.mifamilyhistory.org.

Million, Dian. "Felt Theory: An Indigenous Feminist Approach to Affect and History." *Wicazo Sa Review* 24, no. 2 (2009): 53–76.

Mills, Charles W. *The Racial Contract*. Ithaca, NY: Cornell University Press, 1999.

Miner, Dylan A. T. "Tikibiing Booskikamigaag: An Indigenous History and Ecology of Flint, Michigan," 2016. www.academia.edu.

Ministry of Citizens' Services. "Terminology in Indigenous Content." Province of British Columbia. Accessed July 28, 2022. www2.gov.bc.ca/gov.

Mink, Gwendolyn. "The Lady and the Tramp: Gender, Race, and the Origins of the American Welfare State." In *Women, the State, and Welfare*, edited by Linda Gordon, 92–122. Madison: University of Wisconsin Press, 1990.

Mishkin, Kate. "4th Circuit Orders Temporary Halt to Atlantic Coast Pipeline." *Charleston Gazette-Mail*, November 7, 2019. www.wvgazettemail.com.

———. "The Appalachian Storage Hub Is Mired in Secrecy. Residents Say They're Already Worried about What They Do Know." *Charleston Gazette-Mail*, August 3, 2019. www.wvgazettemail.com.

Mishkin, Kate, and Ken Jr. Ward. "What Happens When a Pipeline Runs Afoul of Government Rules? Authorities Change the Rules." *ProPublica*, August 10, 2018. www.propublica.org.

Mitchell, Audra, and Aadita Chaudhury. "Worlding beyond 'the' 'End' of 'the World': White Apocalyptic Visions and BIPOC Futurisms." *International Relations* 34, no. 3 (September 2020): 309–32.

Mitchell, Timothy. *Carbon Democracy: Political Power in the Age of Oil*. New York: Verso, 2011.

Mitman, Gregg. "Donna Haraway and Anna Tsing Reflect on the Plantationocene." *Edge Effects*, June 18, 2019. https://edgeeffects.net.

Monroe, Robert. "Natural Methane 'Time Bomb' Unlikely to Wreak Climate Havoc." Scripps Institution of Oceanography, August 23, 2017. https://scripps.ucsd.edu.

Moore, Stephen. "Can Red State and Blue State America Coexist?" *Washington Times*, January 6, 2019. www.washingtontimes.com.

Moreton-Robinson, Aileen. *The White Possessive: Property, Power, and Indigenous Sovereignty*. Minneapolis: University of Minnesota Press, 2015.

Morgensen, Scott Lauria. *Spaces between Us: Queer Settler Colonialism and Indigenous Decolonization*. Minneapolis: University of Minnesota Press, 2011.

Morrone, Michele, Geoffrey L. Buckley, Donald Edward Davis, and Jedediah Purdy. *Mountains of Injustice: Social and Environmental Justice in Appalachia*. Athens: Ohio University Press, 2011.

Morrone, Michele, Amy E. Chadwick, and Natalie Kruse. "A Community Divided: Hydraulic Fracturing in Rural Appalachia." *Journal of Appalachian Studies* 21, no. 2 (Fall 2015): 207–28.

Mortimer-Sandilands, Catriona, and Bruce Erickson, eds. *Queer Ecologies: Sex, Nature, Politics, Desire.* Bloomington: University of Indiana Press, 2010.

Morton, Timothy. *Hyperobjects: Philosophy and Ecology after the End of the World.* Minneapolis: University of Minnesota Press, 2013.

Moskowitz, Marina. *Standard of Living: The Measure of the Middle Class in Modern America.* Baltimore, MD: Johns Hopkins University Press, 2008.

Náñez, Dianna M. "A Border Tribe, and the Wall That Will Divide It." USAToday.com, 2018. www.usatoday.com.

Nardella, Beth. "Identity Politics and Resistance: The Social Media Response to the Elk River Chemical Spill." *Journal of Appalachian Studies* 25, no. 1 (Spring 2019): 7–25.

Native Land Digital. "Our Home on Native Land." Accessed June 7, 2019. https://native-land.ca/.

Nazaryan, Alexander. "Methane Gas Crisis: How California's Porter Ranch Became a Ghost Town." *Newsweek*, January 7, 2016. www.newsweek.com.

NBC News, and Greta Thunberg. "Read Greta Thunberg's Full Speech at the United Nations Climate Action Summit." NBC News, September 23, 2019. www.nbcnews.com.

Nichols, Robert. *Theft Is Property!: Dispossession and Critical Theory.* Durham, NC: Duke University Press, 2020.

Nilles, Bruce, and Mary Ann Hitt. "From the Senate to the WV Coalfields, a Pivotal Week for Mountaintop Removal." *Sierra Club Compass*, June 25, 2009. http://blogs.sierraclub.org/compass/2009/06/from-the-senate-to-the-wv-coalfields-a-pivotal-week-for-mountaintop-removal.html.

Noak, Rick. "Why Australia's Prime Minister Just Defended Coal, Even Though the Country Is 'on Fire' and Voters Fear Climate Change." *Washington Post*, December 23, 2019. www.washingtonpost.com.

Norgaard, Kari Marie. *Salmon and Acorns Feed Our People: Colonialism, Nature, and Social Action.* New Brunswick, NJ: Rutgers University Press, 2019.

Nuzum, Lydia, Carly Runquist, and David Perry. "Man Camps from Natural Gas Boom Cause Headaches for Local Officials." *Mountaineer News Service*, May 2, 2013. http://mountaineernewsservice.com.

O'Brien, Jean M. *Firsting and Lasting: Writing Indians Out of Existence in New England.* Minneapolis: University of Minnesota Press, 2010.

O'Connor, James. "Capitalism, Nature, Socialism a Theoretical Introduction." *Capitalism, Nature, Socialism* 1, no. 1 (1988): 11–38.

O'Connor, Martin. "The Second Contradiction of Capitalism: The Material/Communal Conditions of Life." *Capitalism Nature Socialism* 5, no. 4 (December 1, 1994): 105–14.

Ohio Valley Environmental Coalition. "Appalachian Storage Hub/Petrochemical Complex." Accessed January 8, 2019. https://ohvec.org.

———. "Deep Shale Oil & Gas." Accessed October 3, 2017. http://ohvec.org.

O'Leary, Sean. "Impacts of Gas Drilling in Wetzel County." West Virginia Center on Budget & Policy, April 2014. www.wvpolicy.org.

———. "A Win-Win Marcellus Shale Tax Incentive." West Virginia Center on Budget & Policy. September 23, 2015. www.wvpolicy.org.

Omi, Michael, and Howard Winant. *Racial Formation in the United States.* New York: Routledge, 2015.

O'Neil, Rob. "In 1800s, De Celis Owned Most of the Valley." *Los Angeles Times*, July 9, 1997. www.latimes.com.

O'Neill, Jesse. "Kansas Cleans Up from Record Keystone Pipeline Spill." *New York Post.* December 11, 2022. https://nypost.com.

Oostling, Jonathan. "Study: Michigan School Funding Getting 'More Unequal.'" *Detroit News.* June 28, 2016. www.detroitnews.com.

Ortiz, Eric. "'Trouble in Paradise': Why Death of World's Coral Is Alarming." *NBC News.* April 21, 2018. www.nbcnews.com.

Pachirat, Timothy. *Every Twelve Seconds: Industrialized Slaughter and the Politics of Sight.* New Haven, CT: Yale University Press, 2013.

Palmer, A. Laurie. *In the Aura of a Hole: Exploring Sites of Material Extraction.* London: Black Dog Press, 2015.

Parry, Emily, Ami R. Zota, June-Soo Park, and Tracey J. Woodruff. "Polybrominated Diphenyl Ethers (PBDEs) and Hydroxylated PBDE Metabolites (OH-PBDEs): A Six-Year Temporal Trend in Northern California Pregnant Women." *Chemosphere* 195 (March 1, 2018): 777–83.

Parsons, Talcott. "The Kinship System of the Contemporary United States." In *Essays in Sociological Theory*, 189–94. New York: Free Press, 1954.

Parvani, Sarah, and Tony Barboza. "SoCal Gas Relocates Hundreds of Porter Ranch Residents While Trying to Fix Leaking Well." *Los Angeles Times.* December 2, 2015. www.latimes.com.

Pasternak, Shiri. *Grounded Authority: The Algonquins of Barriere Lake against the State.* Minneapolis: University of Minnesota Press, 2017.

Paterson, Leigh. "Could Drilling Rigs Pop Up in Bears Ears National Monument in Utah?" Marketplace. December 4, 2017. www.marketplace.org.

Pearson, Stephen. "'The Last Bastion of Colonialism': Appalachian Settler Colonialism and Self-Indigenization." *American Indian Culture and Research Journal* 37, no. 2 (January 1, 2013): 165–84.

Penn, Ivan. "Atlantic Coast Pipeline Canceled as Delays and Costs Mount." *New York Times*, July 5, 2020. www.nytimes.com.

Penniman, Linda. "The Gift of Ecological Humility." Yale Forum on Religion and Ecology, February 16, 2021. https://fore.yale.edu.

Perry, Imani. *Vexy Thing: On Gender and Liberation.* Durham, NC: Duke University Press, 2018.

Pieratos, Nikki A., Sarah S. Manning, and Nick Tilsen. "Land Back: A Meta Narrative to Help Indigenous People Show Up as Movement Leaders." *Leadership* 17, no. 1 (February 1, 2021): 47–61.

Plumwood, Val. *Feminism and the Mastery of Nature*. London: Routledge, 1994.

Polanyi, Karl. *The Great Transformation*. Boston, MA: Beacon Press, 2001.

Pulido, Laura. "Geographies of Race and Ethnicity I: White Supremacy vs White Privilege in Environmental Racism Research." *Progress in Human Geography* 39, no. 6 (December 1, 2015): 809–17.

———. "Rethinking Environmental Racism: White Privilege and Urban Development in Southern California." *Annals of the Association of American Geographers* 90, no. 1 (2000): 12–40.

Radin, Margaret Jane. "Property and Personhood." *Stanford Law Review* 34, no. 5 (May 1982): 957.

Rainforth, Dylan. "How Aborigines Invented the Idea of Object-Oriented Ontology." *Un Magazine*, 2016. http://unprojects.org.

Reardon, Jenny, and Kim TallBear. "'Your DNA Is Our History': Genomics, Anthropology, and the Construction of Whiteness as Property." *Current Anthropology* 53. no. S5 (2012): S233.

Redoubt News. "Video: Cliven Bundy—First Press Conference." January 10, 2018. https://redoubtnews.com.

Reeve, Elspeth. "Just How Racist Is the 'Obama Phone' Video?" *The Atlantic*, September 2012. www.theatlantic.com.

Reid, Herbert, and Betsy Taylor. *Recovering the Commons: Demcracy, Place, and Global Justice*. Urbana-Champaign: University of Illinois Press, 2010.

Renick, Sharelle. "Attack on Fort Donnally, West Virginia Daily News." *West Virginia Archives & History*, March 3, 1969. www.wvculture.org.

"Revolution." (@Revolution). The Official Profile for Revolution. Facebook. Accessed April 5, 2023. https://www.facebook.com/Revolution.

Rezal, Adriana. "The States Where the Most Native Americans Live." *US News & World Report*, November 26, 2021. www.usnews.com.

Rice, Waubgeshig. *Moon of the Crusted Snow*. Toronto, Canada: ECW Press, 2018.

Rifkin, Mark. *Beyond Settler Time: Temporal Sovereignty and Indigenous Self-Determination*. Durham, NC: Duke University Press, 2017.

———. *Settler Common Sense: Queerness and Everyday Colonialism in the American Renaissance*. Minneapolis: University of Minnesota Press, 2014.

Roberts, Alaina E. "Who Belongs in Indian Territory?" *The Journal of the Gilded Age and Progressive Era* 20, no. 2 (April 2021): 334–37.

Roberts, David. "Why Coal Has a Hit on 'America's Got Talent.'" *Grist*, July 22, 2013. https://grist.org .

Rostow, W. W. "The Stages of Economic Growth." *The Economic History Review* 12, no. 1 (1959): 1–16.

Rutherford, Stephanie. *Governing the Wild: Ecotours of Power*. Minneapolis: University of Minnesota Press, 2011.

Sadler, Richard Casey, and Andrew R. Highsmith. "Rethinking Tiebout: The Contribution of Political Fragmentation and Racial/Economic Segregation to the Flint Water Crisis." *Environmental Justice* 9, no. 5 (2016): 143–51.

Saldaña-Portillo, María Josefina. *Indian Given: Racial Geographies across Mexico and the United States*. Durham, NC: Duke University Press, 2016.

Sandoval, Chela. *Methodology of the Oppressed*. Minneapolis: University of Minnesota Press, 2000.

"Save Porter Ranch." Accessed February 27, 2017. www.saveporterranch.com/.

Schneider, Gregory S. "Virginia Regulators Approve Permit for Pipeline Compressor Station." *Washington Post*. January 8, 2019. www.washingtonpost.com.

Schneider, Lindsey. "'There's Something in the Water': Salmon Runs and Settler Colonialism on the Columbia River." *American Indian Culture and Research Journal* 37, no. 2 (January 1, 2013): 149–64.

Schneider-Mayerson, Matthew. *Peak Oil: Apocalyptic Environmentalism and Libertarian Political Culture*. Chicago: University of Chicago Press, 2015.

Schwartzman, Gabe. "Anti-Blackness, Black Geographies, and Racialized Depopulation in Coalfield Appalachia from 1940 to 2000." *Journal of Appalachian Studies* 28, no. 2 (2022): 125–43.

Scott, James C. *Seeing Like a State: How Certain Schemes to Improve the Human Condition Have Failed*. New Haven, CT: Yale University Press, 1999.

Scott, Rebecca. "Dependent Masculinity and Political Culture in Pro-Mountaintop Removal Discourse: Or, How I Learned to Stop Worrying and Love the Dragline." *Feminist Studies* 33, no. 3 (Fall 2007): 484–509.

———. *Removing Mountains: Extracting Nature and Identity in the Appalachian Coalfields*. Minneapolis: University of Minnesota Press, 2010.

———. "The Sociology of Coal Hollow: Safety, Othering, and Representations of Inequality." *Journal of Appalachian Studies* no. 1/2 (2009): 7–25.

———. "Structures of Environmental Inequality: Property and Vulnerability." *Environmental Justice* 11, no. 3 (2018): 137–42.

Seawright, Gardner. "Settler Traditions of Place: Making Explicit the Epistemological Legacy of White Supremacy and Settler Colonialism for Place-Based Education." *Educational Studies* 50, no. 6 (November 2, 2014): 554–72.

Semple, Ellen Churchill. "The Ango-Saxons of the Kentucky Mountains." (1901). In *Appalachian Images in Folk and Popular Culture*, edited by W. K. McNeil, 145–74. Knoxville: University of Tennessee Press, 1995.

Senier, Laura, Phil Brown, Sara Shostak, and Bridget Hanna. "The Socio-Exposome: Advancing Exposure Science and Environmental Justice in a Postgenomic Era." *Environmental Sociology* 3, no. 2 (2016): 107–21.

Sherman, Jennifer. *Those Who Work, Those Who Don't: Poverty, Morality, and Family in Rural America*. Minneapolis: University of Minnesota Press, 2009.

Shiva, Vandana. *Earth Democracy: Justice, Sustainability, and Peace*. Berkeley, CA: North Atlantic Books, 2015.

Shorter, David Delgado. "Spirituality." In *The Oxford Handbook of American Indian History*, edited by Frederick E. Hoxie, 433–52. New York: Oxford University Press, 2016.

Sierra Club. "Beyond Coal." Accessed March 2, 2018. https://content.sierraclub.org.

———. "Sierra Club Home Page: Explore, Enjoy and Protect the Planet." Sierra Club. Accessed February 28, 2018. www.sierraclub.org.

Silverstein, Ken. "Bloomberg: Coal Is Dead in the Ground While Renewables Will Rise. But That Could Change." *Forbes*, June 20, 2018. www.forbes.com.

Simpson, Leanne Betasamosake. *As We Have Always Done: Indigenous Freedom through Radical Resistance*. Minneapolis: University of Minnesota Press, 2017.

———, ed. *Lighting the Eighth Fire: The Liberation, Resurgence, and Protection of Indigenous Nations*. Winnipeg, Canada: Arbeiter Ring Publishing, 2008.

Singer, Merrill. "Down Cancer Alley: The Lived Experience of Health and Environmental Suffering in Louisiana's Chemical Corridor." *Medical Anthropology Quarterly*, 2011.

"Skill Shortages Hamper Fracking Operations." *Marketplace*, July 17, 2017. www.marketplace.org.

Smith, Barbara Ellen, Stephen Fisher, Phillip Obermiller, David Whistant, Emily Satterwhite, and Rodger Cunningham. "Appalachian Identity: A Roundtable Discussion." *Appalachian Journal* 38, no. 1 (2010): 56–76.

Smith, Linda Tuhiwai. *Decolonizing Methodologies: Research and Indigenous Peoples*. New York: Zed Books, 2012.

Smith, Mitch. "Flint Water Crisis: Prosecutors Drop All Criminal Charges." *New York Times*, June 13, 2019, sec. U.S. www.nytimes.com.

SoCalGas. "Aliso Canyon Natural Gas Storage Facility." SoCalGas website. Accessed June 14, 2019. www.socalgas.com.

———. "Return Home Information: Frequently Asked Questions." SoCalGas website. Accessed March 10, 2017. www.alisoupdates.com.

Solum, Tracy. "2022: A Year in Review." *Rainforest Action Network*, February 13, 2023. www.ran.org.

St. John, Paige. "Regulators Conclude Aliso Canyon Could Reopen Even Though Cause of Massive Gas Leak Still Undetermined." *Los Angeles Times*, January 17, 2017. www.latimes.com.

Starblanket, Gina. "The Numbered Treaties and the Politics of Incoherency." *Canadian Journal of Political Science/Revue Canadienne de Science Politique* 52, no. 3 (September 2019): 443–59.

Starblanket, Gina, and Heidi Kiiwetinepinesiik Stark. "Towards a Relational Paradigm—Four Points for Consideration: Knowledge, Gender, Land, and Modernity." In *Resurgence and Reconciliation: Indigenous-Settler Relations and Earth Teachings*, edited by John Borrows, Michael Asch, and James Tully, 175–207. Toronto, Canada: University of Toronto Press, 2018.

Stark, Heidi Kiiwetinepinesiik. "Criminal Empire: The Making of the Savage in a Lawless Land." *Theory & Event* 19, no. 4 (2016).

Stein, Rachel, ed. *New Perspectives on Environmental Justice: Gender, Sexuality, and Activism*. New Brunswick, NJ: Rutgers University Press, 2004.

Steinberg, Theodore. *Slide Mountain, or, The Folly of Owning Nature*. Berkeley: University of California Press, 1995.

Stelloh, Tim. "Judge Approves $626 Million Settlement in Flint Water Crisis." NBC News, November 10, 2021. www.nbcnews.com.

Stevens, Matt. "After Prodding from City, SoCal Gas Commits to Faster and Broader Plan to Relocate Porter Ranch Residents." *Los Angeles Times*, December 23, 2015. www.latimes.com.

Stewart, Kathleen. *Ordinary Affects*. Durham, NC: Duke University Press, 2007.

———. *A Space on the Side of the Road*. Princeton, NJ: Princeton University Press, 1996.

Stockton House Museum. "Stockton House Museum." Accessed June 8, 2022. www.stocktonhousemuseum.com.

Stoll, Steven. *Ramp Hollow: The Ordeal of Appalachia*. New York: Hill and Wang, 2017.

Stroud, Angela. "Good Guys with Guns: Hegemonic Masculinity and Concealed Handguns." *Gender & Society* 26, no. 2 (April 1, 2012): 216–38.

Sturm, Circe. *Becoming Indian: The Struggle over Cherokee Identity in the Twenty-First Century*. Santa Fe, NM: School for Advanced Research Press, 2011.

Suggs, Ernie. "Mari Copeny: Activist, 11, Is Face, Voice of Flint Water Crisis." *The Atlanta Journal-Constitution*, February 27, 2019. www.ajc.com.

Sullivan, Esther. *Manufactured Insecurity: Mobile Home Parks and Americans' Tenuous Right to Place*. Oakland: University of California Press, 2018.

Swaine, Jon, and Amanda Holpuch. "Ferguson Police: A Stark Illustration of Newly Militarised US Law Enforcement." *The Guardian*, August 14, 2014, sec. World news. www.theguardian.com.

Sweet Springs Resort Park. "Sweet Springs Resort Park." Accessed September 25, 2019. www.sweetspringsresortpark.org.

Szasz, Andrew. *Ecopopulism: Toxic Waste and the Movement for Environmental Justice*. Minneapolis: University of Minnesota Press, 1994.

———. *Shopping Our Way to Safety: How We Changed from Protecting the Environment to Protecting Ourselves*. Minneapolis: University of Minnesota Press, 2009.

Sze, Julie. *Noxious New York: The Racial Politics of Urban Health and Environmental Justice*. Cambridge, MA: MIT Press, 2006.

Takei, Carl. "How Police Can Stop Being Weaponized by Bias-Motivated 911 Calls." American Civil Liberties Union, June 18, 2018. www.aclu.org.

TallBear, Kimberly. "Beyond the Life/Not Life Binary: A Feminist-Indigenous Reading of Cryopreservation, Interspecies Thinking and the New Materialisms." In *Cryopolitics*, edited by Joanna Radin and Emma Kowal, 179–202. Boston, MA: MIT Press, 2017.

———. "Caretaking Relations, Not American Dreaming." *Kalfou* 6, no. 1 (May 30, 2019). tupjournals.temple.edu.

———. "Feminist, Queer, and Indigenous Thinking as an Antidote to Masculinist Objectivity and Binary Thinking in Biological Anthropology." *American Anthropologist* 121, no. 2 (2019): 494–96.

———. "Making Love and Relations beyond Settler Sex and Family." In *Making Kin Not Population*, edited by Donna J. Haraway and Adele Clarke, 145–64. Chicago: Prickly Paradigm Press, 2018.

———. *Native American DNA: Tribal Belonging and the False Promise of Genetic Science*. Minneapolis: University of Minnesota Press, 2013.

Tankersley, Steve. 2018. "Meanwhile in West Virginia." Facebook, August 16, 2018. www.facebook.com/steve.tankersley.92/videos/1857123521002311/.

Taylor, Dorceta. *The Rise of the American Conservation Movement*. Durham, NC: Duke University Press, 2016.

———. *Toxic Communities: Environmental Racism, Industrial Pollution, and Residential Mobility*. New York: NYU Press, 2014.

Temin, David Myer. "Remapping the World: Vine Deloria, Jr. and the Ends of Settler Sovereignty." PhD dissertation, University of Minnesota, 2016.

Theodori, Gene. "Paradoxical Perceptions of Problems Associated with Unconventional Natural Gas Development." *Journal of Rural Social Sciences* 24, no. 3 (December 31, 2009): 97–117.

Thoenen, Eugene. *History of the Oil and Gas Industry in West Virginia*. Charleston, WV: Education Foundation, 1964.

Tidwell, Christy. "The Problem of Materiality in Paolo Bacigalupi's 'The People of Sand and Slag.'" *Extrapolation* 52, no. 1 (2011): 94–109.

Todd, Zoe. "An Indigenous Feminist's Take on the Ontological Turn: 'Ontology' Is Just Another Word for Colonialism." *Journal of Historical Sociology* 29, no. 1 (2016): 4–22.

Trillin, Calvin. "U.S. Journal: Jeremiah, KY. A Stranger with a Camera." *New Yorker*, April 4, 1969. www.newyorker.com.

Trip, Gabriel. "50 Years into the War on Poverty: Hardship Hits Back." *New York Times*, April 20, 2014. www.nytimes.com.

Trotter, Jr., Joe W. *African American Workers and the Appalachian Coal Industry*. Morgantown: West Virginia University Press, 2022.

———. *Coal, Class, and Color*. Champaign-Urbana: University of Illinois Press, 1990.

Tsing, Anna Lowenhaupt. *Friction: An Ethnography of Global Connection*. Princeton, NJ: Princeton University Press, 2005.

———. *The Mushroom at the End of the World: On the Possibility of Life in Capitalist Ruins*. Princeton, NJ: Princeton University Press, 2015.

Tuck, Eve, and K. Wayne Yang. "Decolonization Is Not a Metaphor." *Decolonization, Indigeneity Education and Society* 1, no. 1 (September 8, 2012): 1–40.

Tully, James. "Reconciliation Here on Earth." In *Resurgence and Reconciliation: Indigenous-Settler Relations and Earth Teachings*, edited by John Borrows, Michael Asch, and James Tully, 83–129. Toronto, Canada: University of Toronto Press, 2018.

United Church of Christ. "Toxic Wastes and Race and Toxic Wastes and Race at Twenty." 2007. www.ucc.org.

US Census Bureau. "Table B25077. Median Value (Dollars) Universe: Owner-Occupied Housing Units. 2011–2015 American Community Survey 5-Year Estimates. Zip Code 91326 (Porter Ranch, CA)." 2011–2015 American Community Survey 5-Year Estimates. Zip Code 91326 (Porter Ranch, CA)., n.d.

"U.S. Census Bureau QuickFacts: United States." 2019. www.census.gov.

"U.S. Census Bureau QuickFacts: West Virginia." 2022. www.census.gov.

US EPA National Center for Environmental Assessment, Immediate Office. "Hydraulic Fracturing for Oil And Gas: Impacts from the Hydraulic Fracturing Water Cycle on Drinking Water Resources in the United States (Final Report)." Reports & Assessments, 2016. https://cfpub.epa.gov.

USGS: Science for a Changing World. "How Much Water Does the Typical Hydraulically Fractured Well Require?" US Geological Survey. Accessed June 10, 2022. www.usgs.gov.

———. "USGS Estimates 214 Trillion Cubic Feet of Natural Gas in Appalachian Basin Formations." US Geological Survey. October 3, 2019. www.usgs.gov.

Vaidyanathan, Gayathri. "How Bad of a Greenhouse Gas Is Methane?" *Scientific American*, December 22, 2015. www.scientificamerican.com.

Vance, J. D. *Hillbilly Elegy: A Memoir of a Family and Culture in Crisis*. New York: Harper, 2016.

Varinsky, Dana. "Here's Every Piece of Land Obama Has Put under Protection during His Presidency." *Business Insider*, January 16, 2017. www.businessinsider.com.

Vasel, Katherine. "You Can Buy a House in Flint for $14,000." *CNN Money*, March 4, 2016. http://money.cnn.com.

Vimalassery, Manu, Juliana Hu Pegues, and Alyosha Goldstein. "On Colonial Unknowing." *Theory & Event* 19, no. 4 (2016): 1–13.

Voyles, Traci Brynne. *Wastelanding: Legacies of Uranium Mining in Navajo Country*. Minneapolis: University of Minnesota Press, 2015.

Walters, Karina L., Michelle Johnson-Jennings, Sandra Stroud, Stacy Rasmus, Billy Charles, Simeon John, James Allen, et al. "Growing from Our Roots: Strategies for Developing Culturally Grounded Health-Promotion Interventions in American Indian, Alaska Native, and Native Hawaiian Communities." *Prevention Science: The Official Journal of the Society for Prevention Research* 21 (November 6, 2018): 54–64.

Ward, Ken. "China Gas Deal with WV Generates More Questions than Answers." *Charleston Gazette-Mail*, November 9, 2017. www.wvgazettemail.com.

———. "West Virginia Is Grappling with Cost, Benefit of Natural Gas Industry. Some See a Warning in State's History with Coal." *State Impact Pennsylvania*, April 30, 2018. https://stateimpact.npr.org.

———. "West Virginia Paid for a CEO to Go on a Trade Delegation. . . ." *ProPublica*, June 15, 2018. www.propublica.org.

———. "WV's Largest Coal Operator Fighting Back against Growing Natural Gas Industry." *Charleston Gazette-Mail*, September 18, 2018. www.wvgazettemail.com.

Washington Post Staff. "Woman Dies after Shooting in U.S. Capitol; D.C. National Guard Activated after Mob Breaches Building." *Washington Post*, January 6, 2021. www.washingtonpost.com.

Waterfield, Sophia. "Out of Control Australian Wildfires Merge as People Face Extreme Fire Danger Conditions." *Newsweek*, January 7, 2020. www.newsweek.com.

Watts, Michael. "Petro-Violence: Community, Extraction, and Political Ecology of a Mythic Commodity." In *Violent Environments*, edited by Michael Watts and Nancy Peluso, 189–212. Ithaca, NY: Cornell University Press, 2001.

Weaver, Jonathan. "Passenger Killed in Sunday Crash on U.S. 50 in Salem, WV." *WV News*, November 25, 2018. www.wvnews.com.

Weise, Robert S. *Grasping at Independence: Debt, Male Authority, and Mineral Rights in Appalachian Kentucky, 1850–1915.* Knoxville: University of Tennessee Press, 2001.

West Virginia Public Service Commission. "Coal Transportation FAQ." Accessed April 5, 2023. www.psc.state.wv.us.

West Virginia State Legislature. WV Code Chapter 22. Environmental Resources, 22-13-5 Article 13. Natural Streams Preservation Act § (2011). www.wvlegislature.gov.

White, Ed. "Court Hears Challenge to Grand Jury in Flint Water Cases." *AP NEWS*, May 4, 2022. https://apnews.com.

Whyte, Kyle Powys. "Our Ancestors' Dystopia Now: Indigenous Conservation and the Anthropocene." SSRN Scholarly Paper. Rochester, NY: Social Science Research Network, September 8, 2016. https://papers.ssrn.com.

Willey, Angela. *Undoing Monogamy: The Politics of Science and the Possibilities of Biology.* Durham, NC: Duke University Press, 2016.

Williams, Evan C. *Combined and Uneven Apocalypse.* Washington, DC: Zero Books, 2011.

Williams, Patricia J. *The Alchemy of Race and Rights.* Cambridge, MA: Harvard University Press, 1991.

Williams, Raymond. *Marxism and Literature.* Oxford, UK: Oxford University Press, 1978.

Wolfe, Cary. *What Is Posthumanism?* Minneapolis: University of Minnesota Press, 2009.

Wolfe, Patrick. "Settler Colonialism and the Elimination of the Native." *Journal of Genocide Research* 8, no. 4 (December 2006): 387–409.

———. "The Settler Complex: An Introduction." *American Indian Culture and Research Journal* 37, no. 2 (January 1, 2013): 1–22.

———. *Traces of History: Elementary Structures of Race.* London; New York: Verso, 2016.

Wray, Matt. *Not Quite White: White Trash and the Boundaries of Whiteness.* Durham, NC: Duke University Press, 2006.

WV Center on Budget and Policy. "Who Owns West Virginia in the 21st Century?" 2018. www.wvpolicy.org.

Yagelski, Paul R. "Federal or FERC Pipeline Condemnation or Eminent Domain." Rothman Gordon, Attorneys, December 11, 2017. www.rothmangordon.com.

Yee, Gregory, Tony Barboza, and Leila Miller. "SoCalGas Agrees to Pay Up to $1.8 Billion in Settlement for 2015 Aliso Canyon Gas Leak." *Los Angeles Times.* September 27, 2021, sec. California. www.latimes.com.

Young, Charles. "Antero's Clearwater Facility: Setting Environmental Standards for Oil and Gas Industry." *Exponent Telegram*, March 29, 2018. www.wvnews.com.

Zimring, Carl A. *Clean and White: A History of Environmental Racism in the United States*. New York: New York University Press, 2016.

Zwick, Austin. "Comparison of the Coal and Fracking Industries in Northern Appalachia." *Journal of Appalachian Studies* 24, no. 2 (2018): 168–84.

Zylinska, Joanne. *The End of Man: A Feminist Counterapocalypse*. Minneapolis: University of Minnesota Press, 2018.

INDEX

ABOUT THE AUTHOR

Rebecca R. Scott is Associate Professor in the Department of Sociology at the University of Missouri–Columbia. She is the author of *Removing Mountains: Extracting Nature and Identity in the Appalachian Coalfields.*